Coping with Aging ∷

Coping with Aging

Richard S. Lazarus

and

Bernice N. Lazarus

2006

OXFORD
UNIVERSITY PRESS

Oxford University Press, Inc., publishes works that further
Oxford University's objective of excellence
in research, scholarship, and education.

Oxford New York
Auckland Cape Town Dar es Salaam Hong Kong Karachi
Kuala Lumpur Madrid Melbourne Mexico City Nairobi
New Delhi Shanghai Taipei Toronto

With offices in
Argentina Austria Brazil Chile Czech Republic France Greece
Guatemala Hungary Italy Japan Poland Portugal Singapore
South Korea Switzerland Thailand Turkey Ukraine Vietnam

Published by Oxford University Press, Inc.
198 Madison Avenue, New York, New York 10016

www.oup.com

Library of Congress Cataloging-in-Publication Data
Lazarus, Richard S.
Coping with aging / Richard S. Lazarus and Bernice N. Lazarus.
p. cm.
Includes bibliographical references and index.
ISBN-13 978-0-19-517302-4
ISBN 0-19-517302-3
1. Older people. 2. Adjustment (Psychology) in old age.
3. Aging—Psychological aspects. I. Lazarus, Bernice N.
II. Title.
HQ1061.L39 2004
305.26—dc22 2004009734

1 3 5 7 9 8 6 4 2

Printed in the United States of America
on acid-free paper

To R.S.L., my knight on a white horse

—B.N.L.

Foreword

This book is historic. It represents the last publication of its senior author, Richard S. Lazarus, who died of one of the environmental hazards he spoke of in this book—a bathroom fall. It also marks the culmination of a remarkable career of creative contribution to behavioral science.

I witnessed the conceptualization, gestation, and birth of this work. In a modern-day variant of *Tuesdays with Morrie*, Professor Lazarus and I would have an extended lunch every Tuesday, sharing braised Chinese fish—a dish he relished but to which his wife, Bernice, was allergic. During those unforgettable meetings, we would discuss intellectual issues, university politics, and, above all, our personal aspirations.

Professor Lazarus was one of the giants of twentieth century psychology. He was a giant precisely because he did not fall victim to allegiance with preexisting theoretical movements. He stood for himself and his ideas. He studied emotion when emotion was (rather surprisingly) considered an unsuitable area of investigation for psychology. He argued for the importance of cognition in emotion at a time when psychologists believed that what mattered was behavior and association of behavior with rewards and punishments. He studied the unconscious when it was considered a ridiculous assertion, beyond the realm of proof. He helped open the fields of stress and coping and health psychology, both of which are now considered critical subareas of behavioral science. And he added simple but convincing clarity to our understanding of the nature of emotion. In 1991, he was awarded the Distinguished Scientific Contribution to Psychology Award by the American Psychological Association in recognition of his creativity and the courage of his convictions.

But despite this and other awards, Professor Lazarus revealed a longing in our Tuesday meals—a longing that led to the writing of this book. He felt dissatisfied with his treatment of emotional development in his classic book

Emotion and Adaptation (1991). He felt he had not done justice to the nature of emotion in the human infant and toddler, and he almost entirely left out treatment of emotion at the other end of the spectrum, in aging. He felt that both areas of development—early life and the end of life—held secrets about what the nature of emotion is, and both areas provide means of confirming or disconfirming what he had written to date about how emotions work. However, he did not draw on these areas for inspiration or self-criticism.

Great and creative figures draw from their own experience the creative wellspring of new ideas and important concepts to share. Indeed, Fellini's movie *8 1/2* deals with precisely this topic of self-experience as the source of creativity. For Professor Lazarus, early life was too distant in time to provide creative sources, but aging was upon him. He had fallen victim to many of the diseases and deteriorations he describes in this book, and he lived the emotional consequences of these changes every day. Thus was conceived the book on aging and emotion that you are about to read.

I believe it is appropriate to review some of the revolutionary ideas about emotion that Professor Lazarus propounded, and that form the core of the thinking of this book. Let us start with the nature of emotion itself. Emotion has been considered ineffable, unfathomable, impossible to define. Indeed, a common starting point in psychological treatments of emotion is that "everyone knows what an emotion is until they are asked to define it." Not so for Professor Lazarus. With the clarity and cogency characteristic of the great mind, Professor Lazarus says convincingly and succinctly: *Emotions reflect the fate of one's motives*. That is the first "commandment" (or more appropriately, the first principle) of emotion. For Professor Lazarus, the understanding of emotion begins with the identification of the goals that one wants to attain. Emotions can be goal-congruent, and thus positive (regardless of what the goal happens to be), or goal-incongruent and hence negative (whatever the goal happens to be). From this principle follow corollaries that explain the occurrence of all emotions.

A second major principle of emotion for Professor Lazarus was *the relational principle*. This principle holds that it is not an event that produces an emotion (the way behaviorists and many others believe), nor is it the self that generates emotion (the way many contemporary scientists and pop psychologists propose). Rather, an emotion is created by how an event relates to one's strivings. Consequently, there can be no single indicator of an emotion (such as a facial expression), nor can there be a single way of behaving characteristic of an emotion (such as aggression in anger). Virtually any event can produce a given emotion, depending on the relational and motivational context, and virtually any response or set of responses can be in the service of an emotion, depending upon what function that behavior is serving in the adaptive life of the person. Consider, for instance, how doing nothing can constitute a potent manifestation of anger. In this book, Professor Lazarus makes clear that it is a mistake to think of any emotion as good or bad—it all will depend on context, on the operation of the relational principle. Professor Lazarus did not think much of "positive psychology" precisely because of its uncritical acceptance of some emotions as intrinsically good, and others as intrinsically bad. His views about emotions as relational are now rapidly becoming the standard view in the field—at last, Professor Lazarus would say.

So far, this discussion has centered on the first author of the book. However, Professor Lazarus's wife, Bernice, represents a powerful force who helped shape his thinking throughout his life. Those Tuesday lunches drove home to me his acknowledgment of her contributions again and again. Bernice did so not only by making it possible for Richard to be free of care and concern to concentrate on his work, but also by providing an argumentative foil for his emerging ideas. It has been said that behind every successful man stands a woman. In this case, behind the intellectual success of Richard Lazarus was a keen-thinking, witty, cheerful, enthusiastic, and intellectually insightful partner. For much of his career, Bernice played a silent role. In later years, Richard made sure that she received the credit long due her. His 1994 book *Passion and Reason* was but one of several of Richard's later publications that justly shared authorship. Moreover, Richard insisted that at any conference in which he was the invited speaker Bernice share the platform as an equal contributor to the power of his ideas. Bernice's contributions to this book are especially noteworthy, because she, like Richard, not only has suffered many personal setbacks in health, but also has drawn on her personal experiences to inform her intellectual and creative contributions to what is said in the pages that follow. What a pair worthy of emulation.

I feel sad in writing these words—sad in not having Professor Lazarus to discuss ideas on Tuesdays, sad in not being able to expect new insights from this remarkable husband-and-wife team who next month would have celebrated, remarkably in these days of divorce, their sixtieth wedding anniversary. However, my sadness quickly dissipates once I consider the admirable and enduring contribution Richard has made, and Bernice has made possible. Would that each of us would leave a comparable legacy for the rest of mankind.

Joseph J. Campos, Ph.D.
Professor of Psychology
University of California, Berkeley
Berkeley, California
August 1, 2005

Preface

We have already said to potential readers all we wanted to about our objectives in writing this book and our outlook on aging. Thus the only function of a preface is to express our thanks to those who have helped us in this venture.

Five special people have graciously and without recompense read and commented usefully on a draft of our book, and they deserve our warm expressions of appreciation. They are as follows: Joseph J. Campos, professor of psychology at the University of California at Berkeley; Yochi Cohen-Charash, a new assistant professor of organizational psychology at Baruch College of the City University of New York; Alan Monat, professor and chairperson in the Department of Psychology, California State University at Hayward; Inger Hilde Nordhus, professor in the Department of Clinical Psychology, Outpatient Clinic for Adults and the Elderly, at the University of Bergen, Norway; and Bob G. Knight, professor in the Andrus Gerontology Center, School of Gerontology, at the University of Southern California.

Each of these outstanding individuals brought special expertise to the task of giving us advice about this book in the making. Their help was of great importance to us and added greatly to what we were trying to do. Naturally, we the authors take full responsibility for what is written, and if we have slipped up in some ways, these advisers bear no responsibility for our gaffes.

In addition, we thank Catharine Carlin, our editor at Oxford University Press, with whom we have published previously. She deserves a very special thank-you for her support and graciousness in the handling of this book's publication. A special thanks also to Stephen Holtje for many hours of work on this project.

Most of all, we hope our eventual readers gain from reading our book in both enjoyment and intellectual stimulation, and perhaps even in their own personal lives.

Contents

I ∷

INSPIRATION AND OVERVIEW

Introduction: Aging, Once Over Lightly

If we have been lucky to stay alive long enough, all of us age. Although there can be important gains, the most troubling feature of aging has to do with the physical, social, and psychological losses and deficits it commonly brings, as well as our increasing nearness to death. And this gets us to the classic sardonic joke of the elderly, which goes something like this: "They say these are the golden years. To believe this, all we have to do is consider the alternative."

We all need to be concerned today about the elderly and those just getting there, because demographers estimate that the growing numbers of the elderly will exceed the young of the world in about fifty years. Our loved ones, indeed everyone, could ultimately need help and forbearance to survive and flourish. There is now widespread societal interest where once was only concern for older family members.

Affluence and good health care, both prevention and treatment, help some folks to live to a much older age than in the past and to function adequately, indeed sometimes surprisingly well, in spite of substantial physical decay. On the other hand, the elderly have become more vulnerable to life-threatening and handicapping ailments, such as heart disease and cancer, because of the self-indulgent lifestyles that wealth can bring, or simply because we live longer and become subject to diseases common to old age.

At over eighty years of age, Richard is approaching the end of his life after a long professional career and family life, which began during the Great Depression followed by World War II. His wife, Bernice, is only three months younger. We have major life-threatening and handicapping ailments. Our experience is not atypical from that of many educated and financially comfortable people, though not all. Some have not yet reached the stage of major sudden, rapid, or dangerous decline, but if death does not come first, their decline surely will occur eventually. These differences in rates and kinds of aging are very important because they help us understand why some people, if they are honest in what they tell others, would speak with genuine satisfaction about their elderly lives while others would complain bitterly.

We are keen to present an accurate portrait of what aging is like, but our most important objective is to examine what we can do to minimize the waste of lives later in life and to maximize the prospects for a successful old age. This is not a textbook but a personal treatment of the nature of aging for the interested layperson.

Most textbooks are filled with the findings of scholarly research. They often fail to yield a useful portrait of getting old for reasons we hope will become obvious to the reader as we proceed. By this we mean that they do not provide a clear idea about what it means to an individual person to be old or to be getting old and what it often takes to remain cheerful, active, and fully engaged in living in the presence of physical and mental decline.

One of the most important reasons for this is that scientific observations about the elderly are expressed typically as statistical averages rather than as descriptions of individual variations, and the information can become overwhelming and ultimately boring. Academic textbooks center on the search for generalizations about aging that fail to give sufficient and detailed attention to individual variations. To anyone who deals clinically with people needing help, this is one of the most striking facts of professional life. The variations deprive the professional of automatic, reliable, well-worn formulas for treatment. Clinical practice becomes as much an art as a science.

The educational commitment of a textbook to cover every topic of aging leaves little room to examine closely what aging is all about in depth, rather than superficially, in our individual lives. We value the interesting issues and human dilemmas of the field of aging, especially the confusing ones, but are turned off by books that try, compulsively, to cover everything but go deeply into nothing. They become large collections of research questions and findings without a soul. We do not avoid research data in this book, but we abjure becoming dependent on statistical averages to describe the aging process.

Our focus is more on aging *as it is experienced* by different kinds of people living under divergent life circumstances. We have written a personal view of aging that adopts the standpoint of various kinds of people who are coping either well or badly with the stresses of aging. It is a psychological rather than a sociological or population (demographic) approach. These latter approaches deal more with people in general than with individuals like you or me.

Because we are writing about our lives and those of selected other persons for illustration as well as about the complex abstraction called aging, we hope the reader will experience less of the usual distance from the author than is typical of a purely academic work. We would like you to react empathetically to the struggles of later life in numerous case histories, including our own, even if these struggles have not yet reached you. To understand them accurately, aided by your own empathic feelings and intuitions, provides the best rationale for offering practical help.

Yet we avoid the maudlin, doom-and-gloom outlook that honest portrayals of human existence can sometimes provoke. And because of our growing physical problems, we want to get our message, which we believe has never been more needed in a coarsened and increasingly indifferent world, across to the lay public while we are still able to work. The potential readers that we hope will find this book to their taste are, first, the aging who want to know the specifics of what they might have to face as they get really old. But we are also writing for the two younger generations that are inexorably moving toward our life stage. Our children, and perhaps our grandchildren as well, are far enough along to begin to think about their own aging. They recognize that their parents are aging and ailing and may ultimately need increased care. What once was easy has now become difficult for us. However, in addition to making the most of their lives, right now they must deal with the present.

We, as their aging parents and grandparents, want to maintain our own independence, which seems to be the norm for our generation, and protect them from spoiling their own lives by being excessively embroiled in helping us. We also need their support, help, and encouragement at this time of our lives. But being able to live more or less independently is the prime value of the very old. We shall later deal with issues having to do with the physical and mental competence that this goal requires. In any case, this book is for the young, too.

Life always seems very short, especially if one looks at it backward from the present. In the course of a few more decades, our children's middle years will have passed in what seems like the wink of an eye, just as it happened to us. They, too, will be entering the late stages of their lives barely comprehending how they got there. We often ask ourselves, "How did we get to be eighty?" It seems to have just happened while we weren't watching.

We were inspired to write this personal account of aging by *My Voyage to Italy*, an unusual movie produced for television by the distinguished film director Martin Scorsese, whose family origins are Sicilian. In it, he reviews Italian films directed by Visconti, Fellini, De Sica, and Rossellini, including some of those that exemplify the neorealist films that thrived immediately after World War II. He believes they have had a tremendous influence on his own films and those of other American directors.

We know many of these highly realistic, simple stories, which we saw initially during the postwar years. We marveled at the extent to which such movies as *The Bicycle Thief* and *La Strada* clobbered our emotions by portraying small human tragedies. Although it was difficult not to become tearful as we watched them, they do not deserve the term of opprobrium *tearjerker*, because they seem real and natural and are presented objectively and sympathetically, without artifice. Later moviemaking in Italy became increasingly more complex and ambiguous, including such films as *La Dolce Vita*, *8 1/2*, and others.

The reason we were inspired is that Scorsese, as a result of his own directing experience and artistic mastery, was able to convey what it was like to be a director of films and participant in the creative trends over many decades since that time. He showed us that one person's personal account of a complex arena of human experience is capable of being far more distinctive, informative, and moving than any distanced academic treatise reflecting the need of the writer to maintain acceptable scientific credentials.

Science values cool analytic detachment, but in our judgment this is not the best way to convey what aging is all about to nonacademic readers, which in addition to the raw facts has an important and potentially widespread emotional impact. Modern science focuses mainly on the causes of what we observe, but it lacks interest in rich description. We shall say no more about this here, because chapter 2 is devoted to a troubling look at what is wrong with aging research and why, in the main, it does not give us adequate description.

Why should you want to read what Richard Lazarus has to say about the topic of aging? I have, of course, some impressive credentials that qualify me, but most readers would not know about that. It is the fact that I can apply what I learned over the course of my career to the harsh lessons of aging that first appeared in my life when I was about sixty-five and grew progressively worse that gives me special qualifications.

At that time, I found the activities of my life were becoming ominously and greatly narrowed by my wife's illness and, subsequently and relentlessly, by my own growing ailments, which were both life-threatening and to some extent disabling. And at eighty these have become major obstacles to satisfaction and what I want to do with the remainder of my life. Nevertheless, you are reading a product of my efforts during this tough period, which are themselves a product of my determination to manage these obstacles and age as successfully as I can, given my circumstances.

A vigorous and youthful-looking man before this time, I began to see the handwriting on the wall. My wife thought I should not write about my own medical history; this might be taken as a plea for sympathy. I thought, however, that it gave me added credibility in portraying the personal experience of getting old, which might be more important than possible embarrassment about a spurious claim for sympathy. Who can portray what aging is like better than someone who both is experiencing it and knows something about the research literature?

Besides, my emphasis in getting at the truth of aging does not have the purpose merely of demonstrating how distressing its rigors can be; it was intended to reveal how a person might cope effectively with the stresses of life, thereby transcending them somewhat in seeking meaningful sources of satisfaction. To this I add without modesty that I am also considered to be an expert on the coping process.

If there is any special pleading here, it is not the desire for sympathy—which can quickly seem empty—but a desire for regard and appreciation for having transcended somewhat the added handicaps of old age. Let me, however, not succumb to the phony game of false modesty. To wish to be admired is hardly sinful, and most of us think we have something worthwhile to say. Big deal! Therefore, I have decided to make one of the major case histories in this book my own, which appears pseudonymously in the chapter on the ailments of aging titled "A Different Doctor for Every Organ." I wanted this book to be a personal document, and I have gone that route.

Allow me tell you a few relevant things about my family and myself. My wife and I have lived together as a married couple for more than fifty-seven years. We were married on the day on which the war with Japan officially ended, September 2, 1945, which is when the treaty of surrender was formally signed. I had been in the army for three and a half years; I then went back to graduate school to obtain a doctorate in psychology. We have two adult children, both born in the 1950s and now each married almost thirty years. When, many years later, we discovered we had a son who was fifty years old, we were astonished. How could that be? We now have four grandchildren, three of whom are young adults; the fourth is seventeen years of age at this writing.

I am a retired professor of psychology from the University of California at Berkeley after more than fifty years of teaching and research, most of them at this university campus. The American Psychological Association certified me as a clinical psychologist in 1955. It announced to the world that I was qualified to engage in the practice of psychotherapy, though as a researcher and teacher, I did a somewhat limited amount. I thought it would be better for me to get the feel of people in trouble and struggle to help.

Just as important to this book, I was an early pioneer in the emerging field of psychological stress, coping, and the emotions and have published research and written quite a bit about aging. I first became interested in this topic when I began to realize I was aging, which reminds me that personal and emotional concerns often direct one's choice of research topics.

Because we got along so well over the years and had such respect for each other, Bernice and I took the chance of working together on a book, a commitment that has broken up other successful marriages. We published a book about the emotions that is being used in many colleges and universities throughout the world.[1] We still get along well, and she contributes her good sense to the present book on aging by reading and criticizing what I write and by making suggestions that help make this book better. (Whenever *I* is used in this book, the voice is Richard's; when *we* is used, it is often to reflect the combined thoughts of both Richard and Bernice, usually in discussions of our life and experiences together.)

We live in a community of older people known as Rossmoor. The minimum age for living here is fifty-five. It is probably representative of many such communities, though it is also heavily weighted on the side of affluent and educated adults who are mostly white. This population is hardly representative of the economic, educational, and social circumstances of a large proportion of our national population. However, much that has to do with aging still applies because most of us grow old, and there is a more or less typical, if not uniform, course of physical aging despite variations in social class.

Rossmooreans comprise more than nine thousand people over age 55, or nearly one-quarter of the population of the East Bay suburban city of Walnut Creek, which is situated not very far due east of San Francisco. The average age of the residents is 77, and the age distribution at this writing is roughly as follows: 95 and older: 2 percent; 85 to 94: 25 percent; 75 to 84: 43 percent; 65 to 74: 24 percent; and 55 to 64: 6 percent. We have drawn heavily on the experiences of people we know here, including our own. Richard also wrote about his attitudes toward work and death in a recent autobiography.[2] However, our medical status and life conditions have changed quite a bit since then, which was only a few short years ago. So what we write here about our life struggles is updated.

We are committed to speak absolute truth about aging, at least as we see it. Why should we make such an odd-sounding statement? Doesn't everyone who writes about aging describe it accurately? The answer is no. Often, in a sincere effort to accentuate the positive, the portrait of aging presented to the public is seriously distorted by the constant use of upbeat aphorisms about aging, such as the one about the golden years we presented in our opening paragraph. Another states, "You are only as old as you feel," which is often a competitive claim that imposes social pressure on others to live up to an outrageously optimistic stance.

This statement would be considered foolish by those who are seriously impaired by an incapacitating or life-threatening illness, such as cancer, diabetes, congestive heart disease, emphysema, asthma, autoimmune disorders, loss of hearing and vision, rheumatoid arthritis, and so forth. Elderly people with these disorders often regard gung ho statements about aging as being out of touch with reality, though they are not likely to argue the point because of social pressures to always sound upbeat. And they, too, would prefer to view old age in the most positive light possible, though they might not be as sanguine about it as they might say publicly.

A softer and more realistic way to express the idea that you are only as old as you feel—yet still remaining positive in tone—is the affirmation that many, perhaps most, old persons are able to preserve commitment, verve, and good spirits and accept the hateful realities of adversity. Consider, for example, this comment by Kenneth Gergen and Mary Gergen that emphasizes the positive side of aging: "As survey research . . . [has] indicated . . . approximately 90% of the people over 65 feel satisfied with their lives, feel they have contributed positively to society, and claim to be in good health. However . . . not all sectors of the aging population are equally satisfied. There is enormous heterogeneity within the aging population."[3]

About this and with greater evenhandedness because we should not accept at face value everything people say about themselves, Neal Krause writes in the same collection:

> One of the most important contributions of social and behavioral gerontology has arisen from efforts to counteract negative stereotypes of aging. It is indeed true that there was a time when late life was viewed in unflattering terms that did not accurately portray the situation or the potential of the later years. But we must be careful not to swing too far in the opposite direction by painting portraits of aging that are too glowing and overly optimistic. Instead, it is important to begin by acknowledging the inescapable facts—people get old, they get sick, and they die. Then, taking this as a point of departure, the goal should be to carefully examine how people confront these critical issues.[4]

Many years ago, Richard was interviewed about coping with stress on *Over Easy*, a now defunct public television program on aging hosted by Hugh Downs. A troubling feature of that program may have contributed to its ultimate demise: the tendency of the producers to emphasize only examples of extraordinarily fortunate aging and to ignore more typical cases. This seemed to us to be a serious mistake for an educational program on aging. No doubt many viewers who were worse off than the fortunate elderly who were paraded each week gave up watching because the program made them feel discouraged and depressed about their own condition. Some people are much luckier than others in the way they age.

The solution is not to patronize old people but to help them learn about, accept, and manage the varied realities of their lot in life and, by all means, to think as positively as they can about it. Here we treat aging with a certain amount of sadness and regret about its losses and deficits, yet we emphasize the many ways old people can cope successfully and compensate for deficits and losses. We didn't really want to grow old, but it is a reality of life, and one must make the best of it.

1 ::

The Typical Course of Aging

The study of aging cannot be divorced from the rest of life, because growing old merges gradually with one's beginnings in childhood. Most diseases of old age can also be found in the young, though not nearly as frequently. In other words, diseases that are life-threatening or that create serious handicaps are not infrequent even in the very young and represent heartrending tragedies. A child's struggle with cancer is even more poignant than the same struggle in an aging person.

Therefore, ill health is not a valid criterion of aging, though certain diseases, such as heart attacks, strokes, and cancer, and various forms of severe dementia, such as Alzheimer's disease, are much more frequent in the old, so we tend to think of them as diseases of old age. Aging itself is not a disease, but it does promote life-threatening and disabling diseases.[1] But becoming old does have special features that make it a topic all its own.

The direction in which we are heading toward the end of life is the gradual or abrupt dissolution of our physiological and psychological structure and the energy it sustains. We all ultimately experience a downward spiral of loss of function until death, regardless of the particular details and how long it takes. One potential publisher of this book wanted me to delete that statement. How can you sell a book, he asked pointedly, with that dour message, even if it is the truth? But just because it is true, it becomes all the more essential to arm ourselves against our likely fate by finding ways to cope, which is the essence of successful aging. This is a central theme throughout this book, but it needs expansion and more detail.

How long do people live, and how many years can science add in the future? The average life span in advanced countries is roughly the mid-70s, and relatively few people live to the 90s and 100s. Humans are by no means the longest living species. The elephant, crocodile, parrot, and crow all outlive us. Sea tortoises appear capable of surviving 150 years or more. Dogs live only about 10 to 16 years, cats somewhat longer. Longevity is to a great extent influenced by species inheritance and individual genes. It also depends on many other factors, such as accidents, diseases, medical treatment, and more general aspects of living, including stress and emotion.

There is an active controversy today about the number of years people can live. As we were writing this chapter, a local newspaper gave an account of a major debate on this subject. The discussion took place in San Francisco at a special session of the American Association for the Advancement of Science (AAAS) on February 18, 2001. One biologist who spoke was optimistic that in time longevity drugs could lead everyone, at least potentially, to become centenarians—that is, to live one hundred years or longer.

The other biologist on this session's program was highly skeptical, and in the news story he was referred to as the pessimist. He expressed the belief that processes at the atomic and molecular level gradually wear down life-sustaining cells, organs, and metabolic activity. Even if we learn to control life-threatening diseases, he said, this pervasive bodily deterioration will win out in the end because one or more parts must ultimately fail. Perhaps, he said, people could gain at best an average of fifteen years of extra life. So you can see that even distinguished experts disagree on how long people might be able to live in the future.

Recently, however, a collection of distinguished scientists expressed alarm at the burgeoning trend to sell treatments aimed at stopping or reversing aging. They wrote a strong attack on the idea that the process of aging can be significantly changed.[2] The main message of these scientists was that those who claim they can stop or reverse the aging process are lying (pretty strong language, we would say). Rather, it is the genetically programmed wearing down of organs and essential systems sustaining life that results in most of the signs of aging, such as loss of muscle and bone, sensory impairment, and greater vulnerability to disease. Even if age-related diseases were cured in the future, our bodies would still age as a result of their inability to repair themselves. The key point is that this is what we can expect, but that does not mean we must give up our efforts to make the best of our declining years. It is not youth we should be seeking but the opportunity and ability to make the best of our declining years when they begin, which would still be important regardless of any changes in the life span average.

For reasons we do not yet fully understand, women on average live about seven years longer than men do. We cannot explain this discrepancy, though there has long been speculation that the stressful and aggressive working life of men over the course of their lives impairs their health. However, for women now routinely working and competing outside the home while also raising children at the same time, the difference in life span might well equalize, though this has not yet happened. Many scholars take more seriously another hypothesis: that the difference in longevity for men and women is genetic in origin, though exactly how and why is unclear.

To understand the life course of the human animal, one must think of the progression from birth to death. In the years before adulthood, this progression is called *development*. This word implies a change from a relatively primitive and disorganized biological and psychological structure and the limited functional capacities it makes possible to a more mature or advanced structure and function. In effect, we progress by becoming more fully organized, complex, skillful, and knowledgeable and better able to reason and control our minds and bodies. It seems sad to us that so much of what we learn as individuals is lost to the community with death.

Just think of the human infant. Its arms and legs flail about in an uncoordinated way. It is forced to remain wherever it is placed, unable to approach or pick up attractive objects or to move away from that which is harmful, though it can cry or wail to attract attention to its plight. It takes quite some time for the infant just to become capable of crawling, walking, and talking, activities which facilitate the learning of children, and adults later, about the world in which they live.

Eventually, the relatively helpless infant becomes capable of extraordinary accomplishments—for example, being able to plan and direct its life, cope with change, and act morally and responsibly—on the way to becoming a distinctive and self-consistent being with its own recognizable personality. Less advanced animals, such as chimpanzees, horses, cows, and ducks, can do much more to take care of themselves at birth than the human infant, but they cannot advance nearly as far. In sum, development is a forward progression in which we gain an impressive degree of mastery over our lives.

Aging, however, is quite another matter. Mostly it seems to move in a direction opposite from development, though we can gain wisdom and even acquire important new skills and creative coping processes to compensate for losses. These gains enable older people to remain effective at dealing with the requirements and opportunities of living even when they are ailing physically and exceeding the young in important respects.

Certain words and expressions for what occurs during aging have a harshly negative sound, but they are also unhappily accurate. For example, we speak of *regression* (going back to an earlier, more primitive condition) or *second childhood*. Shakespeare, in *As You Like It*, gives the famous, though somewhat dour, poetic account of the seven stages of aging in archaic English. Part of the scene describes the last stage, the return to childishness:

> Last scene of all,
> That ends this strange, eventful history,
> Is second childishness and mere oblivion,
> Sans teeth, sans eyes, sans taste, sans everything.
>
> (act 2, scene 7)

This portrait of our condition near the end of life contains considerable truth but applies more to the seventeenth century, when it was written, than to today. Modern medical standards in the developed world, for example, mitigate the negative portrait at the end to some extent, though not altogether. The features of aging we encounter depend on the luck of the draw, how far along we are in the aging process, how we evaluate what is happening, and how we manage aging.

In any case, the main features we must consider if we want to examine aging fully are its negatives and positives. Any listing of negatives and positives is bound to be incomplete with respect to particular individuals and groups. Also, what constitutes a negative or a positive is, to some extent, an individual judgment. But we must not follow the usual disposition of psychologists to take dichotomies too seriously. Negative and positive cut both ways. For example, retirement is in one sense a boon, but it often presents a new problem—that is, what should I do with myself now? How can I make up for the loss of work that defined me as a person in our society? How can I keep busy and engaged? Negative and positive are almost always conjoined.

The Negatives of Aging

A list of major negatives includes the following:

- Awareness that the time of *one's own death* is growing near is universal and most commonly a source of dread, though this is often avoided or denied. Unlike other animal species, people recognize they have a past, present, and future. We anticipate our ultimate death and must cope with it.
- Because of social changes during one's lifetime, older people often experience a *changed and still changing society*. Well-established values and ways of living have vanished or been reversed. Social change results in what is often referred to as a *generation gap*.
- *Death of family members and friends* becomes increasingly frequent as we age. The older we get, the more we watch in distress as a member of our family, a friend, or a neighbor becomes increasingly ill, infirm, and dies. We may also note growing lists of celebrities and colleagues whose lives have ended.
- *Impairment of health* is another important negative experience of old age, though it is likely to be more serious or disabling for some than for others.

- Another negative is the loss of one's opportunity to *sustain a useful function in life*, which is often referred to as our work or, in an earlier day, our calling. We think that paid work may be overvalued in our society, and evidence suggests that on the average, reported life satisfaction does not decline after people retire as long as retirees remain vigorous, active, and reasonably healthy, and especially if what they are doing seems useful to others.

Still, to a great extent, as we intimated earlier, work has long defined us as individuals. It contributes to our sense of well-being and to the well-being of our loved ones, society, and the world. Whether such work is performed outside the home or as homemaking and child care, its loss is sometimes a major blow. It usually requires finding a suitable substitute, even if the new work does not produce anything that is highly valued by others.

The Positives of Aging

Although outnumbered by the negatives, if only in quantity, a reasonable list of major positives includes the following:

- *The satisfactions of retirement* are enjoyed by most of the elderly as long as there is something adequate to take the place of work. For these elderly, being retired could bring the absence of pressure to earn a living; available time for travel; participation in sports and other activities; increased opportunities to get together with family, friends, and acquaintances; and, if one desires, continuing professional involvement. Above all, not having to work for income provides the opportunity for freedom of choice to decide how to spend one's time and new kinds of activity in which to be engaged. In a society that is obsessed with money and efficiency, it is good to be able to cast aside working for a livelihood and choose how to live in one's late years. None of us, however, is entirely free of obligations to others. They come with the territory.
- For many there are also the joys of *caring children and grandchildren*. If they live nearby, as our family does, they can be seen reasonably often, and and families can celebrate holidays together. For others, children living at some distance provide the opportunity for travel to their homes. Children can, of course, be a headache and heartache—indeed, a mixed blessing.
- Another positive comes from the potential for making desirable *changes in oneself*. For example, the things that seemed important in our youth and midlife may no longer be regarded as such. We can, if

we wish, abandon or soft-pedal the values and goals that are now counterproductive or no longer relevant for our happiness and, perhaps, never really were.

- To be able to abandon goals that are no longer suitable requires *wisdom*, which should be considered to be still another positive, though it is by no means guaranteed by age any more than it is by being smart or educated. There is some weak evidence of a greater ability in old people compared with the young to accept painful realities philosophically and laugh at them.
- There can be a *special pattern of communication between spouses* who have had the great good fortune to live together for many years. Each seems to know what the other is thinking even without being verbally explicit about it. The things that have happened to them while together carry emotional meanings *no one else shares or understands*. Something will occur that connects them to the past, and they look at each other and instantly understand without a word having passed between them. It takes many years to attain this level of communion. Although this close communication is by no means universal, when it does happen, it is surely one of the great positive experiences of growing old together. This, by the way, is one of the main reasons the death of a spouse is so often terribly wrenching and a source of loneliness; the person who shared large portions of one's life firsthand is no longer present. The good and the bad are always fused. This will be seen throughout the individual case histories presented in later chapters, which deal with family and friends, medical status, and work.

The extent and kind of negative and positive consequences of aging depend greatly on where one is in the aging cycle and on one's individual good or bad fortune. Edwin Shneidman,[3] who was a pioneer in research on suicide, published a study of a small sample of gifted septuagenarian men (those in their seventies) who were originally studied by Louis Terman, the creator of the highly respected Stanford-Binet intelligence scale. Terman began his study in the college years of this sample at Stanford in 1921 and continued it for many decades thereafter.

In the late 1980s, Shneidman interviewed in depth forty-five men from this sample who were still alive in their seventies and presented preliminary data about eleven lawyers in a number of areas of life, such as occupation, family, friends, culture, community service, and joy in living. He found that most of them were still highly productive, engaged in life with enthusiasm, and generally satisfied with their lives.

To characterize this positive period of life for these men in their seventies, Shneidman used the felicitous expression "the Indian Summer of life."

It was borrowed from *The Education of Henry Adams,* which Shneidman quotes further: "The Indian Summer of life should be a little sunny and a little sad, like the season, and infinite in wealth and depth of tone."[4]

Shneidman also writes about this poetically on his own, with an acute sense of both joy and sorrow:

> Indian Summer is not real summer. During the Indian Summer of life there are premonitions of the imminent winter in which it is embedded, and there is a painful awareness of one's inescapable death-bound plight. (Our plight is that we know our fate, and we feel the turbulent catabolic air-bumps before the inevitable crash.) For this reason, a pleasant stretch of weather in the late Fall is doubly welcome, and we enjoy the rays of the sun while they last, suppressing our certain knowledge of the threat that lies beyond the turn.[5]

Shneidman also observed in some of his subjects that depression began to set in during their late seventies and early eighties, probably because of an increase of ill health and a decline of mental resources. His interviews suggest that the joy of living on the part of these outstanding men declines sharply between the ages of seventy-two and seventy-eight. We need to recognize, of course, that the decline represents an average of those studied; individual variation remains important, as always.

Individual Differences in Aging

In the previous comments on the typical course of aging, the portrait of old age is strangely incomplete. What is underemphasized is an explicit emphasis on and detailed documentation of the enormous variation in the course of aging, which we have hinted at again and again but must address more fully as a dilemma of all human sciences and a recurrent theme of this book. There is variation in when aging seems to begin, the rate at which it progresses, and the particular bodily and mental changes it can bring. Individual differences are the rule rather than the exception, but no challenge can be offered about where everyone will ultimately end up.

We know very little about the struggles that individual persons could be required to sustain at a ripe old age, which we refer to as coping. Aside from good fortune, this effort to manage stress and distress provides the most important basis of successful aging. For any number of reasons, people are not usually very candid about their troubles. For example, age often takes on a competitive quality; we may want to impress others how well we are doing or, to the contrary, how badly we are doing to gain sympathy or to excuse ourselves for not being able to handle the wear and tear. But perhaps most important, others do not want to listen to complaints; they have plenty of problems of their own.

Science is usually defined as the search for general principles. Variation is regarded by science today as a nuisance or as errors that defeat the construction of the broad generalizations that scientists are always seeking about the world and life. This is why all clinical work—for example, in medicine or clinical geriatrics—remains an art rather than a science. The focus is on a particular case when, say, a psychologist, psychiatrist, physician, or social worker takes on the task of helping as much as possible. Much more is said about this in chapter 2.

To portray the typical course of aging does not help us much to predict what happens to any given individual, except as a statement of statistical probability. If we do not grasp this fact, we will never understand aging. There is, in effect, no absolute chronological age when we can be said to be aging or old. This is why we make silly statements like "We are aging from the moment we are born." Without more information than probabilistic statements about the course of life, we cannot say much about what a given older person is like. To know someone's physical and mental condition, we must, in effect, look closely at the individual and not interpret that person's condition on the basis of an average appropriate for a given chronological age.

Some aging experts still like to speak of three levels of aging, the "young old" who are said by one author, for example, to be fifty-five to sixty-five years old, the "middle old" from sixty-six to seventy-five, and the "old old" at seventy-six or above. This has some value as casual communication. However, on the basis of what we have been saying about individuality, these experts have fallen into the trap of creating arbitrary categories that make, at best, only approximate sense. We must also recognize that our sense of the life course changes with the times in which we live and differs among cultures.

What we have been saying is a difficult idea for many people to grasp because we are constantly bombarded by statistics about risk factors for this or that illness and death in general. If we have a blood cholesterol level that is said to be too high for good health, we are presumably in danger of developing heart disease. If we smoke, we are said to be in danger of developing lung cancer, bladder cancer, or emphysema. Such statements may not apply to a particular person, although they represent correct statistical probabilities for a given population in a particular historical period and geographic location. Many people with a high blood cholesterol level or with too much of the bad kind of cholesterol have sound cardiovascular systems, and many who have smoked all their lives do not get the diseases associated with this habit. And still others get lung cancer or emphysema without ever having smoked.

It is a mistake to apply probabilities about illness to particular individuals because they may (or may not) have unmeasured protections against or, perhaps, even greater than average vulnerability to illnesses than others. However, this is not to deny that because of the substantially increased statistical risk, it is clearly unwise to smoke or load up on saturated fats. (For more about the perils of applying general illness probabilities to individuals, see chapter 2, specifically the discussion of cross-sectional research.)

The same applies to aging. Some people display little evidence of mental or physical deterioration for much or most of their lives, experiencing no major illness, working productively—sometimes even more effectively than when young. Some of them die suddenly from disorders that were not evident, dying, as it were, in the saddle. Others live to a ripe old age and take a long time to die.

Most of us, however, notice a loss of strength, energy, and stamina that comes with aging, or realize that we now grow winded while struggling up a steep hill as we walk our dog, a hill that we used to climb almost effortlessly. Changes such as this occur so slowly that they may even not be noticed, except perhaps on certain occasions—for example, when playing ball with our children—when we can remember being physically more capable. Often we do not get the truth about this from peers because it is an emotionally charged issue, and they may have a need to show how extraordinary they are. It is like hearing from friends who recently gambled in a casino; they all came home as winners, according to what they say.

Still others suffer constant or recurrent ailments throughout life and are often ill but may, contrary to expectation, outlive those who displayed robust health most of their lives. Today, large numbers of elderly men and women are kept alive and comparatively healthy by medical care that prevents an illness from becoming terminal. Prompt and effective treatment may allow them to live ten to twenty years longer than if they had not been lucky enough to have had the deadly disease correctly diagnosed when it could still be dealt with. Unless we acknowledge these and other variations, we cannot make sense of aging.

II ::
THEORETICAL FRAMEWORK

2

The Emotions and Research Problems

We are about to embark on a series of chapters dealing with changes over the life course, the role of family and friends, issues of health and illness, the function of work in later life, treatment of emotional disturbances, and principles of successful aging. Looking at this list, the reader might expect us to make pronouncements in each of the next chapters about what aging is like that are based strictly on reviews of the findings of aging research. But no!

We shall, indeed, make statements about aging, but most of them do not deserve to be treated as the appropriate conclusions of formal research. In this I am at variance with a high percentage of my colleagues, how many I cannot say—in any case, what is usually called "the establishment." There is, believe it or not, a poor research base for describing much of what old age is like. I explain why in this chapter, which addresses the most serious problems of the most commonly employed methodologies of psychology in general and aging research in particular.

I ask the reader to be patient. However, if for any reason you can not stand reading about research methods, just pass this chapter by and go directly to the later substance of aging. If you stay with it, however, you could find it interesting and worthwhile, with discussions of the generation gap and several health issues in addition to the research. Reading it with care should help you to distinguish the wheat from the chaff of research. The journey also provides a bonus: it will help you be better protected against the misleading media hype that claims to have a research basis for what the elderly are like and the things that are good and bad for us.

Today a largely self-serving media seems interested only in selling its products and those of corporate America, while public understanding is dramatically distorted. We cannot remember a time when we were so likely to be harangued about what to do and buy to preserve our health. This is hard on everyone, but particularly on the elderly, whose health is more frequently compromised and who depend on too many overpriced medicines that many cannot afford.

I have been a maverick during my long career as an academic research scholar. I like to tell unpalatable truths and embrace controversy. So I expect to irritate, perhaps even to shock, my colleagues by criticizing much of the research on aging and, more broadly, psychology in general. I offer a kind of exposé of insubstantial and misleading research. As you will see, I favor some types of research and say why. I also believe there is much we can say about aging that does not derive from established science but requires more thought and judgment than has been applied to what aging is truly like.

Some of us believe that this unhappy state of affairs is a product of a faulty reward system within which most of us work. Publish, publish, publish, in order to get promoted or to gain the assets and privileges of grant support ("publish or perish," as some say), whether or not what one publishes is junk. Useless findings that few pay attention to continue to pile up like garbage and make little or no difference in our knowledge in the long run. One has only to look at the research that is typically cited in research articles to see that they seldom go back into the past beyond five or ten years. What has been produced in the recent past begins to look like a growing mountain of costly waste to which few pay any attention.

It is downright dangerous for the young and ambitious to complain too loudly about the system. However, in my case, the approach of the end of my life and my solid reputation as a research scholar mitigate the risk. But I know from private conversations that plenty of other psychologists agree with the core of what I am saying. Unease about these problems has increasingly led to debates about how psychology has been doing as a practical science.[1] I defer discussion of how we got into this mess until the end of the chapter, after I have examined the most serious problems that infect aging research and much of psychological research in general.

Science as Description and the Search for Causes

Two of the most prominent values of psychology as a science are central to my arguments. Some social scientists consider it enough to describe, just as an artist or gifted writer might, how people manage their lives, without necessarily attempting to predict their future actions. They are a small minority in an era in which science is almost uniformly defined as the search for the causes of phenomena in which we are interested.

Accurate description is absolutely essential to understanding, and we do not do it enough or as carefully as we should. This and the fact that the research methods employed to identify causes are often inadequate for doing so become valid reasons for why cause-and-effect research should, perhaps, not dominate research as much as it does. Description, however, is clearly not enough either. The world of inanimate and living objects is normally portrayed as orderly. If we want to understand it, not only out of curiosity but also for the purpose of making things better by, say, preventing and curing illness and increasing the general well-being, then cause-and-effect thinking remains an essential requirement of the scientific enterprise.

Causality as a concept turns out to be more complex and controversial than it sometimes has been thought to be. Aristotle, the ancient Greek philosopher who has had such a great influence on us, divided cause into four kinds.[2] *Efficient cause* refers to the agency that produces the effect. *Formal cause* is the means—that is, the instrumentality or process that produces it. *Material cause* is the substance producing it—in other words, our physiology; when it comes to how people behave, for example, this cause is usually presumed to be the brain, hormones, and how they affect the way our bodies work. *Final cause* is the purpose or end for which the effect is produced.

At this juncture, we confront a major dilemma. Because living creatures have minds, they also have purposes or intentions, but this does not translate well into the inanimate physical world. Although debates about the idea of purpose and intention can be interesting, this topic would take us too far afield to be worth pursuing further. It would be more useful, however, to ask about the logical grounds for making a causal inference from what is observed.

There are two main grounds. The first is that we observe an invariant succession in which one variable, which we call an *antecedent*, is followed by another variable, the *consequent* or *effect*. The second ground is that the variables in this succession seem inextricably bound together—that is, if the antecedent appears, the consequent must eventually appear.

Without invariant connections between the antecedent and consequent or the cause and effect, an orderly world would be impossible to conceive.[3] Therefore, a primary scientific task is to discover these connections or relationships among variables to identify the most important sources and kinds of order in the world. When I first came into psychology, I read about the methods of causal reasoning described by John Stuart Mill (1803–73), which made it possible to evaluate a cause-and-effect relationship. Students spoke of these as Mill's canons.

The doctrine of causality, which is that every event is caused by something else, is called *determinism*. Nowadays, however, after Werner Heisenberg's work on the principle of indeterminacy, we recognize that strict determinism cannot be applied even to the physical world, much less to the psychological world where we must deal with personal intentions or will. Besides, with the multiplicity and complex hierarchies of ill-defined causes of mind and behavior, too many to identify for an individual, we begin to recognize that we can predict less well than we have long believed should be possible.

Many psychologists take seriously some variant of free will in which we need not always act and react automatically as the causal conditions of life dictate. We intuit that there must be room to act in accordance with our own individual lights. In other words, not everything is fixed by a strict determinism. We can, in effect, struggle against addiction, control drinking, smoking, and drugs, by acts of will.

This creates a strange dilemma, which is the contradiction between the way psychologists tend to talk informally about causation in our daily lives and the way we presume things work in our research. In research we act as if everything is caused, but at the same time we accept the idea that there is only a modest degree of determinism. We refer to this as *soft determinism*, in which room is left for an individual decision or will. This is a fine line to walk, and I am not sure whether we have in this way resolved the contradiction.

This may all sound abstruse and distant, but it is very important for the main practical thesis of this book, which is to examine how we can cope with the adversity in old age in order to age successfully. To do this, each of us must apply two seemingly contradictory modes of thought as we try to appraise what is happening and what to do about it. On the one hand, we want to appraise the conditions we face *realistically* so that we can cope with them effectively. But at the same time, we want to put the most *positive spin* we can on our judgment in order to retain hope and sanguinity. In every situation that we must struggle to adapt to, we *negotiate* between these two seemingly contradictory modes of thought. I am convinced that both are equally important in permitting us to survive and flourish in our lives, both as a species and as individuals.

The bottom line of all this is that if we want to improve the quality of life for our species, we must be able first to understand and predict human reactions by understanding the ways our minds work and the conditions that influence them. The ability to predict confirms, at least in our minds, that we understand the rules, which follow from the venerable cause-and-effect tradition of science. Only if we can predict the future based on the past can we be convinced that we might exercise some control over the psychological, physiological, and social events that affect our well-being. It is this belief that leads many of us to invest our lives in the ideals of research and teaching.

Research on the Causes of Illness

The practical importance of cause-and-effect thinking can be seen clearly in clinical work that is designed to help us manage the physical and mental losses and deficits of aging. If we know the conditions that might affect illnesses and how we function, we must obtain and draw on reliable knowledge about the rules that lead to order in contrast to chaos in our lives. This might lead to the use of drugs or surgery in medicine. If we adopt a more psychological perspective, we can try to make it easier for handicapped persons to live independently and teach them to cope more effectively.

There is a wonderful story about a pump handle that social epidemiologists love to recite as a reminder to students about how causes of illness can be discovered and illness prevented or cured. It derives from the nineteenth-century idea that a disease can arise from a single environmental condition. It tells a true account of a cholera epidemic in London in 1855, before the discovery of microbes. At that time it was believed that this deadly disease was caused by bad air. Although this is an erroneous explanation, it might be considered intuitively close to the truth, perhaps a step on the way to more complete knowledge.

John Snow, considered by many to be the father of epidemiology, had a better idea. He believed cholera had to do with the presence of fecal matter in the Thames. This is an instance of how important an informed and creative mind is in science. Two companies, one upstream and the other downstream, supplied water to London residents. Mapping the locations of the cholera outbreak by means of a household census, Snow found that cholera appeared in only one of the two sources of water. Thus he performed the first epidemiological mapping of a disease on record.

All that was needed to end the disease outbreak was to turn off the correct spigot—in other words, the pump handle that controlled the source of the polluted water. Snow is a hero in the field of epidemiology, and present-day students in that field hope they will have the opportunity to discover the cause of a new disease that could be figuratively or literally shut off in the same way.

The only problem with this concept of illness causation is that it is oversimple. Usually at least two agencies are required to result in an infectious illness, an external cause—say, a bacterium or virus—and the inability of the host to resist the biological invasion. If host resistance is high, the illness is less likely to occur or kill than if it is low. Thus, not everyone in Europe who came in contact with the bubonic plague during the Middle Ages got sick or died, though it is estimated that between a third and a half of the population lost their lives.

In any epidemic, such as the famous influenza outbreak following World War I, when large numbers of people were stricken and died, many others did not die or even come down with the flu. Their immune systems evidently protected them by successfully fighting off the invasion by the biological enemy. This is true of most diseases.

The key idea I want to get across here is that the *relationship between a person and the environment* is always crucial in illness. This can also change under conditions in which the person's resources are weakened and with age because the immune system is progressively weakened, which is why we get sick more readily when we get old.[4]

This relational principle can be illustrated in the breakthrough research of three pioneers who discovered and proved that microorganisms were the external cause of disease but that the outcome depends on the body's ability to fight the germs. They include Louis Pasteur (1822–95), whose many contributions to modern germ theory are extraordinary: Joseph Lister (1827–1912), who developed antiseptic surgery; and Robert Koch (1843–1910), who discovered anthrax. Reading about these pioneers in Paul De Kruif's book *Microbe Hunters* when I was young greatly inspired me. I was struck with their courage and integrity in persisting in their research and in disseminating what they learned despite attempts to vilify them as heretics.[5] Perhaps you can forgive (or appreciate) a rare moment of cynicism on my part at this point. It is that today, when only money and celebrity are revered in our society, the primary motive for such a commitment is to become rich by controlling lucrative patents rather than by making a lasting contribution to human well-being.

One of Pasteur's major contributions was to prove by an elegant field experiment that a microorganism was the cause of anthrax in sheep and goats. In one experiment, he injected healthy animals with contaminated substances from fields in which sick animals lived. The two groups of animals, those that were injected and those that were not, were separated so that they could not infect each other. In this way Pasteur's research design ruled out other possible causes and provided a strong proof about the causal agent. The infected animals died of anthrax, but the control animals were not infected because they had had no contact with the bacillus.

Pasteur's work demonstrated that microorganisms, which can only be seen under a microscope, could cause a number of deadly diseases. Pasteur also discovered the microbial source of rabies and its treatment, the principle of fermentation, and the pasteurization of milk. He demonstrated the extremely important principle that the virulence of the anthrax bacillus could be attenuated and used to protect the animal from it by inoculation. This is known as *vaccination*, which is a way of preventing infection.

What needs to be most emphasized, however, is that this type of success in preventing and curing microbial diseases has kept cause-and-effect thinking in good repute despite the philosophical concerns I mentioned earlier about whether science is too much preoccupied with cause and too little with description. In recent years, much has been learned about the way our immune system operates, which explains species and individual variations in vulnerability to particular diseases.

One of the great mistakes made by academic psychology when it became a separate discipline that was independent of philosophy departments where it had earlier been housed was to model itself after Newtonian physics. This led psychology down the garden path by the failure to recognize that physics is probably an unsuitable model for the task of understanding living creatures, which, in contrast with inanimate objects, have a mind that inanimate objects do not share.

In the early days, when the new discipline of psychology was being founded, psychologists were claiming their own credentials as scientists by snidely suggesting that philosophy was engaged solely in armchair speculation without a database. This was both spurious and ungracious and a poor way to defend the scientific status of psychology. It suggests that psychology suffered from an inferiority complex about its scientific credentials; I think it still does, which seems to generate rigidity and hypocrisy about how to do research. Throughout its brief history, psychology has argued fruitlessly and often hypocritically about how to be scientific while vigorously denying some of the obvious defects of its favorite methods.

I have long maintained the heretical view that good fiction writers often understand people better than methodologically hidebound psychologists. Because the latter are often arrogant about what constitutes science and at the same time defensive about their scientific credentials, they seem to be unreachable. But by far the worst failing is to claim to be ultrascientific while drawing heavily on one of the weakest methodologies available to identify causes—namely, cross-sectional research. There, I said it and I'm glad. But it is time to look at the major research designs employed in psychological research, including cross-sectional research, and to consider their strengths and weaknesses.

Major Research Designs of Psychology

Psychologists employ four basic research designs or formats as they seek invariant relationships between cause-and-effect variables of interest. The first involves *naturalistic observation*—that is, watching and describing what happens in nature. The second is *cross-sectional research,* in which groups or cohorts that differ from each other in one or a number of psychological or social characteristics are compared. The third is *longitudinal or intra-individual research,* in which the same individuals are compared with themselves over time or across life circumstances. The fourth consists of *performing experiments,* in which procedures that are created in the laboratory are regarded as analogies of real life. (In some cases, existing variables are chosen from nature and compared with respect to their observed effects. This is often referred to as *quasi-experimental,* but it is little different from cross-sectional designs and often suffers from the latter's limitations and defects.)

I touch on all four approaches but center my attention mainly on two—namely, cross-sectional and longitudinal research. Cross-sectional designs are especially weak in demonstrating cause-and-effect relationships and in permitting us to observe when a variable is stable or in flux. Longitudinal research offers much better prospects both for assessing causation and in the opportunity to contrast variables that are stable with those that are in continual flux. In this sense it can be regarded as a possible antidote to the most important limitations and defects of cross-sectional research. Let us look at each format a bit more closely to see where it fails or succeeds in identifying causes and reveals whether the phenomena of interest are stable or in flux.

Naturalistic Observation

Naturalistic observation—in effect, to look and describe—is the oldest of research traditions. Its premise is that if we observe the world as it is, we can derive (*induce* is a more accurate word) an understanding of how things work in nature. One might think here of Leonardo da Vinci, who constantly struggled to describe, understand, and use that knowledge in practical ways. As a format for research, observation provides the richest data, which are usually qualitative rather than quantitative. If we regard quantitative data as the gold standard of research, as many scientists do, how to measure what we are looking at becomes an important issue.

The most serious problem challenging the scientific status of naturalistic observation is that to be accepted as science it must be shown that different observers agree on the fundamentals of what is happening in any given set of observations. This is usually referred to as *observer reliability*, which can be assessed by comparing the observations and conclusions of different observers. Unless especially trained, different observers are apt to attend to different aspects of an event on the basis of their interests and perspectives, and as a result they may offer different interpretations about what the event means.

Nevertheless, they may come up with surprising agreement. Consider, for example, the various meanings that define each of our discrete emotions—for example, anger, anxiety, guilt, envy, jealousy, joy, and love. These meanings are based on the ways individuals evaluate the implications of what is happening for their well-being. I refer to this judgmental process as *appraising*, which in its noun form is an *appraisal*.

As I see it, those who become *angered* have judged that they have been demeaned or belittled by what another person or persons has said or done. *Anxiety*, in contrast, is facing uncertain threat, often having to do with who we are and where we are going in life in general, including death. *Guilt* results from having transgressed a moral imperative. *Joy* is the delight that is aroused by having attained an important goal. In its weaker form, we can speak of happiness or a positive frame of mind. It is usually short-lived, and just making progress toward a goal is often enough to yield such a positive state of mind. After all, often it is the process of striving toward a goal that is exhilarating, not the actual outcome, which may turn out to be disappointing.[6]

I bring up the potential for agreement about these individual subject meanings to suggest that even more or less casual anecdotal experiences that define emotions and the events leading to them can generate remarkable agreement among different theoreticians. Emotions are, I think, best viewed as stories about human relationships, which depend on the history of the relationship and the flow of events in the encounter that brought them about. This flow includes a provocation and the pattern of reactions, with continuous feedback from what is said and done to the other participants as the encounter proceeds.

The appraisals presumed to underlie each of the emotions are individual and subjective in the sense that they depend on what a specific emotion means to a particular person with particular goals, beliefs, and ways of coping with stress and adversity. However, the personal meanings for each emotion turn out to be surprisingly similar in discussions of them by diverse scholars.[7] By the time we become adults, most of us have experienced most emotions, and this provides a common basis for shared knowledge.

Consider, for example, the common experiences of triumph (joy), disappointment (sadness), unfair treatment (anger), treachery (hatred), threat of uncertain origin (anxiety), and so on. There is, incidentally, a growing movement within psychology that emphasizes stories or narratives as the best way of understanding people.[8] Stories provide the substance of what we all understand to be true about human experiences, codifying, in effect, what could be referred to as the collective wisdom of the ages. They must not be denigrated simply because they do not conform to what many psychologists tout as proper science.

Disagreements among observers, can, of course, be found, and they need to be addressed both logically and empirically. They usually arise over details. For example, I consider anger to center on the meaning that one has been demeaned or belittled by another's words or actions. Others see anger as the result of being treated unfairly, even in the case of a person whom we observe but do not know personally. All well and good.

Still, unfairness is a threat to the common need to believe in an orderly and fair society.[9] If the events of life are chaotic and disorderly, we are all in some trouble because we cannot predict what is likely to happen, and we may become victims of an ill chance, too. Therefore, when we observe unfairness, I suggest it makes most of us feel smaller and endangered. The two meanings—that is, being dealt with unfairly and being demeaned—come together in a common theme. When we have this kind of consensus, I think it is quite remarkable despite disagreements about given details.

Cross-Sectional Research

In this research design, two or more groups of people who supposedly represent a cross section of the population are compared on a single occasion with respect to a characteristic of interest. This format for research is solely interindividual—that is, people are compared with each other. Although the researcher wants to demonstrate causality, this, as I said, cannot be proved with this kind of research format because the two groups or cohorts are not only different in age but also were born and raised in different eras. In other words, the groups differ on at least two variables, not one, and so we cannot be sure that it is age or the experiences of growing up that explain the observed group differences. This is a result of the presence of different outlooks, usually referred to as a generation gap, which is what creates the cohort problem. I shall examine this later in the section on the most serious problems with psychological research.

Longitudinal Research

The third basic type of research design compares people with themselves over time and under different conditions. It is, in effect, intra-individual in format. It offers the best chance to make valid causal inferences because the same research subjects are followed over time, which provides an opportunity to observe an antecedent variable—one that comes earlier—in an invariant relationship with a later-appearing variable, the consequent or effect. Longitudinal research, incidentally, does not need to cover long periods of time but only a reasonable time to reveal changes if they occur during the comparison period.

We can, in other words, predict from the antecedent variable an effect that appears later. And because the same persons are involved, we need not worry about the contaminating effects of individual differences. The person being compared is always the same; thus, we have good reason to conclude that the antecedent variable could or must be the cause of the later-appearing variable. Longitudinal research is, therefore, an antidote to some of the limitations and defects of cross-sectional research. Unless age levels are studied longitudinally, study findings cannot be interpreted with any confidence.

Longitudinal research is also referred to as *ipsative-normative research*, which represents a combination of intra-individual and interindividual procedures.[10] When the same persons are studied over time and across different life conditions, it illustrates the intra-individual or ipsative feature. It is possible in this kind of research to compare individuals or subgroups also, illustrating the interindividual feature. Although longitudinal research, per se, cannot demonstrate causality, the fact that it is temporal provides an opportunity to *predict* what follows from the antecedent variable. The ability to predict is commonly employed to confirm that there is a causal connection.

Although I have praised intra-individual research more than normative or interindividual research, representative samples are badly needed to permit such generalization—that is, the issue is whether we can say anything beyond the limited sample that was employed in the study. All research designs, even the best ones, require compromise of some sort to be practical.

In fact, intra-individual and interindividual research strategies, considered separately, actually pursue different questions and often produce contradictory findings. For example, we can ask of interindividual comparisons whether a given life condition results in the same or different emotions in different persons. It is usually found that people who are often angry are also often anxious, so the two emotions are positively correlated. However, if we ask whether the same emotion occurs in a given person, it is commonly observed that the person who is feeling angry is less likely to feel anxious. Here both emotions are negatively correlated. The questions asked are different, as are the answers.

The bottom line is that to know whether and how people change, we need to compare the same persons with themselves over time as they age. It is for this reason that K. Warner Schaie has developed what he calls sequential research designs that combine longitudinal and cohort studies.[11] Age cohorts are studied at one time, and then some years later they are observed again. Thus, any changes that occur from one time to another cannot be cohort effects because people at two different age levels are being compared with themselves.

Laboratory Experiments

The fourth type of research design in the repertoire of research psychologists is the experiment. In this procedure, one creates in the laboratory two different conditions in order to compare their effects—for example, doing a stressful task, which is compared with a benign task that is not stressful. As was done in a clever recent experiment, the researcher could show that the group under stress is more likely to catch cold when subjects are placed in direct contact with a rhinovirus in the laboratory.[12] The natural conclusion is that stress increased the likelihood that a subject will catch cold if exposed to the cold virus.

The difficulty of demonstrating causality applies less to the experimental manipulation of variables in the laboratory than to cross-sectional correlation research. By manipulating a variable and showing a later effect, we can more readily argue that the antecedent might well have resulted in the effect. We have, in other words, predicted the outcome. However, even the laboratory has its own special problems with making causal inferences.

When I began graduate school in 1946, I accepted the dominant wisdom of the times that laboratory experiments offered the best way to test our understanding of how the mind works. Their main virtue is that we have, presumably, controlled all the nonexperimental variables by creating a constant situation for all subjects, and if our manipulation allows us to predict the effect, we have probably unearthed a causal antecedent. All experiments are analogues of real life; that does not mean they are good or accurate analogues, however, and so the reasoning from which our manipulation is derived remains important.

Perhaps the most serious problem with this approach is the assumption that we have controlled all the other possible causal variables in the experiment by creating a constant situation for all subjects. This assumption is quite likely to be false, especially when there are unmeasured variations in the stakes that subjects have in participating.

Most subjects also engage in second-guessing about what is going on in the experiment, and they come up with different ideas about what the experiment is all about. They make diverse interpretations of what the experimenter is trying to find out. This tendency to second-guess belies the crucial assumption that the experimenter has exercised tight control over all other variables. All sorts of psychological processes are going on that may not even be recognized by the experimenter or under the experimenter's control. I soon developed doubts about whether this method was as perfect as claimed and have written about this in detail recently.[13]

Actually, no single research method provides an acceptable demonstration of cause and effect in the absence of what scientists refer to as *replication,* which means the same study should be repeated in a different laboratory. Without replication, careful measurement, and the ability to rule out other potential antecedents of any so-called effects, there are no acceptable grounds for arguing in favor of causality. Prediction is not tantamount to causality, though it is commonly taken to support or refute a causal hypothesis.

What is most needed is for researchers to draw on as many different methods of research as are suitable to the questions being asked. Each method has a tendency to produce certain outcomes, which is referred to as methods variance, which have nothing to do with the question at hand but reflect the particular method that has been chosen by the research scholar.

The Most Serious Research Problems

Four special problems apply to research employing one or another of the basic research designs I have been discussing. One is the *cohort problem,* which arises from what has long been called the generation gap and it applies most strongly to cross-sectional research designs.

The second problem concerns the attribution of a positive or negative *valence* or emotional tone in an effort to compare their effects, say, on health or performance of a task.

The third problem is the widespread *tendency to exaggerate* the importance of group or cohort differences and understate the importance of *individual differences.*

The fourth problem has to do with the *superficial measurement of emotion,* which is endemic in psychological research. Let us look at each of these problems in turn. Except for the cohort problem, which is tied mostly to cross-sectional research designs, the other problems are not tied in this way.

The Cohort Problem

Why is cross-sectional research unable to provide a dependable demonstration that a particular variable of interest, say, chronological age, is an antecedent, hence a cause, of the difference observed between the two groups being compared? In aging research, the term *cohort* means a particular group is being compared with another group that differs, presumably, only in chronological age, which refers only to when its group members were born.

This type of design is especially weak on causality because it does not permit prediction from one time or circumstance to a later time or circumstance for the same research subjects. The comparisons are restricted to different persons or groups and tell us nothing about whether the variables being studied are stable or in flux. Permit me first to take up the issue of causation.

Most readers have probably been confronted many times with television or other media examples of this problem. The correlation that is commonly obtained between exercise and health is highly touted in the health field but does not prove causality or its direction, even though it is constantly implied that exercise helps us live longer. Which direction does the causation go, from exercise to better health or from better health to exercise? It is possible that people who exercise might live longer because of the exercise, which is the interpretation usually given by researchers and the media. However, what is claimed is really only a presumption, based on weak evidence, because we want to believe it, and a growing industry depends on it. But it is equally plausible that people who are healthy are better able to engage in exercise and enjoy it. Or perhaps some other factor in their lives could account for the correlation.

Thus, the difference in longevity (which, incidentally, is very small) could easily be the result of lifestyle, biological factors, personality, upbringing, or cultural outlook, which have not been ruled out. The main virtue of exercise is to make it possible to be more effective and feel better because of improved muscle tone, balance, and flexibility rather than to live longer.

The direction of causality is a problem that seldom surfaces when media people talk about exercise and health, just as it is an almost unmentioned problem when psychologists consider age as a factor in emotions and their effect on health. Yet even when a proper qualification is made voluntarily by the researcher in a publication, the thrust of the discussion is still apt to imply an antecedent-consequent contingency—that is, causation.

As I was writing this material in mid-July 2002, a major public commotion arose that gained full media attention as a result of a remarkable decision by the National Institutes of Health to cancel a large study on hormone replacement therapy for women who had reached menopause. Preliminary findings apparently made it clear to the federal researchers that the two drugs used in the treatment, estrogen and progestin, created added risks that included invasive breast cancer, heart attacks, strokes, and blood clots, though the treatment did reduce hip fractures and colorectal cancer.

This news created major uncertainties for millions of women at this stage of life regarding whether they should continue the treatment or terminate it. They had to weigh the following information about risks. Of ten thousand women who might take the drugs for a year compared with the same number who did not, the drug takers would experience eight more cases of invasive breast cancer, seven more heart attacks, eight more strokes, and eighteen more blood clots. There would also be six fewer colorectal cancers and five fewer hip fractures.

Although at first glance these numbers sound almost trivial, from a public health standpoint this translates into almost twenty-five thousand cases of life-threatening or terminal illnesses for the six million women who are taking hormone replacement therapy. Some officials were quick to point out that the treatment, which is designed to be preventive, is for a normal, universal life change that is not an illness or major dysfunction in itself, although for some women the menopausal symptoms are highly troubling.

Most important for my general argument about the inadequacies of much research is how this decision came into being and why the health risks presented were not clear earlier, before use of hormone replacement therapy had become so widespread. What seems to have happened is that there was at first some theory and a few inadequate, small-scale studies. A body of opinion had emerged on skimpy evidence that made this procedure seem prematurely desirable from a health standpoint. As was pointed out in a series of articles in the *New York Times*, the practice of medicine got ahead of the science of medicine. Reasonable suppositions on which the preventive treatment was predicated were simply not proved by research, and these suppositions were then belied by the large federal study that was suddenly terminated.[14]

This is hardly the first time this kind of thing has happened as a result of the failure to do careful research before instituting major treatment programs. One terrible example is the drug diethylstilbestrol (DES), which was given to pregnant women to prevent miscarriages. It took many years to discover that the drug did not work; worse, many daughters of those who took the drug later developed vaginal cancer.

Arthroscopic surgery for osteoarthritis of the knee is another example. We recently learned that the procedure, which has been widespread, does no good, though it could have a placebo effect for those patients who are believers. I had that procedure, and it made my knee worse for a time. The surgeon was a highly respected physician who, I am confident, was as skilled as they come and sincere in recommending the treatment. But the scientific evidence of its efficacy, as is often the case in the practice of medicine—which is an art, not a science—was lacking. Again and again we see this kind of problem in which belief, wishful thinking, and inadequate research clues mislead almost everyone. The same applies to the roller-coaster recommendations about diet and other health dicta. The tendency to jump the gun on the basis of inadequate information exposes the health sciences and the field of medicine to a serious loss of credibility.

These examples regarding the use and, sometimes, misuse of data and probabilities applied to a collectivity of people rather than single individuals illustrate why I warned at the end of chapter 1 against applying such thinking to aging in individuals (you can refer back to that section for more examples of the flaws in this approach).

The generation gap is the source of the *cohort problem*, which is inherent in *cross-sectional research*. Differences and conflicts between generations arise from the outlooks their members have acquired by growing up in their own time. Most scholars believe that they have always existed. They are mentioned in the Bible and in classical Greek drama and are a major theme in Shakespeare's *Henry IV* and *King Lear*. They are also described in many social science treatises on adolescence, with its turbulence and rebellion.

Conflict between generations is also observed in other countries, such as Japan, a society with extremely strong, unified traditions that have lasted for centuries. Older people in Japan have traditionally been treated with great respect and deference, but many complain today about feeling useless, empty, lonely, and ignored by their children. The same situation has been observed in Western Europe.

Although social change means that each generation grows up in a world markedly different from the one from which it sprang, we must also recognize that some kinds of change are certainly needed, because our social world is far from perfect. Change does not always make our lives worse; it can lead to human betterment, or so we hope.

A generation gap also implies that parents will not know much about the inner experience of their children any more than children will know the inner experience of their parents. Exceptions to ignorance across generations might occur if the ways of thinking and feeling of one generation can be imagined by another generation. This depends on the human capacity for empathy and the existence of human experiences that are shared by everyone regardless of their social class. Even children brought up in the same family can be essentially like different generations if the two cohorts being compared were treated differently or have different genes. These children have actually grown up in different social environments from their siblings.

No generation is uniform in outlook within itself, and rebellion against older traditions is by no means universal. In survey studies of the generation gap among college students during the 1960s, much to the surprise of the researchers, more students than expected were conservative as opposed to radical. Even in the absence of social change, in which case no generation gap would exist, there can still be conflict between the generations because each has different needs and would probably still see some things differently.

When we examine what is said about the generation gap, it is important to understand that the perspective of the observer and researcher can make a big difference in the interpretation of what is observed. This connects with our theme of individual variation and the stakes a person has in whatever is taking place. Referring to the diverse findings of studies of social trends in the 1960s, Martin Grossack and Howard Gardner wrote this comment about perspective:

> Those European analysts who look at America through Teutonic or Gallic or Leninist lenses are likely to interpret a social event like a race riot quite differently from social scientists raised in the Middle West who are ministers' sons. One analyst may infer that violence is becoming rampant in America, another that the proletariat is asserting itself, another that Negroes no longer fear police brutality, another that blacks resent police brutality, a fifth that the Negroes' lot is improving, a sixth that it is desperate. And, in a curious sense, they may all be right for their analyses may apply to different segments of the rioters, or may be applicable at different times.[15]

Bob Knight and T. J. McCallum have written about the cohort problem in a way that is easy to understand from the standpoint of the generation gap. Here is a sample of what they say:

> Another dimension of our understanding of older adults from life span development is the ability to separate the effects of maturation from the effects of cohort membership. Much of social gerontology could be summarized as the discovery that many differences between the old and the young that society (and therefore, psychotherapists) has attributed to the aging process are due, in fact, to cohort effects. Cohort differences are explained by membership in a birth-year-defined group that is socialized into certain abilities, beliefs, attitudes, and personality dimensions . . . (e.g., in the United States, Baby Boomers are between the GI Generation and Generation X).[16]

The older groups in most of the relevant cross-sectional studies of age differences were born at a different time than the younger groups. These groups were selected to be similar in socioeconomic, educational, ethnic, and racial characteristics. Except for age, they could be a cross section of the actual population. Yet people who were born in the early part of the twentieth century tended to denigrate physical and emotional expressions of affection toward children, whereas the advice of later child psychologists and pediatricians about child rearing emphasized the desirability of open displays of affection.[17]

Attitudes about child rearing from era to era have oscillated between strict control and permissiveness. In my childhood, if I did not have a bowel movement on one day, it was castor oil for me. The oil made me sick to my stomach; sometimes it was mixed with orange juice, and I felt nauseated at the smell of orange juice for a long time afterward. My parents believed in strict discipline. All the magazines published expert testimony to the effect that one dare not lose the battle of control with one's children. By contrast, my children believe in warmth and acceptance, though I think there is discipline, too—another example of individual variation. Those who grow up in different periods develop different ways of thinking, feeling, and acting; this has nothing to do with how old they are but reflects what they have learned from their particular period in history.

We should digress momentarily to mention two remarkable books that have emerged from longitudinal and cross-sectional studies that were performed at the Institute of Human Development of the University of California at Berkeley. One is a classic study by Glen Elder showing that people who grew up during the Great Depression of the 1930s had very different outlooks in later life and dealt with problems differently than those who had grown up at other times. In effect, what Elder found was a cohort effect rather than an age effect. Yet there was also substantial stability in personality over these people's lifetimes.

Elder's work reveals that the effects of economic hardship on later life were, however, complex rather than uniform for the children of the Great

Depression. Relationships and emotional patterns in the home made as much difference as income in the subjects' outlook. The effects also differed for sons and daughters, with the sons often having a tougher time, perhaps because the Depression experience threatened their careers.

The experience of downward economic mobility of the women who became accustomed to the hardships of the Depression and World War II also differed from that of women growing up later. The Depression kids became accustomed to economic hardship and learned how to deal with it, whereas those who matured later did not know what they should do when hardship arrived. In the main, the group raised in the Depression wanted more material things than the post-Depression group, who claimed that their deprivation actually helped them abandon a heavily materialistic outlook.[18]

The second book, by John Clausen, looks back at three hundred children of the Great Depression who were born in the 1920s. The main thrust of his book, however, is the individual life experiences and outlooks of six such persons from childhood to old age, which are presented in rich detail. Many of the readers of our book on aging will have been born during this period. They should find the life stories, which will provoke many reminiscences of that era and what followed, fascinating reading.[19]

We who grew up during the Great Depression displayed very different outlooks in later life and dealt with problems differently than those who had grown up at other times. The differences are cohort effects and probably not a result of age. My wife and I (born in 1922), and perhaps most people our age, provide a good anecdotal illustration of this kind of generation difference. We still have considerable anxiety about money even in good times. The Depression was a terrible time for a large proportion of the population, and as children we were greatly influenced by what was happening even though we were too young to understand its full significance and all the ways in which we were affected.

What happened led us to expect that prosperity can suddenly give way to widespread poverty, making us forever wary about investing in the stock market (which to this day still seems to us like gambling). The experience now urges us to protect our children from similar economic disasters if we can. Our children, who grew up in the 1960s, show few of these concerns, having matured in a period of increasing and sustained prosperity. We have found that many others of our generation have very similar outlooks.

Some years ago my colleagues and I used a cross-sectional methodology to do some research on stress and coping as a function of chronological age.[20] It was a mistake I have always regretted, because it limited what we could say from the evidence we obtained. We studied two age-groups or cohorts, one 35 to 44 years of age, one 65 to 74. The younger cohort reported significantly more stress than the older group in the domains of finance, work, home maintenance, personal life, and family and friends. The findings made good sense. Those in the younger cohort were still in the workforce and had families to support. The older group reported more stress about environmental and social concerns, daily life maintenance tasks, and health. They had many more health problems, and some lacked the strength and energy to do what was needed to care for their daily needs.

Although it was tempting to treat age as a casual variable, it was not possible to have confidence that age accounted for the obtained differences rather than when the two cohorts were born and raised as different generations. Although cross-sectional research can sometimes give us valuable clues about possible age differences, it cannot prove that these differences have anything to do with chronological age. We said this in our conclusions. We had chosen a research design that could not make a strong case for causality by virtue of chronological age, which is what we suspected.

The same problem, incidentally, has been found with respect to the intellectual capabilities of different age-groups. In such studies, and there are many, older persons compared cross-sectionally with young ones show considerable intellectual deficit, especially in short-term memory and speed of reaction.[21]

Some intellectual declines are undoubtedly a result of age, but cross-sectional research tends to exaggerate them. If the researcher studies the same people as they progress in age from younger to older, the deficit in functioning turns out to be much more modest than that found in cross-sectional research. Other such differences in intellectual functioning are probably the result of the different attitudes and ways of thinking that are characteristic of younger and older cohorts, not just age itself. Another possibility is that the older cohort might include some persons with dementia, which would bring down the cohort's average.

The difficulty of inferring causation from a relationship between two variables is not the only serious problem with cross-sectional research. Two other very important ones include the *valence problem* and the *individual differences problem*, which could apply to any of the four basic research designs employed in aging studies and psychology in general.

The Valence Problem

We make three mistakes when a valence or affective tone is automatically attributed to an emotion—for example, when love is automatically considered a positive emotion and anger a negative one. The first is the failure to question the basis for attributing a positive or negative valence to a prior-named emotion. Usually the judgment is made without considering which of three distinctly different rationales is being used for a positive attribution. Emotions are regarded as positive (1) when they feel good, (2) when favorable life conditions have brought them into being, and (3) when they have a desirable social outcome. The same principle applies to an attribution of a negative valence, except that (1) the person would feel bad, not good, (2) the emotion would be based on unfavorable rather than favorable life conditions, or (3) the emotion has negative effects.

The second mistake is to combine a number of emotions on the basis of their positive or negative valence for the purpose of comparing them. If we do this, we overlook the advantages of studying discrete emotions. Each emotion conveys a distinctive personal implication or meaning for a given person's well-being. This also implies a different set of causes, subjective experience, and impulse to act. The information that could be provided by knowing we are dealing with anger as opposed to anxiety is lost in the combination. All we get, then, is a hodgepodge, an uninterpretable mixture.

The third mistake in combining emotions into two groups, positive and negative, is the most serious of all. If one thinks about it carefully, positive and negative emotions are not really consistent opposites. The crucial principle is that all emotions have the potential for being either one or the other, or both, on different occasions and even on the same occasion in different individuals. Love can be a source of misery as well as joy or ecstasy, and joy can be subordinated to what a success implies for the future. In other words, gaining an advanced degree, which is likely to be a source of joy, usually means that we shall shortly need to be looking for a job, which can be demanding or threatening.

Let us look searchingly at some examples of this paradox, which should convince you that to regard so-called positive and negative emotions as opposites is a distortion of reality. I touch briefly here on the emotions of hope, joy, pride, love, and anger in making the case for what I just said. All except anger are usually considered to have a positive valence. A comparable case could be made for any emotion not on these lists.

HOPE. Hope is always—oops, that dangerous word—a combination of (1) a wish and a belief that the desired outcome could occur and (2) anxiety that it won't. Consider the following two common scenarios of life, one from the domain of existential threat, the other from the domain of wishful thinking. The existential threat scenario is that, if you are awaiting the results of a biopsy for a suspicious lump, you are likely to hope that the lump is not malignant. However, you will also feel anxious because you cannot be sure about this before the results of careful medical testing are announced. The wishful thinking scenario is that, if you really want the job you applied for, you might believe your chances of getting it are favorable but also feel uneasy because you cannot be sure until the decision is announced.

It is, therefore, not sensible to classify hope as either positive or negative because it is usually both; I believe the qualifying word *always* might be justified in this case. One might suppose that optimism is quite a different case. If you are optimistic, you are said to have few or no doubts about the outcome, so anxiety about it should be absent or minimal. But this may be more of a linguistic than a real distinction; there might well be degrees of optimism, which make the standard either-or approach to measurement of this trait suspect.

JOY OR HAPPINESS. There is little agreement about the psychodynamics of this emotion. An acute emotion, in contrast to a mood or sentiment, is apt to be limited in duration. When we experience a triumph or attain what we want, most of us will experience joy, but we cannot live on it for long. The troublesome realities of life will sooner or later intrude, and often what we thought we wanted turns out to be disappointing.

For example, students who achieve an advanced degree must shortly go on to the next life step, which for many (perhaps most) people would be to get a job. They have little time to bask in their happy frame of mind. As another example, only in fantasy does getting married, which is often but not always joyous—it can be coupled with or dominated by anxiety—imply that we live happily ever after without plenty of intervening struggle and distress.

The joys of a marital relationship can be substantial, but along with them a host of negative conditions and responsibilities arrive, which can create stressful demands. For example, we may be dealing with someone who has different needs and goals or daily tempo, establishing a home, producing an adequate income, having children and caring for them. There can be disappointments, too, such as serious illness, infidelity, or waning sexual enthusiasm. The same used to be said about the honeymoon but is less frequently heard today in the light of the current cultural pattern in which intimacy and living together often start before marriage.

Here we might consider also the importance of the social context for emotions, in this case joy. This emotion in one person may be a provocation for envy, jealousy, or positive identification and modeling in another. Expressions of joy can also be defensive and appear to be Pollyannaish—that is, they may represent a person's attempt to avoid dealing with life's adversities.

PRIDE. Many societies, including our own, are ambivalent about pride. In Western countries it is most often treated as having a positive valence, yet we speak of overweening pride and warn that pride goes before a fall. Other persons may be wounded by a gaudy display of pride because they regard bragging as a put-down. Nevertheless, an experienced pride, which one feels justified about or employs defensively, may be pursued militantly. In Judeo-Christian religious thought, it is frequently considered to be one of the seven deadly sins.

LOVE. This is a positive emotion when shared by the person you love but a great misery when unrequited. In effect, to love is to be *vulnerable to loss*, which points up the impossibility of defining it as solely a positive emotion. To illustrate, love can become a source of threat as a result of the potential of dementia, death, separation, or merely disengagement. Threat is, in other words, an indispensable aspect of the emotion of love, though this is apt to remain in the background of one's thoughts. It could become foreground, however, when something happens to suggest that the threat might be real.

One of the sources of confusion about this emotion is the contrast between love as an emotion and as a sentiment, a distinction that is akin to state versus trait. We can acknowledge that two people have a loving relationship in general—that is, they share the sentiment of mutual love—but at varying times in the relationship there may be negatively toned emotions such as anger, anxiety, guilt, disappointment, envy, and jealousy. Feelings of love are usually in flux.

Depending on the stage of a relationship, when lovers are apart from each other, say, at work, they usually concentrate on all sorts of other things without experiencing the emotion of love, which at the moment is not attended to. In the early stage of a newfound love, however, the couple might have more trouble putting aside this feeling and focusing on other matters. As an emotion rather than a sentiment, love waxes and wanes, and in its place from time to time a host of other emotional states can intervene without necessarily undermining the overall sentiment. A sentiment may even remain quite stable through thick and thin, but it too can eventually change.

ANGER. This emotion is a special case because it is usually classified as having a negative valence when, actually, it is often experienced as positive. The negative classification is probably made because of its potentially destructive consequences for the quality of an intimate relationship or, alternatively, because of the belief that it can be directly damaging to health, depending perhaps on how it is managed.

Anger is experienced as having a positive tone or valence when we act resolutely and forcefully against someone or something by standing up for ourselves rather than shrinking away fearfully and helplessly. The sense of mastery derived from this could make us feel wonderful. Here, too, is an emotion that is capable of having either a positive or a negative valence, and often both. Even righteous anger, which often feels good, may make a person vulnerable to anxiety about its social consequences, or, if we are uncertain about its righteousness, it may violate one's own moral standards and could lead to guilt.

In a number of fields of psychology, grouping the emotions into positive and negative categories for comparison has until recently dominated research, as opposed to the treatment of emotions as discrete reaction patterns. From the standpoint of adaptation to the work environment, for example, what happens when a worker reacts with anger is quite different from other so-called negative emotions—for example, anxiety and guilt.

Anger commonly leads to attempts to undermine what a person considers the external cause of feeling demeaned, such as a faulty management or other workers who have gained more status and pay. Guilt involves accepting blame oneself and often leads to wanting to do better to expiate one's sins. Why lose the considerable information contained in the distinctiveness of each emotion? We can learn much more by studying each of a number of discrete emotions at work or in any other social context than by trying to classify them as positive or negative.

The Individual-Differences Problem

There are huge individual differences in just about everything that exists in nature, even the characteristics of the planets that rotate around the sun, how our bodies are shaped, the sizes of our organs, our mental capacity, the emotions we experience in similar circumstances, and how we cope with stress. Despite the ubiquity of individual differences, however, there is a widespread tendency for researchers to overstate cohort (group) differences but not give adequate attention to individual variations.

Differences between people are often regarded as a nuisance or viewed as getting in the way of the goal of achieving scientific generalizations. They must, nevertheless, be described fully if we are to have an adequate picture because they represent the great majority of people who do not fit into nice, neat categories that scholars create to achieve a rational way to view the world. Aging is a case in point because of the tremendous variation in the functioning of people at different chronological ages.

Even when they are statistically significant, the cohort differences obtained in most emotion research are ordinarily very modest in scope compared with individual differences. The heart of the issue is that most of the subjects being contrasted on some presumably antecedent—read causal—variable cannot be distinguished from one another statistically on the so-called emotional or health outcome variable because they fall within the overlap between the two cohorts.

Only a modest proportion of the research subjects at either extreme of the distribution—that is, those falling outside the overlap—can be truly said to belong to one or the other of the two cohorts being compared. In effect, despite the statistical evidence that an obtained difference probably exceeds chance, individual differences are far greater than the average difference between the cohorts.

I have chosen a study by James J. Gross, Laura L. Carstensen, Monisha Pasupathi, Jeanne Tsai, Carina Götestam Skorpen, and Angie Y. C. Hsu to serve as an example of the failure to take adequate account of individual differences. The study centers on an attempt to show that chronological age affects the emotional life. One reason for choosing it is that the cohort differences it found, though much less impressive than the individual differences, are still more robust than in many other comparable studies. Therefore, no one can legitimately challenge my conclusions by saying I chose a unique case that favors what I am trying to say.

These researchers performed a series of four separate studies, each evaluating a different emotion-related variable. A sample item for the variable of impulse strength is "I have strong emotions." For *positive emotional expressivity*, it is "When I'm happy, my feelings show." For *negative emotional expressivity*, it is "When I feel negative emotions, people can easily see exactly what I'm feeling." And for *emotional control*, a scale ranging from 1 (no control) to 10 (complete control) is presented to all research subjects in the form of the following question: "Overall, how much control would you say you have over your emotions?" Note that these emotion variables have to do with various criteria of emotionality rather than with discrete emotions.[22]

Figure 2.1 shows four sets of normal curves that reveal how the subjects' scores are distributed on each of the emotion-related variables for two cohorts distinguished by chronological age. One is an older sample ranging in age from fifty-eight to ninety-six. The other is a younger sample, aged nineteen to fifty-six. The curves for each variable are generated from the cohort means and standard deviations presented by the authors.[23]

Let us examine the overlap between the two age cohorts for each of the four variables in the figure. You will see on each graph two normal distributions superimposed on each other on the same abscissa (the horizontal axis). The *overlap* between the young and old cohorts is shown in the darkest center section of each graph. As indicated on the graphs, for *impulse strength* the overlap is 76 percent. For *positive expressivity* it is 72 percent. For *negative expressivity* it is 75 percent. For *control* it is 60 percent.

This overlap identifies all research subjects from both the old and the young cohorts who cannot be said to be reliably different on the basis of their age. In effect, these are the subjects from each age cohort whose difference from each other does not exceed chance probability. Therefore, statistically speaking, any score that falls within the overlap between the cohorts must be treated as though it was not significantly different—which means that the difference is merely a matter of chance or accident.

Notice that the overlap on all the emotion variables includes considerably more than half the research subjects. Roughly three-quarters of the subjects in each cohort fall within the overlap in three of the four emotion variables. In other words, most of the subjects, regardless of whether they are in the older or younger age cohorts, cannot be distinguished from each other on the variable of emotion being studied. Only a minority of the subjects

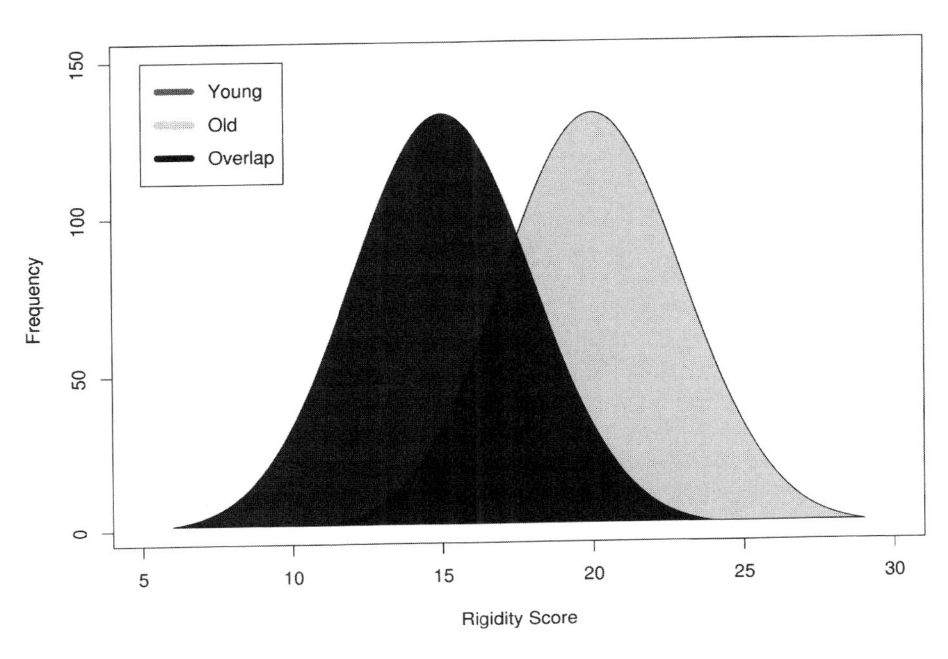

FIGURE 2.1
Overlap between old and young cohorts on four variables of emotionality. The means and standard deviations for each variable are as follows. For *impulse strength*, the mean of the young cohort was 4.85 with a standard deviation (SD) of 1.11; the mean for the older cohort was 4.45 with an SD of 1.13. For *positive expressivity*, the mean for the young cohort was 5.59 with an SD of 0.98; the mean for the older cohort was 5.21 with an SD of 0.93. For *negative expressivity*, the mean for the young cohort was 3.90 with an SD of 0.99; the mean for the older cohort was 3.52 with an SD of 1.01. For *control*, the mean for the younger cohort was 6.05 with an SD of 1.73; the mean for the older cohort was 7.07 with an SD of 1.92.

(roughly 25 to 40 percent) falls within the range of scores that differ from each other beyond chance probability.

All this can be summed up by saying that emotion, as it is measured in this research, is somewhat but not greatly affected by the subjects' age. Another way to say this, as noted earlier, is that individual differences *within* the two age cohorts are more impressive than the average differences *between* the age cohorts. Therefore, for most of the subjects, age cannot be said to be a factor in their emotional lives. My conclusion is that *too much is being made of too little*.

Following the tradition of journal research reports, the authors present an extensive analysis and set of conclusions about what their data show, which they refer to—much too sanguinely, I would say—as "age-related changes" in emotion, thereby implying causality. Given the cohort problem, the modest size of the obtained differences, and the superficial nature of the emotion measurement, to claim age-related changes is a presumption rather than a proven fact. Nor can such research be used *to describe the emotional life of most people at a given chronological age*, which is what we usually want to do with findings like these on aging.

What can we say about age as a causal variable from these data? First, we cannot say with any confidence whether chronological age is the cause of the group differences, despite the fact that two widely different age ranges were built into the study. Yet this is what the researchers wanted to be able to say. Second, we cannot make an accurate descriptive statement about the emotional lives of most old compared with young persons. So when all is said and done, the data are at best suggestive but inadequate.

I do not wish to fault anyone for accepting weaker methodological standards than most of us would desire. As I said, I have done the same myself, with later regret, and I have empathy for the problems of researchers. Nevertheless, the ubiquity of cross-sectional, interindividual research needs to be recognized. The interpretations drawn from such research can readily be misleading. Our field needs to find a way to resolve this problem. The best solution would be to use this kind of research design only as a pilot study to see whether something promising is going on and then to follow up with replication and longitudinal formats.

In the desire to be scientific, which in the eyes of most scientists calls for making broad, elegant generalizations from observations, those who do research stubbornly display a de facto denial of the importance of individual variation and the value of detailed description in science. No one has stated this dilemma of science as eloquently as has David Spiegel in a discussion of coping with cancer:

> Modern psychological science has been biased towards quantitative analysis of data . . . but also toward the goal of platonic simplicity. *We are often caught in the dilemma that our theories are either too elegant to be meaningful or too full of meaning to be elegant*. Coping is an important construct and yet it has become clear that it has a short life span—that we must ask the question "Coping by whom? At what moment, in response to what types of stress, and in what context?" Thus, researchers are beginning to address the common complaint of clinicians, that they fail to adequately take into account the existential reality of individuals in life-threatening situations.[24]

The Emotion Measurement Problem

The two previous problems, one having to do with emotion valence, the other involving cohort versus individual differences, come together squarely on the urgent need to measure emotions fully and accurately. In a sense, measurement is the bottom line of research on the emotions and any other psychological effect of aging, one that is, nonetheless, most commonly given short shrift by employing one-time-only, overly simple checklists and questionnaires without follow-up or with minimal exploration of their adequacy.

In a checklist or questionnaire, the research subjects are asked to list and perhaps rate any emotions they have experienced in a particular encounter or a given time period. But without more in-depth inquiry, it cannot be said confidently what actually happened and what emotions were actually experienced, even though there could readily be more than one. It is like survey research on political opinion, which offers at most a superficial look at attitudes about candidates and issues that are usually complex and cannot provide an adequately nuanced picture of that opinion; thus, what is learned can distort what people are really thinking.

In research on the emotions, there are often social pressures against telling what was actually felt, and not everyone questioned can be counted on to have adequate insight about what they have been feeling. The absence of careful, in-depth measurement also rules out the possibility of obtaining observations about the flow of events in an emotional encounter and the conditions generating the emotions, which must be known in order to pin down the phenomena being observed and to assess their relational meanings.

When considering the factors influencing health and well-being, the role of coping must also be examined, which means asking about what the person did to manage the situation. It is possible, for example, that the coping process contributes all or most of the variance concerning harmful or favorable consequences of any given emotion to bodily health and psychological well-being. The effects of coping, if any, could be mediated by indirect damage done to intimate relationships or by direct hormonal effects on bodily organs, or both.

Which one of these is responsible in any given instance—it may very well be both—and how this works cry out to be addressed by competent research. There is no doubt in my mind that, if we measure emotions or any other property of aging poorly, efforts to answer the important questions will be inadequate or, worse, misleading.

To identify how a correlation between emotion, health, and well-being really works, a distinction must be drawn between a *fluctuating state* and a *stable personality trait*. It is difficult for me to see, for example, how an occasional moment of gratitude or joy could benefit the person importantly in long-term health. The benefit or harm of an emotion, whatever it might be, would presumably apply for only as long or as frequently as a person might feel this way, with the rare exception of an acute stroke or heart attack in an emotional crisis.

I believe we must assume instead that to influence long-term health (in contrast, for example, with acute, short-term infections), there would have to be a general emotional or coping trait. However, this cannot be found by using cross-sectional research design. Only longitudinal studies in which the same persons are compared with themselves over time or circumstances can show whether any given person consistently draws on specific emotions or coping processes.

What I have just said about trait versus state should apply especially to ailments that are slow to develop, such as cancer and heart disease, rather than short-term health outcomes. The case is strong for the thesis that short-term stress can impair immune system functioning and increase the likelihood of infections. To evaluate the trait principle, one could look at, say, happy and depressed or optimistic and pessimistic people, though I am convinced that concepts such as these are far more complex and difficult to assess than has previously been presumed.

To establish the actual mechanism, that is, whether it is a state, trait, or both, one must make very careful measurements of the same research subjects' emotions repeatedly over time and across different conditions. The measures must reflect accurately what the subject is actually feeling under each condition and during each period. Provision should also be made for multiple emotions, which could have either a positive or a negative valence, or both.

How We Got into This Mess

More than a century ago, most scholars and researchers—for example, Darwin—were independently wealthy and did not make a living from research. They pursued their research on their own, sometimes obtaining funding help from special-interest groups. Today probably all scientists do this work as a job, a career from which they make a living, often as university teachers.

The time pressures on scholars have grown alarmingly with this change. There is a severe lack of time to do what a research scholar must do: read, evaluate, plan, and, above all, think. What follows here is probably a reasonable but incomplete list of the most important of these pressures.

At the *graduate level of teaching*, which includes preparing seminars or lectures, giving oral examinations, and making graduate student evaluations, the faculty member is expected to meet often with the students, with whom they work closely in order to supervise their work as apprentices and help with their academic problems. A faculty member is a highly specialized teacher, but the growing competence of the students may soon make them the teacher's colleagues who collaborate with him or her on research. Writing letters of recommendation is another substantial responsibility.

At the *undergraduate level of teaching*, there is the almost constant need to prepare lectures and to keep office hours, which are never enough for the large classes that are endemic these days. At many institutions, work with individual undergraduates is encouraged. I have published considerable research with undergraduates to our mutual advantage. Visits from ex-students are more than welcome, and we usually want to keep track of how they are doing.

At the *departmental level of administration*, committees proliferate, some of which call for extensive efforts to prepare dossiers and recommendations for the hiring and promotion of faculty and meetings to make decisions on departmental policies. There are also committees at the *university level of administration*. Some of these are quite time-consuming and demanding, such as those assigned the task of evaluating a troubled department, those that hold regular meetings on faculty governance, and so on.

At the *field level*, say, psychology or physiology, faculty members must deal with obligations to their discipline. Committee work often involves travel. Active faculty members are expected to help with decisions about journals, reviewing grant applications, awards, and policies. With respect to journals, if faculty members have gained national or international visibility, they are likely to be asked often to review the grant applications of other researchers and papers submitted for publication. These committees can often be interesting and advantageous to participate in, because these faculty members feel more deeply embedded in their field, gain influence, and become better known to their colleagues, but they still take up a tremendous amount of time.

Thus far I have said nothing about *scholars' own research*. To be competitive, academics need funds from some private or governmental agency to finance their research. An application for such funds is a lengthy and complex document that is designed to demonstrate the applicant's competence and describe the research. It is not uncommon to spend a few years revising applications again and again on the basis of peer criticisms. Participating in these committees themselves is a faculty member's obligation and can be an arduous process. It can also be helpful in facilitating one's own efforts to obtain funding.

All these activities increase the scholar's visibility and reputation, but they take up much time. They help to build a dossier (referred to in academia as a vitae, which consists of the details of a life's work) that presents the scholar as a knowledgeable and responsible member of his or her discipline. More than any other criterion of academic success, salary increases and promotions are commonly based on how a scholar has performed the obligation to attain new knowledge. This is the coin of the realm of competitive academic life.

Given this heavy load, career efficiency depends on a type of research in which data can be collected, written up, and published rapidly. Faculty members serving on a promotion committee appointed to review the work of another member face the same pressures. The incentive is strong for skimming articles as rapidly as possible rather than examining them in depth.

If a faculty member who is up for promotion has a solid reputation and publishes substantially, it is less likely that a committee member will nitpick about what the candidate has accomplished, though field or other prejudices and the competitive context might tilt the decision toward a negative or positive decision. The same applies to the conflict of interest that applies to the outside reviewers of a researcher's work on a governmental review committee. By and large, I believe most reviewers are conscientious and ethical in their approach to the task, but backstabbing is hardly rare. In a zero-sum game, it is easy to develop the outlook that anything that helps another harms oneself.

Given the institutional arrangements for research, a faculty member cannot afford to spend years prior to publishing on polishing his or her measures of the phenomena of concern. Even the granting agencies will not pay for a long-term investment in preparatory research and data collection. I have often been unable to analyze useful data because the money to do so was not available. As a result, the data ultimately had to be shelved and never saw the light of day.

It seems unfair to blame researchers for a defective institutional arrangement that is not easily changed. The current incentive system has evolved over many years. Occasionally, one hears about a proposal for change, but nothing ever seems to be done. Longitudinal research, which I have presented as the main alternative to cross-sectional strategies, is expensive and often extends over a long period, sometimes the best part of a professional life. The data collection must be carefully done and can be time-consuming. There can be a mountain of data to analyze and write up when the study is all but finished.

However, longitudinal research also has a host of difficult-to-surmount problems. For example, the common outlook about the proper way to measure the variables and what are considered to be appropriate questions to investigate may change within five or ten years from when researchers begin a longitudinal study. The fashions that dictate what seem like fruitful research problems change rapidly. All in all, there are powerful factors pushing the researcher to do something quick and dirty and to publish frequently. Perhaps no one will notice that few, if any, findings have been replicated. Besides, journals do not relish publishing replications; they are old hat.

A Few Conclusions

What should the reader take away from my account of the methodological inadequacies of some of the most popular and widely used methods in the study of aging and, even more, the entire health care industry? Be wary about accepting what newscasters present as the latest piece of research-generated wisdom. Ask yourself whether causation has been proved, how representative the population is that the conclusions apply to, whether there has been replication of the findings, whether the measurement has been adequate for what is being said, and so forth. If you must make a decision that concerns your well-being, consult if you can with someone who knows something, such as a physician who knows your individual history and characteristics. Just because the information is presented as newsworthy, don't assume anything about its validity.

Remember that in most cases, the effects reported are small, and the media does not give much information about this. The published report might be better, but even here the researchers are looking for publicity for their work to get it spread over the news. They, too, have an ax to grind.

Consider whether the research design is longitudinal or cross-sectional and to what extent the experiment being reported has been well controlled. Is the case for cause and effect sound? Listen to dissenting voices before making up your mind. Has there been a replication? If not, don't jump to any conclusions.

If the public views the outpouring of hasty research and conclusions with skepticism, researchers will quickly get the point that what they are doing lacks credibility. It is like the constant warnings that we get about this or that danger, which, when what is forecast does not materialize, leads us to stop paying attention. Without replication of some sort, most such studies end up in the dust heap of time, flooding the field with findings that make little difference in our understanding, especially when individual variation has been underemphasized.

Finally, those interested should follow the wise old dictum that was around even before the recent corporate scandals and market disasters—namely, caveat emptor, let the buyer beware. It always applies when everyone is trying to sell us a bill of goods, whether deceptively or even sincerely.

3

Coping

In addition to chronic and recurrent problems of living, loss and threat of loss are major sources of stress in the lives of aging persons.[1] And when a major loss appears imminent, it can be a difficult time for that person and others close to him or her. It is not just the amount of stress itself that is important, however, but how one copes with it. Effective coping allows people to keep stress levels moderate and to live with stress without significant psychic and physiological damage.

Because coping is so central to human adaptation and well-being, it receives a great deal of attention throughout this book. It is coping to which we refer even though that term is not actually always employed; it is implied when we speak of managing stress or just dealing with the problems of living. Nowadays, *coping* has become a very familiar word, yet it is not familiar enough for most readers without special training to grasp what it is really about, what we know and do not know. In this chapter, our intention is to provide a portrait of the coping process, just as was done for the emotions in chapter 2. Then the coping process can be applied to aging, as in much of this book.

If we wish to improve the lot of the elderly, one of our most important research priorities must be to study which coping processes work effectively and which do not. This is the tough question. Researchers are not even sure whether people can be readily taught more coping strategies or how best to do so. To do this, we must understand coping effectiveness. We are modestly optimistic that this can be done once we have learned which strategies do and do not work under diverse conditions of life.

A Brief History of Coping

The origin of the English word *cope* goes back to the fifteenth and sixteenth centuries, when it meant a coup, a blow, or the shock of combat. Other definitions mentioned in the *Oxford English Dictionary* include striking, coming to blows with, encountering, joining in battle, and contending with someone in a well-matched fight. It is easy to see why the word, which once had mainly combative connotations, was later adopted by psychologists to refer to the struggle to overcome, defeat, or manage the stresses of living and adapting. The concept first began to be used psychologically in this way in the 1960s and 1970s.

Modern interest in coping began with Freudian ideas about the ways people defend their psychological integrity. Seen from the point of view of the Freudian system, the main threats are said to be primitive biological impulses, such as sex and aggression, which, when made public, are considered unacceptable in many societies. Freud shocked the literate world by suggesting that young children had sexual urges based on the pleasure derived from stroking erogenous (sexually sensitive) zones of their bodies. (This is not, of course, adult sex but an immature yet fundamental aspect of all sexuality.) Middle-class parents especially react negatively to the manifestation of these impulses, forcing the child to learn self-protective devices, which psychoanalysts refer to as *ego defenses*. The ego is said to be the governing agency of the mind. It controls the child's unwelcome impulses, protecting it against potentially punitive social sanctions. The emotion of anxiety is conceived of as a signal to the ego to inhibit socially proscribed actions. In short, the child learns to think before it acts and, therefore, to avoid the threat of disapproval or punishment. Hereafter, we shorten the term *ego defense* to just *defense*.

Many kinds of defense are possible. For instance, *denial* is the disavowal of a desire and the danger it implies—as in "I am not angry." Sigmund Freud's daughter, Anna Freud, pointed out later that denial could arise from external demands as well as internal impulses, and this expanded view became a standard part of psychoanalytic doctrine, as in the statement "I am not seriously ill."[2] *Intellectualization* refers to attempts to gain emotional distance from ideas that are threatening. *Projection* occurs when someone else is accused of having a socially proscribed impulse that one is unwilling to acknowledge in oneself. *Repression* is sometimes said to be the master defense underlying all others, but Freud seems to have regarded it as just one of many types of defensive strategies. It keeps the desire and the danger it presents out of consciousness. As Matthew H. Erdelyi notes, this idea has its origins a half century earlier in the writings of Johann Herbart (1824–25). Erdelyi adopts the provocative position that what is conscious or unconscious is a relative matter. Proscribed desires and thoughts about them slip back and forth between consciousness and unconsciousness, just as our attention is directed at one thing at one moment and something else at another.[3]

Although considerable ambiguity and controversy exist about exactly how defenses work, they are usually regarded as ways of fooling everyone, especially oneself, about one's state of mind. This reduces the anxiety of being aware of these impulses but distorts the person's perception of reality, which can then lead to dysfunction or psychopathology.[4]

The concept of defense helps us understand psychological dysfunction, often referred to as *mental illness*. We would quarrel, however, with the implication of the word *illness* that the problem is necessarily the result of a biochemical neural pathology that only medicine can address. We join those who prefer to view most psychological dysfunction as an unresolved problem of living, a coping failure that calls for a more effective strategy.

In any case, each main type of dysfunction—for example, what used to be referred to as *neuroses* (e.g., obsessions, compulsions, and depression) and *psychoses* (more severe pathologies such as schizophrenia)—is understood in psychoanalytic thought as arising from a different defense. This has been a mainstay of psychoanalytic clinical work ever since Freud.

A problem with this psychoanalytic emphasis is that a defense is only one method of coping with stress, though certainly an important one. It overlooks the many other things we think and do to cope with stresses in managing our everyday lives. Coping processes include the defenses but are much more than that—for example, they depend on appraisals, which are often quite realistic and guide practical decisions about what to do about the stresses we have to contend with in our lives. Appraising, discussed in connection with the emotions in chapter 2, is also a key to the choice of coping strategies. In any case, psychology has gradually adopted the view that defenses are best regarded as a *subtype of coping*, the latter concept being more inclusive.

To illustrate the way psychodynamically oriented clinicians might analyze what is happening in an emotional transaction, consider the following clinical fragment. A young man says to his father with poignancy, a bit of humor, and a shrug of his shoulders, "Pop, in spite of your best efforts, this is how I turned out." The young man seems to be excusing himself to his father in an endearing fashion. He seems to want to relieve his father of having to accept the blame for his son's inadequacies. He is also seeking to ingratiate himself with his father in order to make friends with him at long last.

The father might have been taken aback by suddenly having to recognize that he had been too hard on his son, and this might well have been an outcome for which the son hoped. In all likelihood, the young man did not truly believe he had turned out as badly as his father seemed to think, which is suggested by the brevity and lightheartedness of what he said. Although his statement seems quite humble, he was also making an effort to preserve his self-esteem by not denigrating himself too much.

We do not know for sure what was actually going on in the son's mind. If he was aware of what he was doing, his statement would not constitute a defense in the psychoanalytic sense but was probably a deliberately planned strategy of coping that was applied to his troubled relationship with his father. But this illustration points up the subtlety and complexity of some strategies of coping.

Bear in mind that any action, such as what the young man said to his father, can serve more than one function. In this case, we think it had at least three—namely, mollifying the father, communicating the son's need for acceptance, and protecting his self-esteem. When people examine coping with care and in depth, they need to look below the surface at the multiple functions, goals, and situational intentions of the action, whether or not the person is aware of them.

Interest in coping began to burgeon in the 1970s. When the book *Coping and Adaptation*, edited by George Coelho, David Hamburg, and John E. Adams, was published in 1974, it was the first time a number of visible psychological thinkers with diverse perspectives on adaptation had argued in favor of the usefulness of the coping concept.[5] A spate of more recent books attests to the growing interest in this subject.[6] In one, an ambitious manual on coping published in 1996, C. S. Carver pointed out, "The vast majority of the work done in this area has occurred within the past two decades." In the same book, P. T. Costa, M. R. Somerfield, and R. R. McCrae managed to locate 113 articles on coping from 1974, 183 from 1980, and 639 from 1984, which illustrates the rapid growth of interest.[7] It is clear why our knowledge about this very important topic is still limited; having begun only recently, the field of coping research and theory is still very young.

Coping as a Personality Trait and a Process

Let us get some terms straight. All of science tries to understand the phenomena of life and the world in terms of two basic ideas—namely, structure and process. Everything that exists is made up of structures and processes. *Structure* is the relatively stable arrangement of the parts of things. In an automobile engine, for example, this arrangement makes it possible for a car to run. *Process* refers to the way the car runs, which implies motion and change—for example, the movement of the wheels and the wearing out of parts. Structure and process reflect two different ways of thinking about coping, that is, as a stable trait or a flexible state, each of which deals with its causes differently.

When coping is treated as a *personality trait*, the analysis is structural. It locates the causes of coping within the person—that is, as preferred strategies and styles of relating to events, which, in turn, are based on what a person desires and believes about the self and the world. In effect, the way people cope is determined by the kind of persons they are.

As a trait, the emphasis is on *stability*. People are shown to be consistent in what they do to cope over time and under diverse conditions. A coping trait is a structure that is analogous to an automobile engine, but we cannot view it directly as we can an engine because it resides in a relatively private mind. So we create or imagine the psychological structure in our theory of the mind in order to make sense of what is observed about people. For example, Amy prefers to *avoid* paying attention to threat, whereas David likes to be *vigilant*. Vigilant people try to do everything possible to control the conditions of their lives so as not to be surprised by something dangerous or harmful.

When coping is regarded as a *flexible state*, the emphasis is on *change*. The causes of coping are said to lie in the person-environment relationship, which are always changing. For example, in the early stages of an encounter, Sally tends to be cautious, but later on she is apt to be impulsive. When Sally is fearful, she avoids thinking about the source of her fear, but when she is angered, she broods about it. In effect, what she does to cope—that is, avoiding ideas or images or brooding about what is troubling her—changes over time and with different conditions of life. If we view coping this way, we are treating it as a changeable state or process rather than a stable trait or structure.

Both ways of thinking—that is, as a structure (trait) or a process (state)—are valid and useful, representing two sides of the same coin. When coping is highly stable, there is less room for change; when coping changes greatly, there is less room for stability. To discover to what extent coping thoughts, actions, and strategies change or remain stable, we need to observe the same persons over time and under different life conditions.

Any particular coping thought or action may or may not be successful. In a sense, therefore, coping must be defined as a tentative effort to deal with stress rather than what will necessarily work well. If the effort fails, we usually try something else. That is why we do not use the word *mastery* to define effective coping. Not all problems in life can be mastered, but they can usually be *managed*, which may mean that we can learn to accept and live with an existing troubling situation.

People often examine and reexamine the outcome of a coping effort, hoping that they have soundly evaluated what must be done. (Psychologists call this *rumination*.) We look for flaws in our judgment or in the way we have acted, all the while trying to reassure ourselves that everything is under control or, alternatively, that we must keep seeking a more viable coping strategy. Coping, in effect, is best defined, as said earlier, as a flexible effort to manage stress, a position that favors a process viewpoint.

Two Ways of Coping

Two main classes of coping strategies are solving problems and regulating the emotions that these problems bring about. We refer to these, respectively, as *problem-focused coping* and *emotion-focused coping*. These are not the only types of coping strategies. Others, for example, are maintaining favorable morale under stress, sustaining or restoring positive self-regard, and taking a break from chronic or recurrent demands that are stressful in order to restore our commitment. However, we regard the problem- and emotion-focused functions as the most important, so we stick to them in subsequent discussions and illustrations.

In *problem-focused coping*, a person's attention centers on what can be done to change the situation to eliminate or lessen the stress. For example, when a tree in the next yard sheds its leaves on our lawn every fall, we may cope with this repeated annoyance by speaking to the person who is the source of the trouble. We hope to get the neighbor to trim the branches of his or her tree, which overlap the fence separating the two backyards. This could risk an angry confrontation that might complicate the relationship or turn it sour. If the effort fails—perhaps we come on too strong or in an accusatory fashion, or the neighbor turns out to be uncooperative—we might try again with a softer line.

In *emotion-focused coping*, no effort is made to change the situation, perhaps because we sense it is unlikely to succeed. The emphasis shifts to dealing with our emotional distress, which is recurrent anger whenever the leaves start to drop. Perhaps we have concealed our anger to avoid further unpleasantness, but it remains an irritant in our life every fall when we anticipate the situation will recur.

A more effective solution might be to convince ourselves that the problem is not worth bothering about. We can *reappraise* the situation in a way that reduces or eliminates our distress. Nothing has changed in the external situation. The tree still discharges its leaves on our lawn every fall. However, we now view the situation differently as a result of the reappraisal. It is no longer a big deal. The reappraisal has allowed us to view the situation with less distress. There is no longer any need to feel upset about the tree because we realize it is not very important. We can now live with what we had once considered an intolerable situation.

Assuming this effort at a benign reappraisal is not just a defensive denial and that we are truly comfortable rather than conflicted about the situation, it could be said that we have found a rational and emotionally helpful solution. It is even possible that this newly found relaxed outlook will lead the neighbor to do voluntarily what he or she would not do under duress—that is, cut down the offending tree limbs. Then we would have attained the best of all possible worlds. If not, it should not matter too much.

Notice that the two types of coping, problem-focused and emotion-focused, have different targets of action. One is the offending situation; the other is our emotional state. However, they are normally combined in most stressful encounters, with each supporting the other. For example, we need to feel confident about our ability to gain an advanced educational degree to justify the effort and the required sacrifice. So we psych ourselves up in order to be convinced we have the intellectual resources, drive, and self-discipline to succeed, which is the emotion-focused function. This conviction helps us mobilize the necessary coping actions, which fall within the problem-focused function, and our chances of succeeding are greatly improved. We have, in effect, combined emotion-focused coping (developing self-confidence) with problem-focused coping (going to school).

Most difficult stressful situations depend on both functions, regulating feelings and trying to change the stressful conditions that are about to be faced. The two functions are seldom separated, nor do they compete with each other with respect to their respective usefulness. Some individuals and cultures value efforts to change the environment more than accommodating to it or accepting things as they are. Other individuals and cultures reverse these respective values, favoring accommodation and harmony more than the active struggle to change things.

The following additional coping scenarios illustrate the interdependence of the two coping functions. In the first, we learn we have an illness and must decide what to do about it. Our initial efforts to cope may involve seeking information or professional advice about what to do (problem-focused coping). We also tell ourselves, perhaps a bit defensively, that there is nothing to worry about (emotion-focused coping by denial).

In the second coping scenario, we are offended by someone and react with anger. Whether the anger is expressed or not depends on how we appraise what is happening. Maybe the other person is powerful and threatening, and we do not consider it prudent to display anger. Its target, the regulation of distressing emotions, makes this seem to be emotion-focused coping. But we are also trying to change the actual relationship, so it could be problem-focused coping, too. Therefore, the effort to disguise how we truly feel is a bit ambiguous with respect to which coping strategy is operating. We could reasonably say it is both.

We may without thinking, however, reveal our anger, and if we do, we have to engage in damage control lest the relationship, which is important to us, be seriously disrupted. We tell ourselves we are wrong, which seems like emotion-focused coping. An apology or gift-giving gesture might help, which is an effort to change the way things are, and so it is also problem-focused coping. Here, too, we are drawing on both strategies.

In the third coping scenario, a loved one offends us. If we can get ourselves to see that it was not done maliciously but as a reaction to major personal stress, the anger that might be expected may not be aroused. To create a self-generated *reappraisal*, we look for and find an acceptable way to excuse the other person for the offensive words. One could say to oneself, for example, "She's not feeling well today," or "He's been worried about his business."

If our reappraisal is realistic rather than merely brittle (hence broken or an easily overthrown denial of reality), emotion-focused coping can be a very powerful process for changing or at least controlling negatively toned emotions such as anger, anxiety, guilt, shame, envy, and jealousy. Some people are more able to do this than others; they are more easygoing or are more highly motivated because of interpersonal needs of their own.

Other Important Strategies

Let us examine three other reappraisal ways of coping that further illustrate different intentions in our minds when we cope. They all convey implications for our health. They are denial and vigilance, with which denial is always compared; seeking emotional support from others; and religion as coping.

Denial versus Vigilance

As mentioned earlier, denial is disavowing reality. It was once thought to be a cause or a form of pathology. Now, however, we know better. When we engage in denial, we are defending against a proscribed desire or a painful reality. *Vigilance*, in contrast, is an attempt to confront harm or threat in order to maintain control over what is happening.

Research on these opposing ways of coping provides striking evidence that any given coping strategy can have different outcomes depending on when it is used and the conditions under which it occurs. Sometimes denial is harmful to our well-being, and sometimes it is beneficial. Similarly, vigilance is sometimes harmful and at other times beneficial. The trick is to know when it will be one or the other and why. Let us consider how this works in the context of illness.

Denial has been found to have different consequences during three stages of a heart attack. In the first stage, in which symptoms are first becoming apparent, the heart attack victim may become aware of a dull pain and heaviness in the chest, with the pain extending down the left arm. These are among the classic signs of a heart attack, but frequently there is ambiguity about whether a heart attack is occurring. Other causes of these symptoms, such as indigestion, can create similar discomforts when there is no actual heart attack.

At this juncture, the person must decide whether to seek medical help, wait until the situation becomes clearer, or reject help on the ground that he or she is experiencing not a heart attack but something else that mimics its symptoms. Because this is a dangerous time for a real heart attack, deciding not to seek help must involve some denial.

People in this situation, especially men with a macho outlook, have not infrequently been known to delay seeking medical help for many hours (more than twenty-four), thereby placing themselves at great risk of dying during this uncertain but dangerous period. They do this because of the ambiguity of the symptoms and, to some extent, in an effort to deny the danger. Believe it or not, some of them run up and down flights of stairs or do vigorous push-ups or knee dips. Given the danger, these actions seem crazy, but these people think that if they survive these exertions, they cannot be having a heart attack. They are, in effect, trying to prove to themselves that they are safe.

Some survive these risky experiments—if they had not, they would not be around to tell anyone about their bizarre actions. Others do not survive, but their lives might have been saved by prompt medical attention. Here we see that denial in the first stage of a heart attack is extremely dangerous, often a deadly way of coping with the threat. But vigilance, such as calling an ambulance at the first sign of trouble, might save lives.

During the second stage, while the patient is recuperating in the hospital, it becomes important therapeutically to resume physical activity and engage in a modest amount of exercise. Many heart attack victims experience what is often referred to as a *cardiac neurosis*, in which they are afraid to do anything even slightly strenuous lest it provoke another attack. But to resist exercise impairs the chances of recovery. In this stage, denial of danger could be beneficial, but vigilance about warding off the danger, which is apt to be greatly exaggerated, is counterproductive.

The third stage occurs when patients return home. They are normally obliged to resume typical pre–heart attack activities, such as work, sex, exercise, and maintaining social relationships. At this time, denial of vulnerability can once again put them at risk of having another heart attack by permitting them to take on too much. If they are not to have another attack, they must not return to the same regimen that had originally led to cardiovascular disease. Post–heart attack patients should reduce stress by moderating high-risk activities and lowering the amount of cholesterol-producing foods in their diets. Denial once again becomes an enemy and vigilance a friend.

As a summary of what has been said thus far about denial and vigilance, one can see from this illustration that any given coping process, in this case denial or vigilance, can be harmful during one stage of a heart attack but beneficial during another.[8] If we turn to other medical contexts, such as hospital surgery or different illnesses, such as sciatica or asthma, there are again solid grounds for the principle that both denial and vigilance can be beneficial in some illness situations but harmful in others. Let us first look at hospital surgery.

Frances Cohen and I interviewed surgical patients the evening before three kinds of minor surgery: gall bladder, thyroid gland, and hernia. On the basis of the interviews, some patients were judged to be coping with the threat of surgery by avoidance or denial, whereas others were said to be coping by vigilance.[9]

These coping styles were characterized by the researchers as follows: Those who *avoided or denied* the threat of surgery did not seek any information about their illness and what would happen during surgery. When such information was offered, they would wave it off. This was the basis for inferring that they did not want to hear anything about their illness or its surgical treatment. These patients also spoke as if they believed their surgeons were the most skillful doctors in the world. Sometimes they even claimed this when the surgeon's professional reputation left much to be desired, a conviction expressed by glowing verbal affirmations such as "My doctor knows what he is doing and will take good care of me. I'm in good hands."

In contrast, patients who were coping *vigilantly* already knew quite a bit about their disorder and kept seeking additional information about what was to happen, whether it was offered or not. They were keen to read even complex medical treatises about their disease and its treatment when these were offered. They were wary about what was happening and knew, for example, that surgeons sometimes operate on the wrong organ. They wanted to anticipate any danger and exercise as much control over their fate as possible. Most people, of course, are between these two extremes, sometimes coping by avoiding or denying and sometimes by being vigilant.

Cohen and I found that patients who engaged in avoidance or denial complained of fewer complications as they recovered and were sent home sooner than those who coped vigilantly. The explanation given by these researchers was that those who avoided or denied any concern with the outcome appeared to the surgeons and attending nurses to be more at ease than those who were vigilant. Therefore, they seemed to be in better shape than the vigilant patients and ready to be discharged from the hospital.

The vigilant patients, in contrast, appeared to be more anxious and complaining than those who avoided or denied. This probably led the surgeon and attending nurses to believe they were not yet ready to go home. One needs to realize that vigilance is just about useless in most hospital settings.

Hospitals are generally highly regimented, which means there is little that being vigilant can do to improve one's condition, especially because recovery from minor surgery is routine.

The preceding explanations of the difference in outcomes between denial and vigilance emphasize the way hospital personnel viewed the social behavior of the patient. But there are also now solid empirical grounds for believing that denial promotes *rapid healing* of wounded tissues, which provides a psychophysiological explanation for these findings. We shall say more about this later when we discuss stress, coping, and bodily health. Regardless of the way postsurgical recovery works, however, we can conclude that as people recover from minor surgery, denial is more useful than vigilance. Many years after my research with Cohen was published, another major study along similar lines had very similar findings.[10]

Readers may have noticed that we have constantly used the expression "avoidance *or* denial" rather than just "denial." These two psychological processes, though different, are difficult to distinguish clinically. Often observers interpret avoidance as denial, but a person can avoid looking at, thinking about, or speaking about something without denying it. A true denial is a disavowal of the reality, whereas avoidance is simply not paying attention to certain facts even if they are fully understood and accepted. In the Cohen and Lazarus study described earlier, the assessment of denial was made with care in light of this distinction, as the researchers wanted to avoid falling into this potential trap. Whether or not they succeeded can no longer be judged because of the absence of the interview data, which were not preserved.

With a different medical problem, acute sciatica from a herniated or slipped spinal disk that can produce acute radiating pain to the hip, leg, and foot, the way denial and vigilance works should be comparable to the hospital surgical situation. There is really little that can be done to relieve the pain associated with this condition except to learn how to avoid body movements that aggravate it and to take pain medication. If one waits for a time, perhaps after some days of bed rest, the pain will almost surely ease and eventually disappear. The alternative to bed rest or waiting is vigilantly to seek either an orthopedic or a neurological surgeon, who is likely to recommend surgery. Current evidence suggests that surgery may not be any better for this condition than inaction.

With a strong belief that there is nothing to worry about, however, perhaps supported by denial, the acute pain is likely to get better. This approach would prevent the more risky and probably unnecessary procedure of surgery. What was said here is reasonable, though the authors cannot cite empirical evidence in the case of sciatica. In all likelihood, however, denial should have the advantage over vigilance.

In the disease asthma, however, there is solid evidence that avoidance or denial is harmful and that vigilance is beneficial. Other researchers compared asthmatics who preferred to cope by vigilance with those preferring avoidance or denial. They found that vigilant asthmatics usually take medications at the first sign of symptoms, which usually aborts the oncoming attack. However, asthmatics who avoided or denied the evidence that they were showing early signs of such an attack, and therefore failed to do anything about it, had to be hospitalized far more often for an asthmatic crisis than those who were vigilant.[11]

In recent years, Cohen and her colleagues have followed up the earlier research on avoidance or denial and vigilance, this time in early adolescent children. They looked further at the roles the age of the child, the stage or timing of events, and the type of surgery play in the outcome. Although this research is not directly related to aging, it in no way invalidates the conclusions we have drawn here, but it adds a few variables that complicate the story a bit.

One study, for example, showed that the age of the child and parental behavior made a difference in coping. The older children (close to thirteen) were more vigilant, presumably because their cognitive skills were more developed and they could use information more effectively, which gave them a better sense of control over the situation. Younger children (close to age eleven), in contrast, depended more heavily on avoidance or denial to help them feel less threatened. In addition, parents communicated their own anxiety to the children, increasing their preoperative anxiety.[12] This could also apply to aging persons, who could differ in cognitive sophistication.

With respect to type of surgery, these researchers also compared coping with *minor surgery* (e.g., tonsillectomy) and *major surgery* (e.g., orthopedic repair of scoliosis, a lateral curvature of the spine) in children of similar ages. This study found that the children were more likely to use vigilant modes of coping for minor surgery, whereas avoidance or denial were more common in major surgery.[13]

How might this be understood? In all likelihood, minor surgery, in comparison with major surgery, was a source of less worry, involved fewer physical and psychological demands, and shortened the time the children stayed in the hospital, allowing them to appraise the situation as one they could handle. Minor surgery allowed them to focus on the details of what was happening, so the child's focus of attention was also a factor in the coping process. They could attend to the details of what was happening without having to face additional threats. This, too, could apply to the elderly.

We close the discussion of denial and vigilant ways of coping with the conclusion that, among other considerations, both the stage of a heart attack and the kind of illness are important factors in whether denial or vigilance is harmful or beneficial. We can even go beyond this conclusion by stating a general principle that helps us understand when and why denial or its opposite, vigilance, is beneficial or harmful.[14] The principle is as follows: Denial is beneficial when nothing can be done to improve one's situation, so doing nothing while denying the problem can do no harm and could make the person feel better. On the other hand, when a particular action is necessary to preserve one's well-being but, as a result of the denial, the action is not taken, then denial is harmful. The obverse applies to vigilance, which is useless or counterproductive (harmful) when there is nothing useful that can be done but beneficial when some preventive or remedial action could help materially.

This principle reminds us of the elegant serenity prayer of Alcoholics Anonymous, which goes something like this: "God grant me the serenity to accept the things I cannot change, the courage to change the things I can, and the wisdom to know the difference." A cynic might substitute for the last phrase "and the good luck not to foul up too often in judging the difference." We love this simple but profound statement because of its epigrammatic quality; it packs a wealth of wisdom into a small number of words.

Seeking Emotional Support

It is often helpful in a personal crisis to obtain emotional support from others when we cannot seem to cope adequately by ourselves. Emotional support falls within the broader concept of *social support*, which includes informational and material support, such as providing money, food, or transportation. These three kinds of support are all potentially useful, but we consider emotional support to be psychologically the most valuable in times of personal crisis. It can make a needy person feel less isolated and provide evidence that someone else understands and sympathizes.

Very often a person in need is disappointed when seeking emotional support from others. This can be the result of a superficial social relationship and an indifferent attitude. A more important reason, however, is that even people who are well-meaning—that is, they want to help—may lack the sophistication or sensitivity to give emotional support effectively. When the chips are down, a person in need may discover that the support that is proffered is not helpful and can even aggravate the distress.[15]

One of the most revealing analyses of what we have just said comes from David Mechanic's classic study of graduate students under stress. The students had already invested several years in graduate school and anticipated taking an oral examination in three months. Because this exam would determine whether or not they would be able to proceed toward the doctorate, it generated great stress. Mechanic interviewed the students several times over the three-month period before the exam and made direct observations of their behavior. He sought information about their states of mind, the ways they coped, and their degrees of anxiety, which was the dominant emotion.[16]

In a typical doctoral oral at a major university, five faculty members, one of them from another department, sit down with the candidate for two or more hours. One after the other, they ask questions they think the student should be able to answer adequately. The task of the faculty is to assess the student's qualifications for the doctorate. The task of the student is to demonstrate these qualifications.

At high-powered academic institutions, such as the one at which Mechanic did his research, many of the faculty are distinguished in their respective subfields. They are all obliged to defend the high standards of the university and the department. To do well, the students—all men in Mechanic's sample, as was true almost everywhere just after World War II—had to be able to understand the questions, field them adequately, and give knowledgeable and sophisticated answers. If it went well, the exam could be exhilarating for the candidate despite the stress and could lead the six participants to have an engaging, stimulating, and expansive discussion. If it went badly, it could be a disaster even if the student passed and an embarrassment for the department's faculty, especially the student's mentor.

With respect to the social support provided by the students' wives, the story is mixed. Some wives tried to reassure their husbands by saying something like, "Honey, I know you're a first-rate student and you'll do very well on the exam. You shouldn't be so worried." If in reading this statement you thought it was supportive, you would be wrong. Despite the fact that these wives were actually trying to help, their husbands felt even more anxious after this nice little speech. Why did this statement, which was designed to be helpful, actually have the opposite effect? It did so because what was said created additional pressure on the husband. In addition to needing to pass, he had to live up to very high expectations. The wife's statement also negated the student's judgment that he had good reasons for his anxiety. Actually, many prior students had failed the orals and had to abandon hope of gaining the doctorate.

Other wives, however, were much more successful at being supportive. They would say something like, "Honey, I know you're worried. So am I. But we've had struggles before and managed, and if things don't work out, we'll be okay." This statement not only confirmed the soundness of the husband's appraisal of the threat but also relieved some of the threat itself. The message given was that all would not be lost if he did badly, and the husband was at least reassured that the marriage was not in danger regardless of the outcome.

Faculty members would be wise to avoid saying to their students, as they often do to give encouragement, "Don't worry, I know you will do well."

They should recognize the important truth in Mechanic's observations that, although it usually feels nice to be complimented, this seemingly positive statement only adds to a student's psychological burden. The student, incidentally, still has to deal with the practical need for letters of recommendation in the quest for good jobs. Even passing could not provide much confidence about the career prospects if both the student and the faculty knew his or her performance was marginal.

The point to appreciate here is that supporting someone who is having troubles requires considerably more sensitivity, thoughtfulness, and sophistication than merely the good intention of wanting to help, which is one example of why it is said that the road to hell is paved with good intentions. A softer way to say this is that good intentions are not enough. Those who seek emotional support must be selective about the people from whom they seek it, because what they often receive is just the opposite.

Religion as Coping

Psychologists have not given much attention to the role of religion in our lives, especially as it might apply to coping. A notable exception is *The Varieties of Religious Experience* (1902), the classic book by William James (1842–1910).[17] A more recent exception is a useful chapter in a book by Susan H. McFadden and J. S. Levin, whose interests fall within the topic of aging. Although the word *coping* never seems to come up, it is implicit in much that these authors say about religion, health, and well-being. A great proportion of the research in this field is methodologically inadequate—for example, there is usually no group of nonreligious subjects with which to compare those who claim religious convictions. Nevertheless, McFadden and Levin's chapter does show an increase in interest in what could eventually become an important field of inquiry.

While focusing on how religion shapes and modulates emotion and its outcomes in health, McFadden and Levin point out the pervasive effects of religion in our society via public observances and private meditation. They intimate that evidence has been accumulating about the positive effects of religion on personal, social, and physical well-being, with emotion being a mediating factor, and suggest that this appears to apply also in gerontology.[18]

We believe that there is a high degree of religiosity among elderly adults and that a general sense of spirituality seems to contribute to well-being. It would be interesting to compare different generations in this regard. One of the problems with doing this is that the depth of spiritual commitment is usually unclear because of the surface nature of most inquiries in this area. There is a big difference between claiming a standard religious belief and living it daily with a strong emotional commitment.

These scholars also suggest that most findings point to a salutary effect of religious involvement on health, an effect found across populations, gender, race, and ethnicity, for young and old alike, and regardless of religious affiliation. Thus, despite weak evidence, the role of religion still appears to us to be a fruitful influence on health that is worthy of further study.

McFadden and Levin suggest five reasonable rationales for this possible influence. First, religious commitment is typically associated with a lower incidence of smoking, drinking, and drug use. Second, social support is increased by religious engagement. However, positive social relationships, whether religious or not, have favorable consequences for health and well-being. Third, worship and prayer may engender positive emotional experiences, such as relaxation, hope, forgiveness, empowerment, catharsis, and love. Fourth, most religions specify health beliefs, which, if followed, might have a positive effect on actual health. Fifth, religious faith could contribute to optimism, which might promote physical and emotional well-being. Thus far, however, the empirical case for most of these expectations seems flimsy.

A few efforts have been made to include items that could have religious implications on some coping questionnaires, such as "found new faith," "rediscovered what is important in life," and "I prayed."[19] Nevertheless, not much of value has yet materialized in research on religion as coping. There are some signs, however, that interest in this area is growing, and there are good reasons for believing that religion can play an important role in the coping process.

The Importance of Small Details

Three broad types of psychological stress were distinguished in chapter 2: harm/loss, threat, and challenge. *Harm/loss* refers to when an event has already occurred and the person is facing its consequences. *Threat* is a harm or loss that has not yet occurred but could be imminent. *Challenge* is a stressful demand that exhilarates us because we are pretty confident we can handle it well and that it will result in our ultimate gain.

This typology is useful as a general way of thinking. It also addresses some interesting specific issues, such as the contrast between threat and challenge with respect to both their causal influence and their performance effects. However, it defines the types of stress so broadly that we would be hard put to choose an appropriate strategy of coping with each type. We need to be more specific about the particulars with which we must cope.

Let us illustrate this with threat alone, because the basic issues are the same whether we examine harm/loss, threat, or challenge. We address some of the specifics by looking at examples of threats brought about by being ill.

The analysis would become even more complex, though no more convincing, if we extended the comparisons to highly divergent threats, such as social rejection, the loss of a job, the loss of a loved one, or a minor versus serious slight.

The need for specifics applies even within any given type of illness. Consider, for example, the differences in the psychological impact of life-threatening, terminal, or disabling but no longer deadly cancer that has been successfully removed surgically before it had begun to spread. Although there are many common requirements for coping among these variants of cancer, each also carries its own special psychological impact.

For a life-threatening cancer, effective treatment must eliminate, if possible, the danger of death. This is essentially a preventive task that could require surgery, radiation, or chemotherapy. For a terminal cancer—that is, one that has metastasized (spread) to other parts of the body—we cannot have much hope for a cure, but a postponement of death or disability is possible. For a disabling cancer, as in cancer of the larynx (voice box) that has been removed before it has spread, our life is not immediately at stake. However, the postsurgical patient will be faced with the daunting and prolonged task of learning how to speak again. Some patients do well at this and others poorly. What is mainly at stake consists of how well the person is able to function.

A few other things should be remembered here. Most illnesses are not static but change from one stage to another. In addition, even if the specific threat is narrowed down to a single illness, say, a potentially curable cancer, divergent threats still arise from the fact that cancers attack diverse bodily organs, with different life consequences. They are, in effect, different diseases that have their own particular set of impacts.

Let us examine one particular instance, cancer of the prostate, which is potentially life-threatening and disabling yet curable. Numerous threats are generated in a patient by this disease. The most immediate threat is that urologists are apt to disagree about how to treat it. The surgeon will argue for surgery if the patient is otherwise healthy and the cancer has not metastasized. The radiologist will urge radiation. Still other physicians advise a wait-and-see strategy, which can sometimes make sense because most prostate cancers grow relatively slowly. The patient has a good chance of dying of a heart attack or something else before the cancer does its worst, so how well or sick he is otherwise is an important factor in the decision.

Given this disagreement, and the dilemmas it raises, a major source of threat for the patient is how to choose between several different treatment alternatives. Breast cancer, which is in a sense a female equivalent of prostate cancer, contains similar ambiguities about the choice of treatment, and the same things are apt to be at stake, though the cosmetic and social aspects of the surgery may play a more important psychological role.

Many further threats are inherent in prostate cancer and in other medically or psychologically similar cancers. One commonly occurs after the cancer has been successfully removed surgically. Uncertainty remains about whether some of the cancer cells were missed or might have fallen on healthy tissue during surgery, embedded themselves, and begun to grow. In effect, we might have a new malignancy that could spread to other parts of the body, which is the most dangerous of all possibilities.

A blood test is available that can show with modest reliability how much of a protein antigen (PSA), which only prostate cancer cells produce, is present. If the PSA is undetectable or near zero, the patient could be free of this cancer, but it will take years to feel confident about this. Each time the test is made during the next five to ten years, say roughly six months apart, anxiety is aroused about whether the cancer might still be present. The danger gradually lessens if there is no evidence of cancer from one year to another.

The foregoing does not exhaust the major threats. One must ask, for example, what a cancer patient should tell others about the illness—for example, a spouse, lover, children, parents, friends, or casual acquaintances. Each of these people could, because of their respective personalities, require somewhat different coping strategies.

What should an elderly man with incontinence or impotence from prostate removal say to a potential female friend or wife? Consider an unattached woman of any age who has multiple sclerosis or breast cancer that has been removed surgically. Her lover deserves to know but might decide to leave her if she tells. The right answer, of course, is the truth, but telling the truth, especially immediately, could endanger the relationship. And how do patients manage doctor visits when they have a demanding job or are responsible for child care?

The point is that different threats usually require different coping solutions, whether the person involved is young or old. Age, of course, can make a major difference, but so can a person's lack of mobility, strength, or energy or being in a great deal of pain. If we ask what the threat is that a person is coping with, it is easy to see that the categories for analyzing threat must be narrowed greatly to encompass the specific details. In sum, overbroad classifications of stress, such as harm/loss, threat, and challenge, do not provide enough psychological details to specify adequately the coping strategy choices facing a person who is ill.

Stress, Coping, Bodily Health, and Well-Being

Stress and coping have become important because of their implications for health. This interest has sparked a number of measurement approaches to interrelated concepts such as stress, morale, mood, and life satisfaction. In the 1970s there was great interest in using lists of *major life events* as a measure of stress in an effort to predict stress-induced illness. The principle was that the more life changes people had experienced during the previous six months to a year, the more likely they were to report later illnesses of all kinds.[20] When it became evident that the correlations between life changes and illness were very modest—that is, too small to sustain individual prediction—many efforts were made to modify the approach in hopes of making it more complete and effective. However, when these efforts failed to increase the life change method's ability to predict illness, enthusiasm for this approach waned.

A radically different approach to the measurement of stress was developed later by my own research project at Berkeley. It was based on the realization that while major life changes are infrequent in the lives of most people, there was still plenty of stress. The new approach was based on the idea that relatively minor *daily hassles*, such as traffic jams, troublesome neighbors, inconsiderate smokers, and so forth, might accumulate and cause illness.[21] This approach improved the predictability of illness compared with the major life events method, but still not enough to successfully predict individual health outcomes in clinical settings. A scale of daily *uplifts* or minor positive happenings was also developed on the premise that these might protect against the negative effects of hassles. This approach received some equivocal research support, but the issue remains unsettled.

Numerous scales have been developed to measure morale, mood, and life satisfaction. An example is the commonly used Bradburn morale scale, which assesses affective states such as happy, bored, cheerful, very unhappy, depressed, and vaguely uneasy,[22] and the CES-D (Radloff, 1977) which measures depression with items such as "I was bothered by things that usually don't bother me," "I thought my life had been a failure," and "I felt lonely."[23] Depression is now a very important concern in clinical work and is also a problem in aging, though as we noted in chapter 1, estimates of its frequency and intensity in old age are not very dependable.

Ed Diener has used the term *subjective well-being* in his approach to the measurement of *life satisfaction*, a concept that is divided into a number of domains of life, such as work, marriage, and positive and negative emotional experiences, all of which are combined into a single index.[24] Later, the same research project reviewed extensive research comparing life satisfaction at different life stages and in different countries, which makes this kind of assessment relevant to aging.[25]

Some professionals have assumed that the elderly are unhappy—that is, dissatisfied, isolated, lonely, neglected, and ill. However, based on large sample surveys, this seems not to be the case, if one can believe what people say. Any doubt about this is fueled by the social pressures on people to present themselves positively, which is like bragging about gambling winnings, and there are also reasons for them wanting to believe that everything is going well in their lives. Another source of doubt is that most people report being above average in life satisfaction, which is illogical (obviously, only around half of people could be above average) and suggests that reports about one's life satisfaction have other special agendas, raising doubts about the validity of such data.

In any case, little change is reported in life satisfaction over the life course. Nor is there much correlation between reported life satisfaction and the objective conditions of life. So, unfortunately in our opinion, not much has come of these comparisons of life satisfaction and age, which are extensive. Most of the research is also questionable from a methodological standpoint because it is cross-sectional (the limitations of such data when comparing different age levels was discussed in chapter 2).

Let us take up now the most fundamental question of whether and how stress and coping affect health. We cannot explore it in the depth it deserves. Readers who want to know more can supplement the discussion here with other sources devoted to this question.[26] There are two ways that psychological stress and coping can cause or, even more likely, exacerbate an existing physical illness. One is via direct effects on the body. Stress results in the secretion of many hormones that can have profound effects on bodily processes and vital organs, including the immune system, which protects us against infection from foreign agents and malignant growths. We are beginning to understand in greater depth the way the immune system works. If coping can reduce stress, then the coping route is also direct because the lowered level of stress hormones will be less damaging to the body. Suicide, of course, is also a strategy of coping that has a direct effect on health; when it is successfully carried out, illness is ended forever.

The second way is indirect—that is, by mobilizing coping behavior, such as smoking, drinking, illegal drugs, overeating, and taking risks, which are dangerous or harmful to health. It is an indirect factor because, to the extent that we do these harmful or risky things in an effort to cope with stress, we add to the probability that we will harm our bodies or sustain injuries or death from accidents. Coping is the proximate cause of the bodily harm, but stress is its provocation.

Readers might recall the earlier description of the health consequences of coping by denial or vigilance in heart disease and other illness contexts, such as surgery, arthritis, and asthma. Denial can endanger our lives or be beneficial, and vigilance can do the same depending on the stage of an illness or the actual illness itself. The research cited earlier need only be remembered as further evidence that coping can have important consequences for health and illness. Although much of the research on stress, coping, and physical health has been informative and provocative, the weakest link has always been the measurement of stress itself. It continues to be defined environmentally rather than in terms of the person-environment relationship and the relational meaning constructed by individuals.

Stress and Infectious Diseases

A very strong case for the effects of stress on health and illness has recently been made by combined field and laboratory research on infectious diseases. This research also indirectly implicates the coping process, because to the extent that coping can reduce stress, it is a weapon against these illnesses. One study examined the effects of psychological stress on susceptibility to the common cold.[27] It demonstrated that such stress increases susceptibility to colds, probably by weakening the action of the body's immune system.

These researchers inserted a cold virus into the noses of volunteer subjects. Using a simple measure of psychological stress, they divided their subjects into two groups, one reporting high stress and the other low stress during the past year. The high-stress group had more colds as a result of contact with the cold virus than the low-stress group. The greater the degree of stress, as measured in the study, the more likely were those who received the cold virus to come down with a cold. Those reporting high stress also experienced a loss of T-cell function, which is one of the protective agents of the immune system.

You may recall that we promised earlier to discuss some new findings on the healing of wounds and the role of denial. Many years ago, research evidence was published that indicated wounded dental tissues heal faster in people who cope by denial than in those who prefer vigilant coping.[28] This study preceded by quite a few years the current interest in the study of the human immune system. With its limited evidence about a psychophysiological mechanism for its results, this study did not gain the attention it deserved from social and biological scientists, but it was clearly on the right track.

Very recently, a remarkable study was reported that makes an even more impressive case that stress plays an important role in the healing of dental wounds. These researchers did a combination field and laboratory study in which they made precise measurements of how rapidly two carefully made experimental wounds, 3.5 millimeters in size, made on the hard palates of eleven dental students would heal.[29] The first wound was made to coincide in time with the academic summer vacation, which was presumed by the researchers to be a low-stress period. The second wound on the other side of the hard palate of each of the same subjects was made three days before the first major exam of the term, which was presumed to be a high-stress period. Notice, by the way, that this is an intra-individual research design, in which the subject is compared with himself or herself rather than with other subjects, thereby eliminating contaminating individual differences as a factor in the result. This kind of design is far more powerful in demonstrating causal factors than interindividual ones.

Using daily photographs and a foaming reaction to hydrogen peroxide, which is a sophisticated physical test of healing, the researchers assessed the rates of healing of the two wounds. The wound made during the stressful period took three days (40 percent) longer to completely heal than the wound that was made during the nonstressful period. The immune process appeared to contribute to this difference. This is solid psychophysiological evidence that stress decreases the rate of healing.

But what does it have to do with *denial*, which was not even measured in this research? It is possible to surmise the role of denial from these findings from the evidence that denial reduces stress. It is not a great leap to suggest that the effects of denial cited earlier on recovery from minor surgery and findings on dental wounds could be explained in this way.

In addition, others have shown that persistent stress produces quite different changes in the body's immune response.[30] Furthermore, when stress was persistent, optimists showed more impairment of the immune response, whereas they responded more favorably when the stress was short-term. In effect, optimists pay a price for their positive expectations when negative conditions persist.

This is among many findings that support the point that illness-related effects of stress depend on many factors that interact with person variables in a complex way. To make sense of what is happening, we have to look at both environmental and personality factors. To put this more trenchantly, it is the person-environment relationship that counts in stress and its effects. By now the reader should expect us to add the litany that the relational meaning that is constructed by the person makes all the difference in the stress-illness effect.

Stress and Chronic Diseases That Are Associated with Aging

Can anything be said about the effects of stress on serious *chronic ailments* such as heart disease and cancer? It is certainly plausible that stress is a factor. However, it is difficult to prove a causal relationship because these diseases, especially cancer, take a long time to develop—probably ten to twenty years. This makes it difficult to monitor the way stress might have influenced the immune process in its defense against a malignant growth or the gradual increase of plaque in the coronary arteries. Studying a large group of random subjects to monitor their stress over time and at critical junctures would be impractical, because twenty years later the number of positive cases would be too small to make an adequate interpretation of the causal factors. Because our main focus in this book is on aging, one particular article is especially relevant: It showed that age increases the risk of impairment of the immune system.[31]

Social scientists have also investigated the possible relationship between *depression and mortality* in the elderly. They have wondered about what appears to be a tendency of the bereaved spouse to die prematurely after his or her loss. One explanation is simply that both spouses are similar in age and have shared a long and similar living history. It is tempting, however, to believe that depression over the loss is a causal factor.

The question that must first be answered is whether the widespread impression that depression resulting from spousal bereavement plays a role in the unexpectedly early demise of the survivor is correct.[32] These researchers studied more than five thousand persons aged sixty-five and over and examined the relationship between spousal bereavement and depression. They found that those who had high levels of depression were 25 percent more likely to die within six years than those with low levels. None of this can prove a cause-and-effect relationship, but it should encourage further study that might identify the basis of this intriguing correlation.

Coping with Memory Loss

The elderly must cope with many other problems in addition to those related to physical health. We close this chapter with a discussion of how the elderly might cope with one of the most common complaints of old folks—namely, losses in working or short-term memory.

Many years ago, the distinguished psychologist B. F. Skinner, then in his mideighties, wrote a charming essay in which he described how he dealt with his own memory lapses. We remember one example in particular. It was a cloudy day in Cambridge, Massachusetts, with a forecast of rain. When the thought occurred to Skinner early in the morning that it might rain, at that instant—lest he forget when he actually went out—he hung his umbrella on the doorknob so it could not be missed.[33]

We make a brief excursion now into the way people late in life cope with complaints about short-term memory loss, which are widespread. Gerontologists usually refer to this as *working memory*, in contrast to well-established memory involving knowledge that was acquired long ago and was rehearsed (or overlearned) and used again and again over a lifetime.

Have you ever wondered, for example, why you can still remember the names of some teachers you encountered decades ago or the words to songs that were popular when you were a teenager or young adult, yet you can not remember the name of your next-door neighbor? This is the difference between the two types of memory. Working memory and processing speed suffer more in the elderly than does well-established memory from the distant past.

Although the loss is sensed as psychological, most likely it has its roots in changes in the brain. Therefore, the problem also falls within the realm of neurology and physical health. But brain damage cannot be reversed at the present time except perhaps by natural processes. However, the problem can be eased by many kinds of coping tricks, which we will describe shortly.

In addition to making daily life more frustrating and dangerous, working memory loss often worries the elderly because they fear it could be an early stage of a much more profound loss—namely, a dementia such as Alzheimer's disease. In ordinary aging, the seemingly missing name or word is not really lost but only temporarily difficult to retrieve. Recognition memory is less damaged than the ability to reproduce a name when one wants to.

The most important difference between the average elderly and someone with dementia is that most of us have little trouble managing our affairs despite problems of working memory. With dementia, however, as in Alzheimer's disease, the loss is permanent and profound. The patient with advanced dementia no longer knows who he or his relatives are and never will. An excellent book has compiled extensive observations and interpretations about Alzheimer's disease patients and draws on these observations to advise caregivers in how to deal with the problems of such patients, which arouse major stress in caregivers.[34] A case history of such a patient and his caregiver's efforts is presented in chapter 6.

Many coping tricks are suggested to older persons who suffer from loss of working memory, in which they seem to forget where they parked their cars, the names of people they know well, and words that express knowledge about how the world works. Here are some of them:

- Pay attention; note the location of your car when you park it. Jot it down on paper before you leave the parking lot.
- Repeat to yourself those things you want to remember, which makes the task a more conscious and deliberate one.
- Memorize little bits of information before going on to something else.
- Use written aids, such as lists of things to do, calendars, timers, and notes for posting.
- Always put keys, glasses, and similar items in the same place.
- Use mnemonic devices, such as associating what you want to remember with other memories.
- Laugh at your memory gaps and refer to them as having a "senior moment."

Most of the elderly learn to do many of these things intuitively. To add a few suggestions of our own, when elderly professors lecture, it is prudent to put the names of sources and terms they might forget during their talk on their notes, even if at the moment they write the notes they have no such trouble. This avoids the embarrassment of having an audience observe that they were about to mention someone's name when all they can do is stand there, mouth agape, while the name fails to come to mind. (It will, of course, pop up later when it is not needed. Why it does that is not known.)

What we have been saying illustrates the abundant possibilities for conjoining research with clinical practice to explore the problems most of us face in growing old. Clearly, the coping process is one of the most important topics for increasing our understanding of the problems of aging—not just in the matter of memory but concerning all sorts of losses and deficits—and how best to manage them. There has been much research on grieving over the loss of a loved one, research that has taught us much of value. The major gap in research, however, is the study of coping with garden-variety aging problems to learn which ones are most and least serviceable under a variety of conditions and for various types of people.

This chapter began by saying that you will find references to coping throughout this book. An emphasis on the coping process in aging is one of its most important and consistent themes. In this chapter, we have mainly concerned ourselves with the fundamentals of the coping process, which could apply at any age. We still need to examine the coping issues raised by changes in the physical and social environment and in people as they age. We also provide case histories of the experiences of aging that involve coping. There are eight such case histories, highlighting some of the most important limitations and assets of people who are aging, for example, in the arenas of family and friends, physical illness, and the pursuit of useful work. And in chapter 10, the last, we present eight principles about the ways of thinking, feeling, and acting, which includes coping, that can contribute to successful aging.

III ⁜

STABILITY AND CHANGE

4 ⁘

The Environment

Here we are concerned with *environmental change*, and we address the physical and social environmental changes over the lives of people in general and especially those who are aging. What has changed or stayed the same in the environment during our lifetime remains one of the most confusing and important issues of psychology. It has not been much explored, which suggests it is not easy to do with good sense.

It must be evident that those who are growing up now—that is, the children of today—do not think of environmental change as anything special because they are learning now about what currently exists. However, being old means that we grew up under circumstances that have greatly changed during our lifetime, and so it will be for the young when they begin to experience change. The world that exists now is very different from the one that existed when we were children. Expectations that were created then are no longer appropriate. This aspect of social change increases the discrepancy between the outlooks of the elderly, their children, and their grandchildren, thus promoting the generation gap and producing the cohort problem, as discussed in chapter 2.

Change can be highly stressful, making heavy demands on how we relate to the world and how to deal with it. So to understand old people requires an understanding of what was true when they were young, how the world in which they grew up has changed in their lifetime, and how these changes have affected them, which is bound to differ somewhat from one person to another.

That world—or, to put it differently, that environment—takes two forms, the physical and the social. When either or both change, it is almost axiomatic that people must change, too, in order to adapt. And vice versa, when a person changes, the person-environment relationship is changed, which, in turn, affects that person's thoughts, emotions, and actions (see chapter 2). To some extent also, people create and alter their environments.

Although the person and the environment are interdependent entities, before we can put the two concepts together in the form of a *person-environment relationship*, we must look separately at each. We must reduce the whole, consisting of the combined relationship, to its two separate parts, the environment and the person, in order to analyze the contributions of each to the other and to identify what influences each.

If you remember what we have said in the last two chapters, it is not an environmental event per se that makes a difference in our lives but its personal significance or relational meaning. It is this meaning, which is imputed to any environmental change by an individual person, that counts in our lives. Recall also from chapter 2 that each of us constructs that meaning from what is happening. What is good or bad about change differs among individuals depending on who and what we are as persons. This is a central theme of our book.

Thus, when we (born in 1922) talk to our children and grandchildren about our childhood lives, we can illustrate numerous changes, and they are amused but not much engaged by what has happened to our physical and social world as it was then and is now. We could talk about trucks bringing lump coal for our apartment house furnace and large chunks of ice for the "icebox." There were no refrigerators. We could talk about our parents washing clothes in a tub in the kitchen, scrubbing them on a ridged washboard, then hanging them on a wooden rack over the stove to dry. When you picked up the phone in those days, it was answered by an operator to whom you gave the number you were calling. And physicians made house calls.

We had no television, and in the evening, when we were not reading or playing cards, we sat around the dining room table listening to the radio, which was, early on, usually sputtering with static and was incorporated into a large piece of wooden furniture. We listened to Jack Benny, scary stories, news, and Franklin Delano Roosevelt, the country's only four-term president, reassuring us in "fireside chats" during the Great Depression that we had nothing to fear but fear itself. As the years passed, the radios got smaller, sounded better, and ultimately led to television and computers. Certain changes made life worse in some ways and better in others, often a mixed blessing or curse. We could write more effectively on a word processor but at sixty-five years of age had to give up the electric typewriter and learn a new system with which our minds were not as well matched.

We were struggling to accommodate to the modern world and to take advantage of its technological advances. Many of our friends have not gone this route, which includes cell phones, but our children and grandchildren take things in stride and often help us. Technological changes, however, are probably not as important as changes in ideas, beliefs, and values about how we should live, raise children, enjoy the good life, be a good person, and create a civil society.

The point here is that our children and grandchildren think of all this as quaint but about the distant past. It has little to do with them now. Whatever exists today is what they expect for their time. These changes were not experienced as such by them because they did not live through them. The importance of change is for the people who live through it and react emotionally to it. It can be profound for the older generation.

Many of the environmental changes we experienced were technical, and they occurred over the relatively short period of one lifetime. As Thomas L. Friedman observed in a column in the *New York Times* in 2001, the effect may be quite mixed. He wrote, "In recent years much of the buzz at Davos [the World Economic Forum held in Davos, Switzerland] was about what technology will do for us. This year, more and more, the buzz has been what technology is doing to us. . . . Doesn't anyone here think this sounds like a vision of hell? . . . Stop the world, I want to get off."[1]

There has always been debate about whether things truly change or remain fundamentally the same. The answer to this depends on how well we can distinguish between changes that are superficial and those that are part of the bedrock condition and outlook of individuals and our society. Anyway, the two seemingly contrasting ideas—namely, stability and change—are totally interdependent; as we said in chapter 3, if stability is great, change must be small; conversely, if change is great, stability must be small. They are opposite sides of the same coin. Let us proceed with the physical environment before we turn to the social.

The Physical Environment

Changes in the physical environment take place all the time. Nature itself changes and has changed dramatically since the so-called big bang, which astrophysicists regard as the origin of the universe as we know it. Many of the changes in the physical environment occur slowly; they take place as a result of gradual weathering by wind and rain. Sometimes, however, they are sudden, as in the upwelling of mountain ranges like the Sierra Nevada from the hot magma below the crust of the earth or as a result of earthquakes, tornadoes, hurricanes, and floods.

Even more important to our daily lives are the physical changes that people themselves create. Houses age, new buildings are constructed, traffic increases, the economy expands or contracts, and so on. People also move to different areas of the country, sometimes voluntarily, sometimes out of financial necessity or the need to be near family members. So people can initiate changes in the physical environment rather than the other way around.

Regardless of how they are brought about, environmental changes are apt to be stressful, especially for the elderly, and call for coping efforts on the part of those who are affected. As we said in chapter 2, stress depends on the balance between environmental demands and the ability of people to cope with them.[2] Coping becomes more difficult for the elderly because of physical and mental losses and infirmities, which shift the balance in favor of the demands. But the elderly can also learn new ways of dealing with the problems they now face.

Certain changes in the residences of many old people are badly needed to make them safer physically. Special housing and living conditions are needed to maximize the ability of the elderly to function and to reduce the hazards from existing structures. Only recently have we come to appreciate this problem fully. M. Powell Lawton, now deceased, was a pioneer in bringing it to national attention.[3]

An illustration of how slow we have been in recognizing household hazards for the elderly is provided by Rossmoor itself. This community was designed for people in later life, but most of its homes were built with entry steps that many elderly folks cannot readily negotiate when they need a walker or wheelchair. One reason for this is the location of Rossmoor in a coastal valley with a hilly, rugged terrain. Another is that many relatively young persons (fifty-five to sixty-five or so years of age) moved there when they were still free of serious physical impediments. They did not realize that a time might come when they might be unable to climb or descend stairs. Even those who do not need a wheelchair still require level entryways or elevators for the purpose of bringing heavily loaded shopping carts into their homes. A modest number of buildings have elevators or were built on a level piece of ground, but far too many buildings, even recent ones, present serious problems for those who are disabled. Most surprisingly, it has taken nearly thirty years to provide wheelchair access to one of the most important Rossmoor buildings used for group dinners, the Stanley Dollar Clubhouse.

There is also a need for firm steel bars over the bathtub or in the shower that one can hold onto to avoid falling. Modern hotels are increasingly equipped in this way, which shows a greater awareness of the need, though we have a long way to go to make travel easier and safer for the elderly, especially in airports. Housing is a constant source of injury for the elderly because their equilibrium is often quite shaky. In addition, most buildings and furniture have sharp rectangular or pointed edges that can result in frequent injuries to soft tissue when a resident bumps into them. Considerations of architectural design from the standpoint of the needs and competencies of elderly persons and to understand its role in encouraging or discouraging social contacts have been explored recently.[4]

Broken bones are a major source of disability. Many of the elderly, especially women, suffer from osteoporosis, a condition that is characterized by thin, weak bones that lack calcium. Broken hips become increasingly common as people age and are a frequent cause of disability and death. A substantial percentage of the elderly who have undergone the surgery necessary to repair a broken hip fail to recover adequately. Mobility is very important for the health and well-being of the old. We need to be active to remain vigorous and healthy.

The *Rossmoor News*, which comes out every week in the community, has recently created a list of things to do to "senior-proof" homes. Some common tips illustrate the special problems of the elderly:

- Floors should be kept clear of debris.
- Stairways should be well lit, with handrails and nonskid surfaces.
- Avoid trailing wires, watch load limits, and replace damaged cords.
- In the kitchen, keep often-used items handy but not over the stove, with heavy things on lower shelves. Don't climb on stools and ladders, avoid loose sleeves when cooking, clean all spills right away, and arrange to have good lighting.
- In the bathroom, put sturdy handrails and skid-proof mats in the bathtub, with a bath bench if needed, and don't hang the shower curtain on a tension rod that may fall when grabbed.
- In the bedroom, have nightlights, easily reached light switches, and a phone or clock with large numbers.
- Couches and chairs should not be too deep or low, and tables should be a suitable height.
- Store medicines in original containers.

Transportation is often a serious problem for older people. Nowadays, especially in the West, public transit is grossly inadequate, which forces many to rely on automobiles. Traffic congestion, which has gotten awesome in recent years in most urban and suburban areas, is threatening to many older people who drive a car. This is especially true on freeways, where two to five closely placed lanes are filled with cars that move at very high speeds, requiring great alertness and fast reactions to drive safely. Lane changing is a constant danger, especially when vision is impaired or the capacity for head turning is restricted.

Buses are needed to transport those who can no longer drive because of impaired vision and/or hearing and the lack of agility necessary to do so safely. In Rossmoor, in addition to buses that move around locally inside and outside the community, there are frequent bus outings to theaters in San Francisco and elsewhere. Most such bus trips are completely booked because they make it unnecessary to drive.

On the other hand, it is simply not true that elderly drivers produce more accidents than the young or middle-aged. Automobile safety among the elderly has been dealt with in great detail by Thomas Bryer, who provides more data than anyone can imagine about the characteristics of vehicle crashes.[5] The data that Bryer tabulates show elderly drivers as old as 85 and over have fewer accidents overall than adults between 30 and 59 years of age and many fewer than those 16 to 44 years of age. Of course, they usually drive shorter distances per trip than the young. But the accusation that the elderly are involved in more accidents than the young or middle-aged appears to be false.

The Social Environment

The social environment can be considered from two quite different perspectives, macro and micro. The macroenvironment has to do with the larger society, societal values, customs, politics, economic issues, and ways people in general live. The microenvironment consists of more intimate social relationships, such as family, friends, and casual acquaintances, including the people who live next door or with whom a person does business. Because we devote chapter 6 to the role of family and friends in aging, it is the macroenvironment that we emphasize here. Both, of course, are important, and they influence each other.

Leaving aside the standard hypocrisies of political rhetoric, the social changes that characterize our times convince many elders that they are living in a different world than the one in which they were reared. It is a world most of us have increasing trouble understanding, and it leads many to feel like comparative strangers. It may well be correct that the recent rate of social change has greatly accelerated. This creates, even in many of the children and grandchildren of our generation, a feeling of tentativeness and instability about life. Perhaps this has contributed to an ethos that emerged in the 1960s and seems rampant today, which is centered on the here-and-now rather than the future.

A *New York Times* columnist, Bob Herbert, refered to the present social conditions as "an absurd, crazy world."[6] One hears much of this kind of talk these days, whether people are exhilarated or turned off by change, but mostly from the older generation. Some of this ambivalence is probably widely shared, but it is difficult to say what the individual take is on this kind of issue. And we have the impression that we see this quite differently than our children do, because the psychological significance of what has changed is substantially different. Our children are more affected by recent economic change, which threatens their job or career possibilities.

Permit us to list some of the changes in our society that trouble us, while recognizing that our beliefs, values, goals, and life circumstances—including our age—might shape how we see things. We have a long list but must limit ourselves to a few changes. Most of them are only minor irritants. Those that have the most profound effect on us get us too far into politics and are out of place in a book about aging.

Television is a special source of annoyance. We are, for instance, put off by commercials on TV that seem frenetic and made only for the very young. The images pass by so quickly, and their messages seem so obscure, that we fail even to get the point of the commercial and often cannot identify the product being advertised. Our children have none of these complaints; they grew up with television and, because they are still young, have faster reaction times than we do.

In sitcoms and dramatic programs, the speech of the actors is hard for older people to understand because the sound level constantly rises and falls or is obscured by music or noise; it is often slurred and imprecise, perhaps because of the current emphasis on realism—presumably this is the way people speak in real life. In the past, actors were required to speak clearly and loudly enough to be understood without subtitles. Public television insists on emphasizing mystery programs from England that we cannot understand well because of the accents that add to our hearing and perceptual problems.

One could argue, of course, that these are not necessarily environmental changes but have to do with worsening hearing and age-connected difficulties of speech processing. Probably both are operating here, but the fact that we seldom experience these problems with old Hollywood movies suggests that real environmental changes have taken place in addition to perceptual changes that result from aging.

We are offended by the low quality of modern news programs compared with those of the past, especially the local newscasts. They revel in frightening viewers about medical news, the implications of which are often undigested, overstated, inadequate, or just plain wrong. They spend an inordinate amount of time reviewing crimes, and if there are not enough local crimes to titillate the audience, they find them in other communities or countries. Newscasters and meteorologists act as if they are celebrities, attractive, excessively cheerful, and personable, rather than intelligent, knowledgeable, or interested in informing the public. The distinction between entertainment and news has been severely blurred.

We are troubled that our wealthy country still permits a quarter to a third of our children to grow up in poverty, which mires many of them in inadequacy and crime. And we do not provide adequate health care to a large proportion of our citizens, including the elderly, who deserve better. When Franklin Roosevelt talked to us on radio in the 1930s, most of us listened enthralled. We were not only impressed by his stentorian tones and clear enunciation; we had the conviction that this man was trustworthy and had the concerns of the country and people like us in his heart. In very difficult times, the Great Depression and World War II, we were greatly reassured by what he said.

By contrast, today our government seems to reverse the Robin Hood legend by robbing the poor to give to the rich, creating an increasing gap between poverty and wealth and failing to provide for children and the elderly alike. The society of today seems far harsher in outlook than it was when we were growing up despite the Great Depression. Unregulated capitalism more and more looks like a reversion of civilization to a predatory pattern that closely resembles the primitive tooth and claw of animal life. Greed rather than social responsibility is what is now celebrated.

We confess, however, that these impressions may have little to do with aging, and just about everything we have said has also been said in previous generations. Many others, no doubt, see these from a different perspective consistent with their outlook about government and the way they would like to see the world. There was also a minority during Roosevelt's time who hated what he said, though many of them respected him. The answer, of course, depends on one's political and social outlook and the stakes one has in the outcome.

The problem for the elderly, which is created both by social change and by the generation gap, is that they must modify how they think, feel, and, at the very least, act in order to adapt or live like strangers in a world they no longer understand. Change in our society is apt to come day by day rather than all at once, and we may not even realize our inner worlds are also changing to accommodate to what is happening. Reaction to change also depends on individual variations in personality. Although change usually makes substantial demands on people, it can also be exhilarating and lead to creative new outlooks and ways of living in the old as well as the young.

What Does Not Change

Not everything in the social world changes. There are solid grounds for believing that some things have remained the same as long as people have existed. Some scholars would argue that fundamentals never change. What are some of the human patterns that appear to have remained constant throughout history? Some of them deal with human characteristics that are deemed positive and others with characteristics that are considered negative.

Examples of what we would consider positive human characteristics are empathy, kindness, courage, a high regard for truth and integrity, and the willingness to help others. These qualities never completely disappear despite many instances of human cruelty and indifference to the suffering of others. We either are built this way, live under social conditions that foster these characteristics, or, most probably, both.

Mostly, however, it is the negative human characteristics that are usually emphasized. The most egregious examples have to do with human aggression, violence, and cruelty, which has led many thinkers, including Freud, to conclude that they are inherited by our species and fundamentally unchangeable. A perennial question that has been asked throughout history is how malleable people are in the face of evolution and the genes that we have acquired as a species. This is no esoteric issue for academic discourse indulged in by a few college professors but is a vital, life-or-death concern in a predatory world. When an elderly person walks down the street from house to store, or wherever, he or she must worry about being attacked, especially in the inner cities of our society, just as a female has good reason to fear attack and rape. There are optimists and pessimists about what it is that brings about our ugly human traits.

Optimists believe human violence depends on the social system under which people live, which has the potential for being changed for the better, even if with great difficulty. Some social arrangements are said to promote violence, whereas others make it less likely.

Many years ago, Ruth Benedict addressed this issue from the optimistic standpoint by contrasting Apollonian and Dionysian cultures of the American Plains Indians. These terms come from ancient Greece, whose deities Apollo and Dionysus epitomize the contrast. Apollonians (illustrated by the Hopi tribes) favor harmony, balance, and moderation; Dionysians (illustrated by the Apache tribes) favor conflict, frenzied or orgiastic rituals, and irrational values.

Based on her observations, Benedict suggested that a society constructed on a principle she called *synergy* leads to nonaggressiveness. Synergy, in Benedict's usage, refers to actions by an individual that serve both the individual and the group or community. This does not happen, she argued, because people are unselfish but because a synergistic society treats the two values, personal gain and social obligation, as interdependent rather than opposites.[7]

Benedict argued that the people of a society in which individuals are pitted against each other are apt to be aggressive and violent.[8] Grades in American colleges and universities provide an excellent example. In curve grading, which represent a zero-sum game, a student receiving an A reduces everyone else's chances of earning an A. Competition, which is a nonsynergistic outlook, is highly valued in our society. That Benedict's ideas have been forgotten by most social scientists may reflect the fundamental opposition between the individualistic American social ethos—though, fortunately, this is often honored in the breach—and a more community-centered outlook.

A modern version of synergy is the contrast between societies that are individualistic, as in the West, and those that are community centered, as in Asia. Recent research and theory suggest, however, that any black-and-white typology between societies is oversimple. Two research scholars, Michael Harris Bond and Peter Bevington Smith, gave voice to doubts about the typology when they wrote, "Researchers infer that because culture X has certain [stated] values, individuals within that culture will share those values."[9]

The point is that stated societal values do not necessarily shape all or perhaps even most of the individuals who grow up in the society. We do not pick up cultural values by osmosis but by finding models—for example, a mother or a father—and selectively identifying with some of the ways these potential models act.[10]

Boys are apt to model themselves after their fathers and girls after their mothers, but this is by no means always the case, especially when young people find out that the values their parents claim to have do not conform to the way they act. In such a situation, we are more likely to internalize a model's actions and to reject what he or she says about how one should act. This is why it is so difficult to teach morality to children. To some extent, our children pick up what they see rather than what they hear, giving only lip service to the latter.

Increasing diversity within societies, including Japan, challenges the stereotypical notion that most people within a given society desire, think, and feel about things in the same way. Even in the competitive and individualistic United States, there are those who favor community spirit or who long for it because they think it does not exist.[11]

Aggression and violence are major problems within our society, which is one of the most violent in the Western world, against enemies both on the outside and within. Japanese, too, are aggressive; however, their aggression tends to be directed against outsiders, such as foreigners, and not so much at their own people. Japanese are comparatively peaceable and consensual within their society in the way people relate to each other and make decisions. A great effort is made to reach decisions by compromise in order to preserve harmony. If you deal with Japanese institutional groups, it can drive you up the wall waiting for them to make up their collective mind.

In general, people go along with what the culture demands; it is easier than looking for trouble. Psychologists and sociologists sometimes refer to this as *compliance*. We act correctly in a pro forma way rather than because it is deeply embedded in one's character. Even a sociopath—that is, a person without conscience—can look like a proper citizen by simply giving surface obeisance to the social rules when it suits.

Many of the values of a culture are indeed incorporated into the individual's personality. Psychologists refer to this process as *internalization*. What we learn from the outside world becomes a deeply ingrained feature of our character as a set of values we fully accept, which are very difficult to change even when our well-being is at stake.[12]

In contrast with the optimists, who think aggression, violence, and cruelty would be curtailed if we could only construct a better society, *pessimists* believe that these evils are part of our species inheritance and can be overcome only by evolutionary changes in our genetic makeup. From a biological standpoint, we are a vile—or at least an inadequately evolved—species because we seem unable to transcend our "tooth-and-claw" biological heritage, which seems in conflict with what we call a civilized society. After all, the animal world consists of both predators and prey.

Most warm-blooded predatory animals, however, seldom kill except for food, mating, and survival, and it is an insult to the animal world to speak of aggression, violence, and cruelty as animal-like, as is implied in the metaphor of tooth and claw. Animals of the same species usually back down when they see they are likely to lose a fight for dominance, and the victor usually allows the loser to leave the scene before being killed. Humans, however, retain the memory of the past defeat and often plan to take revenge later, and it seems that only humans enjoy cruelty toward members of their own species. Remember, only humans enslave other humans. The twentieth century has seen widespread war, genocide (usually justified in idealistic terms by the need for final victory over the enemy), and corruption, as well as huge populations displaced from their homelands and seeking refuge anywhere they can find it. Despite optimistic political statements to the contrary, intergroup hatred based on race, ethnicity, and religion abounds and has probably never been greater. It remains a problem in the United States despite the fact that we pride ourselves on being socially advanced, civilized, and fair-minded.

The population of the earth is currently about seven billion people, a figure that is growing rapidly, greatly endangering our planet's future environment. In the late nineteenth century and during a brief period in the 1960s, it was fashionable to be concerned about overpopulation.[13] The writings of Thomas Malthus (1766–1834) about the dangers of overpopulation for civilization have been much satirized. Now, however, fueled by increasing environmental concerns, there seems to be a gradual renewal of concern about the limits of the human carrying capacity of the earth. The dangers are greater today as peoples all over the world seek a Western lifestyle of high consumer demand and productivity.

There is, nevertheless, strong political opposition to this concern about overpopulation, which may prove one day to be unfortunate if changes in our handling of overpopulation and the environment come too late to preserve our planet for future generations. Short-term well-being governs our actions rather than the long-term future of the world. After all, people do not really live very long, and politicians have an even shorter political life. When all is said and done, we cannot offer a simple answer based on the extremes of pessimistic or optimistic explanation, except to express confidence that both our genetic makeup and social systems share responsibility for human aggression, violence, and cruelty.

Interest in improving the lot of humankind has appeared throughout written history. It is expressed in diverse *utopias*, a word coined by Sir Thomas More in 1516 to refer to fantasies and programs about ideal societies.[14] Examples of utopian thought include Plato's *Republic*, Karl Marx's *Das Kapital* (1867; English translation, 1886), B. F. Skinner's *Walden Two* (1961), and Charles Reich's *Greening of America* (1970). In contrast, *dystopias* include nightmarish fantasies about terrifying societies. They include Aldous Huxley's *Brave New World* (1932), George Orwell's *1984* (1949), and Anthony Burgess's *A Clockwork Orange* (1962). Both kinds of fantasy, utopian and dystopian, reflect the consistent hope of humankind for a truly humane, secure, and constructive society and the consistent fear of destructive ones. Many elderly persons find this kind of thinking important as they look back over their lives. Others seem to have little or no interest in speculations about the future.

You may ask what this has to do with aging. It concerns how we, who are the departing generation, feel about our past and the legacy we leave to our progeny. The life stories, memoirs, and autobiographies of older people, which proliferate today, represent an effort to seek serviceable meaning about what a person's life has been about and to influence others in regard to that meaning. In chapter 9, we shall talk about transforming the idea of a life review into a psychotherapeutic procedure for treating the emotional problems of aging. In any case, how we view the present and the future—for example, with respect to our children and grandchildren, and perhaps beyond—is an important part of this meaning for many of the elderly.

When World War II ended, we wanted to return to the world that had existed prior to the war that had disrupted our lives. If our parents had taught us, or if we had listened, perhaps, or realized that most things never stay the same, we might have been better prepared for the furious rate of change that occurred after 1945. But this is a lesson that few seem to understand or take seriously, and it may well apply to each new generation. We must always be prepared for change. The old are more traumatized by change because it violates their expectations about how things should be and calls for learning new ways of coping when we have become set in our ways and less willing at our stage of life to change.

In the wake of the terrorist attacks of September 11, 2001, the United States is in a strange quasi war with religious zealots who hate us so much they are keen to wantonly murder innocent people, Americans and non-Americans alike. Much about what happened in this event and its aftermath is relevant to lessons to be learned about change. This event provides us with an opportunity to sum up some of the lessons about stability and change that we have considered here. We use an examination of these lessons to close this chapter.

First, how people reacted emotionally and will react in the future will vary with how they are personally affected by what has happened and the *relational meanings* they draw from these events. Although the early media talk reflected a sense of common plight and pulling together against the threat, each group in the country and, indeed, each individual person was affected somewhat differently. Among the most widespread, shared emotions were grief, anxiety, and anger. Those who lost loved ones grieved and felt anxiety for themselves, their families, and friends. Many felt anger and even rage. Older people, who are already less secure physically in their lives—perhaps some mentally, too—have been frightened for themselves and their younger families.

Anxiety is aroused by concern for one's own safety and for that of our loved ones, and by the existential implications of what happened for our life in general—for example, relevant to government, historical freedoms, what our country and the world is all about, our overall sense of security, minor inconveniences, increased obstacles to travel, and so forth. Things will ultimately settle down unless there is another attack.

Anger comes from the sense of being demeaned unjustly, and it is apt to oscillate with anxiety, guilt, shame, and pride. Our country has been attacked, and to the extent we identify with it, this is a powerful basis of shared anger. But if we have also lost loved ones, the anger has a highly personal quality because we as individuals have been assaulted and our lives changed in the process.

We look to our government to act wisely and effectively to restore our lives as much as possible. If the government fails to act, or if we find that it has been irresponsible before the event—for example, creating only the illusion of airport security—the anger could turn against it. It could also turn against groups who seem to have ties with the killers. The most important lesson here is that we as individuals and those who operate our government must achieve, through the process of realistically yet hopefully *appraising* the situation, our needs and resources, and what can be done that is effective considering the long as well as the short run.

Because ours is a large and diverse population, many of us have at worst been inconvenienced by not being able to fly home immediately from somewhere. Most of us have been horrified that this could happen but have suffered little. We wait for what is yet to happen. Some are afraid to fly again;

if they do fly, they may experience considerable anxiety. Those flying can also experience considerable delay at airports. Some may feel uneasy crossing vulnerable bridges or even traveling by train or car.

If there is a succession of terrorist events, each perhaps taking different forms, we will experience chronic or recurrent anxiety and anger, as happens during any period of uncertain threat. If a long period elapses without attack, these emotions will abate until they perhaps are once again aroused by a further attack. It is somewhat like the way we feel when a cancer has been removed and we must be tested every so often to check for any recurrence.

Second, both our government and we as individuals must find ways of coping that are appropriate to the circumstances being faced. The most important lesson in all this, however, is that we will cope with what is happening in diverse ways, learning to live with what has changed, becoming resilient in the face of the new realities. Most of us will cope successfully. The way we cope with change is apt to depend on each new adaptational requirement. For some of us, there also may be some stability in the strategies with which we cope as a result of our personality preferences for avoidance, denial, vigilance, actions to solve problems, or things we tell ourselves to help us feel better.

All that we have said here applies to both young and old. The young have more strength and stamina than the old, many of whom will find the new demands more severely taxing of their resources. Their problems and conditions of life have changed. This is an issue that we take up in chapter 5, where we deal with stability and change in the person in contrast with the environment as each of us ages.

5

The Personality

Having dealt with environmental change, we now come to the important question of whether the personality of an individual changes over a lifetime and, if so, in what ways. If we consider personality development from birth, it should be obvious that early childhood psychological and physical changes are rapid and dramatic. Until a personality has been thoroughly established, the way an individual looks at things, beliefs about the self and the world, skills, and whatever that individual desires in life are still forming and changing. That individual will ultimately develop into a more or less stable and distinctive person.

The question of interest, therefore, consists of how stable or capable of change adults are. When adulthood can be said to take place is by no means certain and probably varies from individual to individual. Changes, even as late as the college years, are still fairly evident to those who know the teenager. In a limited research effort to measure human motivation, it was observed that college students begin to establish stable life goals toward the junior and senior year, after they have learned more about their abilities and interests.[1]

During the late adolescent years, many college students shift away from goals that do not fit their emerging adult minds, psychological resources, and conditions of life. Parents are often concerned observers of this and wait impatiently for their children to grow up so that they will not make poorly conceived, sometimes disastrous, decisions that will forever affect their lives. Even older adults may give up long-standing goals that are no longer feasible to attain or serviceable in their lives.

Most of us believe with justification that we are basically the same persons over our entire adult lives. We have a past that we can describe within limits (some of it accurately, some inaccurately), and we have ideas about how the past contributed to what we are today. If we continue to change, we are apt to do so slowly, and we are less likely to notice it.

But now comes the hard part, which has to do with details—that is, which components of personality remain the same, which change or are capable of change, and in what way changes are brought about. Stability and change in personality are not a simple either-or issue. Both apply, but it is very difficult to find credible evidence to document the details. This means that much of what we say about this topic must be speculative. A substantial amount of research has tried to tackle this issue, with mixed success in our opinion, leaving the issue of stability and change in some doubt. There are at least five reasons for this.

First, relatively few studies have been longitudinal.[2] In chapter 2 we pointed to one of these—namely, the extensive Berkeley research on children of the Great Depression.[3] We also spoke at length about the cohort problem of cross-sectional research in that chapter, saying that when different age-groups are compared, the cohort problem makes many of our suppositions about aging and change impossible to prove.

Second, a personality is made up of characteristics that operate on many different levels of analysis. Some of these characteristics are superficial and responsive to environmental demands and constraints—they shift like a will-o'-the-wisp with changes in the physical and social circumstances a person faces. Other characteristics lie at a deeper level—that is, in the interior of one's being, so to speak—and we assume that they are less accessible to both the person and the observer. They include emotional conflicts and defenses that are unconscious or dimly or fleetingly conscious. Which of these characteristics should be regarded as deep and refractory to change depends on one's theory of personality. There is by no means much agreement about this among personality psychologists.

Third, measuring personality, especially the characteristics that lie below the surface, presents a major challenge. Much of the research in this area employs what we would call superficial questionnaires that depend on how people answer questions about themselves. They are carefully formulated with sophisticated statistical issues in mind rather than being ad hoc scales created on the spot, but there is reason to doubt that this approach covers the ground adequately. (Recall the discussion in chapter 2 under the heading "The Emotion Measurement Problem.")

Those who emphasize questionnaires defend their strategy vigorously and would deny that their data are limited to surface aspects of personality. We believe, however, that to get at deeper levels requires a different assessment strategy, more akin to the clinical method that is employed in psychological treatment. This method requires making inferences from a combination of what clients say about themselves and their experiences on repeated occasions and what is observed about them in the interview sessions.

These inferences are likely to be about personal goals, goal hierarchies, resources, the self-concept, conflicts, and defenses, and they are always of uncertain validity. Not every observer would necessarily make the same judgments, say, about the relational meanings that are said to underlie how a given person thinks, acts, or feels. This is more of an art than a science, though many personality psychologists would deny this vigorously. In our judgment, however, the requirement applies just as much to all measurement approaches.

Some researchers have used questionnaire data obtained at one point in time and correlated with answers to the same questionnaire at a later time. Others have employed projective techniques (e.g., the Rorschach inkblot test or the Thematic Apperception Test). Still others employ in-depth interviews.

Some studies, such as the previously mentioned Berkeley research on children of the Great Depression, studied the same persons from youth to their seventies. In that longitudinal research, many different assessment procedures were employed, including observer ratings and efforts to integrate these procedures into a coherent portrait of each individual person. This research produced evidence of considerable stability over a lifetime.

While we are speaking of diverse approaches to personality assessment, mention should be made of the distinguished personality psychologist Gordon Allport, who among other contributions to psychology is celebrated for his thoughtful and in-depth examination of the use of personal documents in the science of psychology.[4] His writings also include an example of this kind of assessment focus, a set of letters written by a woman, which he edited and interpreted.[5] This approach adds richly to the potential biographical sources of knowledge about the personalities of diverse individuals. Since then, many others have drawn upon such sources for the purpose of personality assessment.

Fourth, when we rely only on what a person says about the past and its personal significance, most of the time it is not what has actually happened that is being addressed but rather reconstructions of past events that change at different times in a person's life. Only on rare occasions do we have an objective record of what actually occurred, especially when a person is recalling highly emotional experiences rather than simple objective facts. These reconstructions are based on suppositions we have about our lives and selves. At each stage of our life, memories are likely to change in detail and sometimes even in meaning because, as our minds develop with life experience, we are apt to view the past quite differently.

It is not that we necessarily lie about our past, though we may do so on various occasions, but that we differently frame what we think happened according to changes in our idea of self, especially when we are thinking about our early developmental years. Consider a woman we know who said in psychotherapy, "I once believed my mother hated me, but I can now see that we had too limited an understanding of each other to grasp what was really happening. Her efforts to control me—probably for my own good—led to resentments on my part that distorted how I interpreted our relationship. And the same probably applied to her." This woman was on the verge of acquiring a powerful insight into her past and present that could greatly improve her emotional life and social functioning and would, in the long run, probably change many of her memories.

As we have argued throughout the early chapters, the personal significance of what happened in the past—that is, its relational meaning—is far more important and indicative of how we view the past than the actual details. These grow more obscure with time, though some of them may still seem very real. Just as a person who is suffering from dementia confabulates in order to fill in mental gaps and confusions, we all do the same with what remain as obscurities about the past. In other words, we make up credible stories that we come to believe. These stories are not usually created out of whole cloth; instead, they involve changing the emphasis and interpretation here and there to fit our present self-image or one we would like to believe. Sometimes we do not succeed in creating a satisfactory story, in which case we may have difficulty discarding what seemed ugly in the past, and which from time to time comes unbidden to mind, to remain a source of distress we never quite escape.

This brings us to a thoughtful and well-crafted article by Tobias Wolff. He was responding to the distress reported publicly by Bob Kerrey, the U.S. senator who played an important role as an army officer in a tragic accident in the Vietnam War (not to be confused with Senator John Kerry, the presidential candidate, who also served in Vietnam). An unarmed group of women and children in the Vietnamese village of Thanh Phong were killed. Different versions of what happened have surfaced along with Kerrey's version.

The reason for mentioning this story is not to speculate about where the truth lies in this traumatic event. Who can say now after so many years and considering the terror and moral conflicts of the moment? Rather, we are concerned with what emotional memories from the past represent. The following passage from Wolff's article, as far as we are concerned, has it right and is instructive about the issue of memories:

> We tend to think of memory as a camera, or a tape recorder, where the past can be filed intact and called up at will. But memory is none of these things. Memory is a storyteller, and like all storytellers it imposes form on the raw mass of experience. It creates shape and mean-

ing by emphasizing some things and leaving others out. It finds connections between events, suggests cause and effect, makes each of us the central figure in an epic journey toward darkness or light.[6]

Fifth, you will recall that in chapter 2, in the description of our theoretical outlook on psychological stress and the emotions, we took the position that our emotional lives depend on how we appraise and construe what is happening in our relationships with others. Emotions are the result of the outcomes of our goals and beliefs as we view them. It takes two forces to create an emotion, the person *and* the environment. The relationship between them, as we appraise its significance or meaning for our well-being, is what counts.

We do not question that there is such an entity as a personality, which can be said to include a number of discrete characteristics, such as goals, beliefs, thinking styles, resources, and a concept of oneself. We are not convinced, however, when trying to understand the way a person thinks, acts, and feels, that it is desirable to divorce the person from the environment or, more to the point, to ignore the person-environment relationship and its relational meaning.

In the discussions that follow, it is clear that the proponents of the position that we are either stable or changeable over our lives are really talking about personality as the unit of choice rather than the person's relationship with others. Few seem to have adopted a relational perspective, which we think is a better unit. The issue gets defined in their thinking as stability or change in the theoretical entity that is referred to as the personality. To think relationally means that the issue of stability and change arises for a particular person who is living in a particular life context—that is, a world of other people, things, and events. We are convinced that we will not fully understand the issue until we adopt a relational perspective.

Ongoing Arguments about Stability and Change

As we were revising this chapter, two very interesting articles appeared that address personality stability and change. What best describes the current status of the issue is that two highly respected theorist-researchers came out on such opposite sides of the fence that it would be difficult to find any basis for agreement between them.

Let us examine what the two protagonists have to say about stability and change. Avshalom Caspi and Brent W. Roberts emphasize a high degree of stability and take the position, which is traditional in developmental psychology, that the child is father to the man, meaning that there is a strong causal connection between early life and later personality. Although they emphasize stability more than change, Caspi and Roberts still allow for change and comment approvingly about the claim that the probability of change decreases with age but does not disappear.[7]

In contrast, Michael Lewis argues that there is very little stability in personality over time; the obtained correlations between measures of personality at one time of life and a later time are really quite low overall, he says, and we believe he is generally correct about this. He also states that earlier events in a person's life do not substantially affect later events, which is a somewhat radical position. In his view, the situational context is the most important factor influencing how we think, feel, and act.[8]

Permit us to quote from another pair of authors who have been heavily involved in this controversy. That personality is stable is strongly affirmed by Paul T. Costa and Robert R. McCrae based on longitudinal data from personality questionnaires. Their position seems far more extreme than that of Caspi and Roberts. Costa and McCrae write:

> The personality traits that characterize the middle-aged man or woman are still likely to be present decades later. Those with the chronic emotions of anxiety, depression, or anger ought not to suppose that they will "mellow" with time; instead, they should perhaps consider psychotherapeutic intervention. Conversely, middle-aged people whose current emotional life can be described in such terms as calm, cheerful, fascinated, affectionate, and determined need not fear the loss of these feelings in old age. *Whatever the vicissitudes of life*, people's emotional responses remain an expression of their enduring dispositions.[9]

The extremeness of this position is reflected in the almost throwaway phrase we have italicized. Costa and McCrae come down hard on the idea of stability in the adult personality and appear to leave no room for change. To bring this home, we also cite another statement that illustrates their tendency to overstate. They begin a chapter on emotionality and aging as follows:

> How will you feel two months and three days after your 78th birthday? After some thought, this odd question is likely to elicit one of two answers. The first is that you will feel "old," meaning tired, apathetic, irritable, and lonely. The second is that the answer depends on a host of factors that cannot be foreseen—your health and your spouse's, your financial situation, recent life events, daily hassles and uplifts (Kanner, Coyne, Schaefer, & Lazarus, 1981); there is thus no meaningful way to make such a prediction.
>
> Both of these answers are wrong. Gerontologists and psychologists are perhaps less aware that affect is predictable years in advance, not from a foreknowledge of the situations that induce affective responses,

but from an understanding of the enduring dispositional basis of affect: personality traits.[10]

The problem here is not that these researchers argue for stability over the years of our life in affective dispositions, even substantial stability. Few would argue against this, though as we have seen, Michael Lewis does.[11] It is Costa and McCrae's denial that the conditions of life are also important in a person's affect pattern. This is an extreme position that is almost certain to be in error. Later in this chapter we shall speak of life events that greatly increase the chances of major changes in personality.

There are also those who believe that people generally become mellow as they get old. My experiences in living in an elderly community convince me that older people do not routinely get mellow, though they may get too tired to care. My children tend to believe this about me. But don't you believe it; I am just as feisty and ornery as ever. Maybe they only have come to think I am mellow because they want to, or because they themselves have matured and can see more diverse facets in their parents than they could when younger.

In any case, this kind of casual impression does not have much of a scientific basis, though it could be a hunch that has merit if anyone wanted to find out through programmatic research. An even better guess is that as people get older, they become more like they were earlier; those who were mellow become more so, and those who were nasty get nastier. This too, however, has not been subjected to serious empirical research.

There are two problems with the empirical basis of the Costa and McCrae claim of high stability in personality. First, most of it is based on questionnaires that we think have limits on what can be learned. Subjects also probably remember something of what they answered on the same questionnaire earlier, which could inflate the impression of stability. But far more important, what is missing is the deeper, less accessible level of personality, such as defenses. This would also include areas of ambivalence and unstated but proscribed patterns of motivation and overall life plans that can power and direct a person's life without that person being willing or able to acknowledge them.

Second, as we have already said, Costa and McCrae tend again and again to overstate the significance of small or modest degrees of correlation that define stability over time and circumstance. We are inclined to believe, along with Caspi and Roberts, that there is, indeed, substantial stability in personality over most of a person's lifetime but plenty of room for change, too, especially when events in a person's life are traumatic or reflect crises of beliefs that have been sustaining in the past. We shall come back to this point later.

Programmatic Research on Cognitive-Emotional Change

Let us move on to others who have addressed the issues of stability and change in our cognitive and emotional lives. A book by K. Warner Schaie and M. Powell Lawton brings together the work of a number of influential research scholars who examine what happens to thinking and emotion as we move from adulthood to aging and old age. Interviews are often used to make these assessments.[12]

Many of the authors in this volume—including Gisela Labouvie-Vief, Carol Magai and V. Passman, Fredda Blanchard-Fields, and Laura Carstensen, James J. Gross, and Helene Hoilam Fung—provide provocative and interesting ideas and observations about changes in cognition (referring to thinking) and emotion over the life course that appear to have the ring of truth. The work of Carstensen and her colleagues on the roles of marriage, families, and friends as people age is included in our summary of general themes, but it is taken up separately in chapter 6.

These authors are not all saying basically the same things about cognition, emotion, and aging. If we take a few liberties and overlook possible differences, however, there appear to be three important overarching themes in their work on cognitive and emotional change with age.

First, as people grow older, the complexity of their thinking appears to increase. Cognitive complexity means that a person can see many facets of a given problem or a relationship with another person. In the light of Gisela Labouvie-Vief's ideas and data, it would be more accurate to say some people become more mature cognitively as they get older, though this is quite variable from person to person.

A second theme is that, if patterns of thought in later life grow more complex, the emotions of these persons are also affected because they depend on how people think about themselves and the world around them. For example, older persons are said to be more sensitive than young ones in anticipating how others will react. They can put themselves more readily into the shoes of others and understand their feelings. This should result in better control over their emotions. Older adults are said to be just as emotional as younger adults, but they manage to regulate their feelings better than the young.

Third, older persons are said to accept adversity better than the young and to be able to remain cheerful in the face of unpleasant realities.[13] On the basis of longitudinal data, George Vaillant reported that as they mature, his college subjects use fewer primitive defenses, such as denial or avoidance, and fool themselves less about the realities. They cope with their troubles more philosophically than the young, can see the humor in what is happening, and use humor to distance themselves from emotional distress.

Unfortunately, the studies on age differences discussed in Schaie and Lawton's book share two basic limitations. The first is the cohort problem, which is inherent in cross-sectional research. As we pointed out several times in chapter 3, this problem plagues most of the research on aging. All the authors cited here from the Schaie and Lawton volume recognize this limitation and rue the absence of longitudinal studies that could confirm the principles they assert. As we also said earlier, we must remain wary about any generalizations about age or developmental differences that are made from cross-sectional research designs.

The second limitation, which may be even more important than the first, is that the actual differences obtained in aging research are really very modest in size. This is not so widely acknowledged by research scholars in this field. It is even more likely than the cohort problem to mislead those who read about this research.

We discussed this at length in chapter 2, using a study (by Gross, Carstensen, Pasupathi, Tsai, Skorpen, and Hsu) as an example of research that makes too big a deal of small differences, showing with a graph how problematic the results were.

This problem of speculative generalizing from modest findings is widespread in social science research. In their desire to be scientific, which in the eyes of most scientists calls for making broad, elegant generalizations from observations, those who do research stubbornly display a de facto denial of the importance of individual variation. This is a major theme in our book. We are reluctant to talk about what old people are like in general because they are so different from each other. The alternative is to describe particular cases as accurately as possible, which is why we have presented case histories in some detail in chapters 6 through 8. *Description is proper science, too.*

How Major Personality Changes Might Occur

We acknowledge the difficulties of obtaining an accurate answer about stability and change in personality and attribute some of the confusion to lack of agreement about how to measure personality. We think Lewis is right to argue for contextual influences. On the other hand, we consider the quotation from Caspi and Roberts to have merit, too. It points modestly to increased stability with age but recognizes that change can occur even though it is difficult to point to credible quantitative evidence. If they are right about this, the next step is to examine how personality change might occur and the conditions that could favor it. The concept of *change events* in psychotherapy is a good place to start.

Change Events in Psychotherapy

Personality change is particularly important to psychotherapists. They have a vested interest in the idea that therapy can help troubled people abandon unrealistic goals, dysfunctional outlooks, and ineffective coping and learn more effective ones. This vested interest could prompt them to see change even when it is barely detectable or modest. Psychotherapists also deal with a select population, people who are failing in their lives in some way, and are also likely to influence these clients in the course of therapy.

Nevertheless, this interest in producing therapeutic change may also be one of the reasons that psychotherapists have written more about the topic of personality change than most social scientists.[14] We shall say more about psychological treatment in chapter 9.

Psychotherapists accept the premise that people can change and treatment can facilitate it. In psychotherapy, such change is promoted or facilitated by certain life events, which some think of as change events, and which push the individual to recognize that the old ways of functioning are not working adequately and a reorganization of the personality may be necessary. But although people resist it, we believe they can and do change. Powerful and destructive conditions of life can sometimes overwhelm this resistance.

Psychotherapy is also a major context for the longitudinal exploration of deeper layers of personality and unconscious processes. In intensive psychotherapy, sessions with a client take place at least once each week and may continue for months or years. An enormous amount of information about given persons can be accumulated in this clinical context.

Psychotherapists also emphasize the individual meanings, as we do, that such events convey to the person who is facing them. Their perspective, like ours, is relational—that is, it is focused on how their clients construct meaning from what is happening in their ongoing relationships. Even shorter psychotherapies, which are more the fashion these days, provide much in-depth information about a person over time and diverse life circumstances. The therapist is there to observe and second-guess what clients say about their goals and emotions in everyday life.

In our judgment, more of the important insights about personality dynamics have come from psychotherapy and from field observations of human behavior than from the laboratory, with its formal personality assessment procedures. This does not mean that personality psychologists should abandon their research, or that there are no methodological difficulties in what can be learned from psychotherapy. Rather, we should somehow take into account both sources of evidence when we deal with the question of personality stability and change.

Vittorio Guidano suggests that change is not possible without the involvement of our emotions. Emotional crises are not simply external events but depend on the discovery that to deal with them the person must undergo a reorganization of personality to function effectively. The old ways of relating and coping have ceased to be adequate.[15]

To this we would add that emotional experiences must be thought about and evaluated by the person in order to become change events.[16] The provocative event, which the person can no longer handle, must be appraised as such. This urges the person to cope with the event and others like it differently. Emotion is crucial to change, but so is the cognitive process of appraisal, which involves a search for a more serviceable relational meaning and a different way of coping that can translate this insight into action.

Laura N. Rice and Leslie S. Greenberg illustrate this theme with a client who described an emotional change event leading to therapy as follows:

> One client described an incident in which he replied to a seemingly friendly comment with an antagonistic response, while another client described a situation in which he suddenly felt small and insignificant. The implications of such incidents are often ignored by therapists, who view them as merely the recounting of stories. The significance of these stories lies in the fact that the clients are aware of some discrepancy between their view of an appropriate or self-consistent reaction and their own actual reaction, and are thus motivated to explore and understand it [in therapy].[17]

Although the theory presented here seems sound, we find the example of a change event presented in the preceding quotation somewhat weak if we think in terms of a personal crisis as the life event that provokes change. We would not, however, want to deny that it could have contributed to the therapy by motivating, along with other personal issues, an effort to change.

Two conditions of change seem eminently reasonable to us. One is the experience of personal trauma or crisis. The other is religious conversion. Examples of crises might be loss of a loved one, a near-death experience, seeing a comrade's terrible death in battle, rape, destruction of one's home by earthquake or fire, or an instance of treachery by a friend. In the case of conversion, people must be dissatisfied with their spiritual outlook, but even a wonderful epiphany might also bring about a major religious conversion.

Although the data are insufficient to make the case firmly, clinical observations on change are sometimes quite provocative. The section that follows reflects our own tendency to trust in-depth clinical work with people in trouble as one of the best ways of looking at the issue of personality change. Because so many elderly people struggle with the crises of aging in the form of bereavement, life-threatening or disabling illnesses, and the active search for a more serviceable meaning in life, we think there are observations about this that should be taken into account.

So we proceed as follows: First, we compare the concepts of crisis intervention, stress, and trauma, because they present the best possibility of inducing change. Second, we turn to what is known about religious conversions. Finally, we offer some brief thoughts about personality change with age.

Crisis Intervention, Stress, and Trauma

The need for help in a crisis is the reason for the development in recent years of *crisis intervention* theory and practice. One modern impetus for this development was the growing awareness after the Vietnam War of what is now referred to as *posttraumatic stress disorder*.[18] A person afflicted with this disorder may need professional help, not necessarily because of long-standing neurotic problems but because of having experienced an extreme trauma that he or she cannot seem to manage adequately.

An experience is traumatic when it is shattering psychologically for a person. Everything that person has believed about life has been seriously challenged or assaulted. This may never happen to most of us, but it does to those who are vulnerable, and they experience a severe psychological crisis for which professional help is needed.

Interest in crisis intervention actually had its beginnings long before the Vietnam War, after the Cocoanut Grove nightclub fire in Boston, Massachusetts, on November 28, 1942, in which 493 people died. Eric Lindemann, a local psychiatrist, took on the task of studying how the survivors of this disaster grieved.[19] His work yielded the concept of "grief work" and public support for short-term help for people who were in crisis. Karl Slaikeu has presented a good statement of the rationale for crisis intervention:

> Very few people avoid crises altogether. Adult life, whether neurotic or normal, healthy or ill, optimistic or pessimistic in outlook, is a function of how we have weathered earlier crises, whether these be changing schools, surviving the divorce of parents, dealing with life-threatening illness, or surviving the loss of a first love.
>
> It is a time when "Everything is on the line," so to speak. Previous means of coping and managing problems break down in the face of new threats and challenges. The potential for good or bad outcomes lies in the disorganization and disequilibrium of crisis. A wealth of clinical data suggest that some form of reorganization will begin in a matter of weeks after the onset of crisis.[20]

The problem of crisis intervention, then, is to prevent a worse psychological disorder from arising by providing what clinicians refer to as *secondary prevention*, which involves effort to strengthen the resources of the person who has been traumatized. In contrast, *primary prevention* is the effort to prevent trauma and disorder from occurring.

The objective of those who pursue crisis intervention is to return people to their preexisting level of functioning. This treatment is not concerned with producing or demonstrating major personality change unless it seems necessary. There are, however, good grounds for believing that major personality changes do occur as a result of the trauma and the struggle to deal with it.

But what should be said about stress and trauma? Normally we do not think of *stress* as producing major personality change. What, then, is the difference between these two closely related concepts? Certain life events in particular kinds of people are said to be so destructive of their prior way of looking at life that they force major transformations in their outlook. This is *trauma*, and the person is apt to experience what we referred to as a crisis. We still know little about the rules that help us say when and how this will happen.

An event that does not seem awesome enough to one person to have a profound effect may be truly overpowering to another. In other words, the reaction will vary greatly from one person to another. In one person, we may see little evidence of more than minimal, short-lived distress. An observer is apt to interpret this as disinterest, coldness, or toughness of spirit. However, without knowing that person well, it is dangerous to say which interpretation is sound. In another person, we observe overwhelming and long-lasting distress, which some observers might interpret as weakness or neuroticism. Given the ambiguity of human behavior, observers can easily misread what is going on in the person's mind.

Remember that it is not the event itself that is primary in producing trauma but the *meaning* or lesson a bereaved person draws from it. Of course, the more terrible the experience, the more likely it will be capable of producing a traumatic reaction. But the critical feature of such an event is its significance or meaning for the person who experiences it. It challenges what the person once believed to be true.[21] This is easiest to see after a trauma that leads to a struggle for new meanings to sustain the person in the future.

Stress is, in effect, a weaker source of distress and dysfunction than trauma. It is, as we have noted (see chapter 2), an inevitable feature of normal living, though it can have positive consequences and may never reach traumatic or crisis proportions. Stress requires coping, but it does not normally overwhelm the person. The difference between stress and trauma, therefore, lies in the extent to which a person is *overwhelmed* by what has happened. This may never happen to most of us, but it does happen to those who are vulnerable, and they may experience a severe psychological crisis for which professional help is needed.

We can use bereavement and grief to bring home the point. Grieving is a prime example of a major coping struggle. Most people are not completely shattered (traumatized or overwhelmed) by the loss of a loved one, though they may experience and/or display considerable emotional distress and dysfunction. Some are hardly distressed at all. Others have a much more difficult and prolonged period of grief. All this depends on the person, the quality of the relationship, the details of the death itself, and the coping resources that person can draw on.

Grieving usually requires that the bereaved person reconcile the past with the present and a future that is difficult to foresee.[22] Doing so is likely to be very difficult psychological work. The bereaved person may have to cope with guilt over past anger felt or displayed toward the deceased person. Just the effort to get on with one's life and establish a new relationship of importance without being burdened by the past may provoke guilt because it seems disloyal to the person who is gone.

Bereavement creates the necessity of change in the way one lives one's life, but we must ask whether it results in major personality change or merely a superficially changed lifestyle. Research has not thoroughly established what has been changed by the grief work. Those who have studied the process of grieving usually think of it as a way to restore the person's previous level of functioning and emotional integrity rather than as producing major personality change.

Important changes of some sort are likely, however, if not inevitable. The main problem with all our suppositions about change is that we have little except anecdotal data to reveal what has changed in the person as a result of grieving or some other stress or trauma. Nor do we have much data about the effects of psychotherapy because of the methodological challenges that are involved in assessing change.[23]

Religious Conversion and Personality Change

Precisely the same set of issues arise with respect to religious conversions. We have long assumed that a major transformation of one's spiritual outlook must be accompanied by major personality change. Ray Paloutzian, James Richardson, and Lewis Rambo have reviewed research in this area, analyzed the issues involved in personality change, and raised doubts about this assumption. They write thoughtfully and with enthusiasm about the issues involved; the following passage points to our lack of consensus about what we mean by personality and what it means for personality change to take place:

> One of the biggest questions in the history of intellectual work concerns knowledge of how to change a human being. If we were to fully

understand what constitutes a person and how to change a person from one condition to another, how to transform a personality, we would have accomplished one of the greatest achievements, filled with the greatest potential for good and ill, that the human mind could hope for. The potential for both freeing and controlling each individual follows straightforwardly from such knowledge.[24]

These authors add that people seek meaning, belonging, and identity, and they draw on religious commitments as a way to attain what they seek. Buddhism, Christianity, and Islam are among the major religions of the world (Paloutzian et al. leave out Judaism, appearing inappropriately to assimilate it to Christianity). They are (except for Judaism) missionary religions, and most religions want to attract adherents to their beliefs and practices. It is widely believed that religious conversion is a transformational experience that changes one's life in a profound way.

The frequency of religious conversion is apparently high if we consider reports of born-again experiences and evidence from new converts. We do not know much about how many give up the new religion after a time or lapse from their original enthusiasm. One would think, as Paloutzian et al. suggest, that personality psychologists could learn something useful from these phenomena about what it takes for personality change to take place.

The primary questions that can be raised, say these authors, are twofold. First, what provokes religious conversion? Second, what are its effects on personality? With respect to the first question, it would appear that many who are ultimately converted are looking for a new approach to life that will serve them better than what they had before, which is similar to the way change events are conceived of by cognitive therapists. Certainly stress and dissatisfaction with life are high on the list of precursors to seeking and finding a new spiritual outlook with which to guide living.

As to the second question, about the effects of conversion on personality, it is obvious that behavioral changes will occur, many of which have to do merely with following the tenets of the newly adopted religion. Paloutzian et al. suggest that there is evidence of modifications in the way one defines one's self, confidence, and sense of purpose. They quote William James as saying in 1890 that by the age of thirty the human character is "set like plaster." They further write, "The popular claims of dramatic changes in basic personality structure . . . do not seem to be warranted by the evidence. Instead, people with certain personality types may seek those groups that attract and reinforce those types within the culture of the group."[25]

In effect, people who were extroverts before religious conversion remain so, and people who are introverts remain introverts. The authors' review of research shows little evidence that these personality traits and basic structure change after conversion. People with certain attributes and attitudes are more prone than others to convert. Presumably, as they deal with the daily issues of living, they need to find personal expression through the religion they choose. That is, conversion influences beliefs, goals, strivings, and identity, but it seems to have little effect on extroversion or introversion.

Here we have a major disagreement with these authors, which has to do with their treatment of surface and depth in personality. In their comments, these authors appear to reverse what we consider to be the basic and superficial features of personality. For us, beliefs, goals, strivings, and identity, especially those that are conflicted and defensive, are basic, whereas traits like extroversion or introversion, though important, are superficial. They deal with a temperamental quality of persons rather than the relational meanings on which our emotional reactions rest.

But it is these meanings we are always searching for. They have the power to influence our will to live, the commitments on which our life is vested and from which our joys and tragedies arise. Whether we are socially outgoing or more reserved has to do, in our view, merely with temperamental styles by means of which we address the truly important struggles of our existence that form the important substance of our lives.

Therefore, we see the evidence that these scholars review as providing positive support for the idea that religious conversion can, indeed, change basic aspects of personality, just as we claimed with respect to trauma or crisis. It all depends on what one considers basic or superficial. It seems to us that the answer to this difficult question about the change effects of religious conversion remains unsettled.

Aging and Personality Change

Does aging promote fundamental changes in personality in the absence of signs of dementia? We cannot make such a claim on the basis of programmatic evidence. According to what we have been saying, however, when the magnitude of losses is great enough and it becomes impossible to live in accordance with well-established patterns from the past, basic changes should be possible, if not likely.

As we said, most of the observations about such changes are anecdotal and clinical rather than programmatic. But they do encourage the view that, although most of us are who we are forever, so to speak, major traumas in late life can be change events depending on how they are viewed by the person in crisis. Do traumatic losses increase the potential for change in important characteristics of personality? Our speculative answer is yes. How often, in what ways, and how close to the end of life they occur, no one yet knows.

The combination of stability and its counterpart, change, which must be discussed together, constitutes a rich but perplexing topic for psychology and social science in general. We have barely scratched the surface of it here, as is also true of research in this area. We seem to have a long way to go to find a sound resolution of the issue of whether and how personality changes in adulthood. However, we hope we have stimulated your curiosity and provoked you to think about it, especially as it might apply to your own life and those you care about.

IV ::

CENTRAL EXPERIENCES OF AGING: CASE HISTORIES

6 ::

Family and Friends

The central questions for this chapter are whether, how, and to what extent family and friends play a role in the quality of life and well-being of aging persons. We are inclined to think this role can be both positive and negative, a source of joy and of distress. Social scientists have great interest in these questions, as should the elderly, and there has been considerable recent research attempting to address the way family and friends might contribute to or detract from the lives of people who are growing old. We examine ideas and research about this in the first half of the chapter. In the second half, we present a case history of a wife who takes on the role of caregiver for a husband with Alzheimer's disease.

Looking at family and friends in aging people involves, as does the issue of personality stability and change, a difficult dilemma for anyone who wants to summarize what has been learned. Because most research is cross-sectional, we are left in doubt about whether the effects observed result from chronological age or the time in which the research cohort grew up. It is awkward to present this research when a definitive answer remains in doubt and then complain incessantly about faulty methods. Yet just ignoring the problem does not seem like the sensible thing to do.

The ideas and speculations about the roles of family and friends in aging are plausible, interesting, instructive, and provocative. They could even be, in the main, correct though not proven, so we should not discard altogether what is said about this topic. Our solution requires that we explain at the outset what we need to be wary about, particularly for those who are not familiar with the rigorous demands of good science. Here are three recommendations about what can be said about the findings of cross-sectional research.

The first recommendation is that the concepts of appraisal, coping, and relational meanings are needed to help us understand individual variations in the emotional relationships between people, especially intimate ones. This applies to everything important in one's life and certainly, therefore, to what happens with family and friends.

Second, it is only when comparisons are made of two or more age-groups, say those in their fifties and those in their seventies, that we run into the cohort problem with respect to age and our relationships with family members and friends. Other aspects of this research can still be enlightening. For example, attempts to describe the social and psychological dynamics operating within an age cohort can provide valuable information not about aging but about the ways people of that particular cohort think, feel, and act. Careful description is just as important in science as are simplifying generalizations or principles. In other words, to study family life and friendship in septuagenarians (those between seventy and seventy-nine years of age) is perfectly defensible so long as no comparisons are made using younger cohorts to identify the effects of age. For the latter question, we need longitudinal research designs.

Third, if the differences found between age-groups are modest in size, which is the usual finding, we may be making too much out of too little in our conclusions. In other words, most of the subjects cannot be distinguished from each other on the causal variable in question, as we pointed out in chapter 5. Then we should avoid speaking as though we know what people are like at any given chronological age. Researchers should be obliged to describe the data fully enough so that the reader can judge what has validly been demonstrated. Most often they do not. Scientific journal editors should require this but typically do not.

If you follow these recommendations, it should be possible for you to judge for yourself whether the research justifies the generalizations made about different age cohorts. From the standpoint of our concern with the experience of people who are aging, most of the research we discuss in the following provides mainly statistical averages of this or that group, but it sometimes contains dependable knowledge about individual variations or the role of family and friends as people age. Let us look a bit more closely at some of these ideas and research, to which we add some anecdotes that focus on individuals.

Family

Families come in many varieties, such as single-parent families, nuclear families, and extended families. What are called families these days consist of a much larger variety of living arrangements than in the past. The so-called *nuclear family* consists of a mother, father, and children; the *extended family* consists of parents, grandparents, grandchildren, siblings, aunts, uncles, and cousins. As a couple grows older, their parents, and certainly their grandparents, have less chance of still being alive, but they are likely to remain important influences nonetheless.

The 2000 census in the United States shows that for the first time in our country's history, the proportion of nuclear families dropped below 25 percent of all households. This is thought to be the result of several other social changes, such as delay in the age of marriage and having children, the fact that more couples live longer after their children leave home, and a faster increase in the number of single-parent families than married couples.

Marriage is among the most important and intimate of social relationships. Although there are common patterns in marriage, we must always think of individual differences among couples. They include, for example, the similarities and differences between marital partners, their expectations, values, degree of harmony and disharmony, and the intensity and duration of spousal relationships, which are always substantial.

There has been surprisingly little systematic research on the topic of marriage. What there is has looked mainly at marital satisfaction, the factors involved in it, and the impact of marriage on health and the emotional life. The variety of marital relationships and how they work have not been major topics of research. Laura Carstensen and her colleagues are among some of those to view marriage from the standpoint of the adult life course.[1] Noting the scarcity of studies of marriage among aging couples, one article states, "The nature of marriage as it unfolds across adulthood remains relatively uncharted territory."[2] Except for one study (Carstensen, 1995), this research is all cross-sectional.

Carolyn Pape Cowan and Philip A. Cowan studied couples over time, but their research had little to do with aging unless resentment about an imbalance between spouses is assumed to carry over into later life or the changing cultural roles for men and women affect well-established marriages as couples age. They report that marital satisfaction, including passionate love, is highest in the newly married but declines after that, especially after childbirth. The division of labor between husband and wife is apt to be a major factor in marital conflict during the period of child rearing, and wives typically carry a disproportionately heavier burden.[3]

They also suggest that marital satisfaction makes a comeback in later years: "Studies . . . suggest that marriages that survive into the twilight years are often satisfying and emotionally close."[4] They add, "In retrospective accounts of marriages that had lasted for more than 50 years, the childbearing years were viewed as both the most satisfying and least satisfying periods of marriages; and in old age, the presence of adult children is strongly predictive of emotional well being."[5]

Citing Robert Levenson et al. (1993) as a source, Carstensen et al. summarize some important observations about the conflicts between marital partners and what happens at different ages. In middle-aged married couples, disagreements tend to be centered on children, money, religion, and recreation. None of these topics appeared important, however, in older couples. According to what older couples say about their marital relationships compared with midlife couples, more pleasure is derived from talking about children and grandchildren, sharing their dreams, doing things together, and vacations.

It makes sense that the sources of stress change over different life stages.[6] Considering the total life course, Carstensen et al. conclude that older couples experience more pleasure and less conflict in their marriages than young or midlife couples. The older ones also show more affection and lower levels of anger, disgust, belligerence, and whining. These ideas are provocative, but as we have said more than once, we must always be wary of cross-sectional comparisons and the generalizations derived from them. (On this point, we are beginning to sound like nags even to ourselves.)

Theory and research had once suggested a crossover of gender roles that occurred as married people age, with women supposedly becoming more aggressive and dominating and men more nurturing.[7] If these data were correct, as was once thought, then men and women would constantly be out of phase with each other's developmental trajectory. This would be frustrating and could account for notorious gender battles, sometimes stereotyped as two opposing camps, Mars and Venus.

However, the gender differences in Carstensen et al.'s data were constant in the different age cohorts. Midlife and older wives expressed more emotion, both positive and negative, but husbands controlled their emotions rather tightly. This male effort at control—one might call it overcontrol—is referred to as "stonewalling."[8] That is, when pressed by their wives to confront emotional conflicts, the men avoided doing so, a behavior pattern that often greatly aggravated their wives.

One of the serious traumas of long-lasting marriages is the virtual certainty that one or the other spouse will become ill and die. A striking consequence of old age is that women tend to live longer than men. On this theme we are undoubtedly on solid empirical ground. The last data we have for Rossmoor indicate that 63 percent are single occupancies and 37 percent are doubles. Most of these singles are women, because men die sooner, but this difference is compounded by the fact that women tend to marry older men. By the age of eighty-four, 62 percent of women and only 20 percent of men have lost their spouse as a result of death.[9] It is patently obvious that in Rossmoor, as in other living settings for the elderly, a large proportion of women residents become widows and that they outnumber male widowers.

Death of a spouse is apt to be emotionally devastating for husband or wife, even when the marriage has been troubled, though gender seems to make a big difference. Wives seem to do better than husbands in coping with spousal loss. There is nothing new in the idea that the death of their wife is especially stressful for men, leading to greatly increased risk of mortality. After becoming widowers, men are four times more likely than women to remarry.

The typical explanation for the greater problems of men who have lost a spouse is that the wife, especially in the older generations, has for a long time taken charge of the couple's household and social life. Husbands are likely to rely on their wives for emotional support and social activity, whereas women tend to have female confidants. The loss of the wife typically leaves the surviving husband without a social network that could supply such support. Men often remarry to replace it.

For either husband or wife, living with their children after the other spouse dies sounds like a lovely idea, but it is fraught with peril for both the bereaved and the children. We are not aware that this issue has been studied programmatically in research on aging. Most of the bereaved persons we know say they prefer to live alone and control their own life patterns if they can.

A high percentage of caregivers of ailing or dying spouses become clinically depressed.[10] When a husband is ill, the wife is likely to become the caregiver. When a wife is ill, a female relative or friend often becomes the caregiver, or the husband might hire professional help. Women tend to be more reluctant to seek help, and men less often feel comfortable with the caregiving role, which probably tells us why more women become caregivers than men do.

Carstensen et al. offer some useful thoughts in summarizing their view of the role of family in the emotional life and health of those who are aging. They suggest that close relationships can provide benefits in later life—for example, by buffering the mental and physical problems associated with illness. They believe that these relationships provide emotionally meaningful experiences and help people master the art of regulating their emotions.[11] This is an important idea, even though we do not know whether age brings with it greater skill at handling one's emotions and those of others who are important in one's life. And, we would add, along with the benefits of such relationships can come considerable stress. We need to look closely at both.

What, then, can we safely say about the social dynamics of family life as applied to aging from this analysis? The data clearly show that among the elderly, women are much more likely than men to be living alone because men usually die before their wives. There is no methodological problem in this instance because the generalization refers to a given cohort, and although there are individual differences that should be given more attention, the average gender difference in longevity is large, consisting of about five years. Decline of passionate love and the discrepant burden of child care are also fair game to cite in young couples who report this. This pattern seems to characterize early marriages, but it says little about sex, love, and conflict among aging or old couples.

Statistical references to the emotional lives of the elderly constitute a questionable way of understanding the actual experience of old age. Although we are still together and over eighty, both of us can anticipate a time when one of us will die after a marriage that is now of more than fifty-seven years' duration. Our thoughts and feelings about this are probably similar to those of many others and provide the experiential aspects of aging and the anticipation of loss that statistical data cannot. Thus we try to describe them here.

Though each has his or her own independent activities outside the home, so much of our lives and history are interdependent that it is difficult for either of us to contemplate the loss when it happens, as we know it must. The signs that it is coming are serious ailments that leave us both vulnerable, though there is no way to predict which one will go first. Richard is trying to learn how the household is run so he can cope with it if Bernice goes first. Bernice may be on firmer ground in this regard because she has protected Richard's work all these years. When we see a movie or read a book that brings up this kind of wrenching loss, it is difficult not to become tearful, anxious, and sad, if not depressed. We do not talk much about it, but it is always there in the background.

Our children, and we think our grandchildren, too, have begun to realize that the ends of our lives are coming close. Our daughter-in-law lost her mother to cancer only two years ago, and there was much suffering involved. We notice the individual youngsters in the family try to find more time now to have lunch or dinner with us, and our grown-up children telephone often to check on our medical diagnoses and treatments. They offer to drive us now because they worry about our having an accident, but we prefer to do what we have to as much as possible. But they are well aware of where we are in our life cycle, and we are fortunate to have a close, loving family.

We suspect that the biggest problem associated with the loss is loneliness and, even worse, emptiness. We had some good friends; the woman died of a heart attack. Her husband confided to us about a year later about the terrible loneliness he experienced despite having a concerned and loving family. Children and grandchildren are not adequate replacements for a deceased loved one from a long marriage.

Soon after the death of his wife, our male friend began to date another woman whom the children resented, seeing her as controlling and competitive. The husband's firstborn daughter was particularly hostile toward her. Most of the rest of the family were horrified and obviously resented this intruder into the family circle. In their eyes, she may have posed an economic threat, but their hostility was probably based on much more than this.

This resentment of our friend's companion made his adjustment to his loss even more difficult. We never said anything to the children—we were not close enough to them to intrude. If we had, we would have chastened them about the selfishness that kept them from accepting that their father needed to relate to someone of his generation. We felt that they should have been glad he had someone he enjoyed being with. We have heard similar stories from others about family resentments that added to the grief over a lost loved one and interfered with the necessary grief work and the rebuilding of a life that did not have much further to go.

Friends

Friends are people with whom a person has a voluntary social relationship. They may be limited to a particular time period or continue throughout life. A Chinese fortune cookie we recently saw said portentously, "A friend is a present you give yourself." That statement implies, of course, a good friend, but not all friends are equally good. The life satisfaction of older adults depends on the *quality* of friendships rather than their quantity.[12]

Some friends offer a casual though relatively stable social connection that can add greatly to life satisfaction, though it can also add stress. Other friendships are fleeting and superficial and, accordingly, are best thought of as acquaintances. They remain transient and peripheral, often disappearing as people move from one place to another. There is no challenge, however, to the general idea that, like family, friends play a very important role in the lives of most people, older ones included.[13]

When it comes to its place in aging research, the cohort problem is just as relevant to friendship as it is to family. Most generalizations about friendship are based on modest age- and gender-based differences and cross-sectional research designs; they are subject to the same doubts we raised with respect to personality change and the role of family in aging. Whenever age comparisons are implied, as we said, it is best to be wary.

When necessary, most people—not just the elderly—reduce their circle of friends depending on other obligations, but this may be temporary and occur under special circumstances. For example, young adults curtail their social lives for a time while they are raising children or attending to career development. Midlife adults may do so when they must care for aging parents. The elderly do so on a more permanent basis because of physical limitations and illness, which increase their need to prioritize their activities. In aging research this is known as the *selectivity principle*.

Carstensen, who has emphasized this principle, reanalyzed an intergeneration growth study from the University of California at Berkeley. The study, which was longitudinal, showed that from late adolescence to middle age, there is a gradual and selective reduction in social contact with acquaintances, with this trend peaking between ages eighteen and thirty.[14] This does not deal with the elderly, but it provides support for the life course principle of selectivity (see also chapter 9).

There is also an obverse relationship between the comparative investment in family or friends because of the limits of time and energy in the elderly. Involvement with one limits the time available for the other. For this reason, the study of the social and emotional lives of all people, especially the elderly, should include *both* family and friends.[15] These relationships serve overlapping but somewhat different functions in life.

The contrast between family and friends has been expressed in the oft-quoted aphorism that "God gives us our relatives, but thank God we can choose our friends." This is a put-down of family because of its obligatory demands. A contrary aphorism about family loyalty, however, is that "blood is thicker than water." You cannot win this aphorism game. For every positive statement, there is always a negative one, and vice versa.

Anger is more commonly felt and more intensely expressed toward close family members and friends than strangers.[16] Guilt feelings are also more likely in family relationships than in other relationships. This is probably the case because the most important and intimate relationships are much more likely to produce both joy and misery as a result of their potential for both benefit and harm. No doubt all emotions are apt to be more intense with intimates than with mere acquaintances. The same probably applies to all the emotions in every adult stage of life, but we are not aware of relevant data.

Different ways of attempting to reconcile competition over which to be engaged with, family or friends, as a person's main social involvement have been proposed. Although the two areas can overlap, these researchers compared the different functions that family and friends play in a person's psychological economy. Zena Smith Blau suggests that an elderly person with a good friend can deal with the losses and challenges of old age better than one who has a dozen grandchildren but no peer-group friends.[17] Barbara J. Felton and C. A. Berry report that the elderly feel better if their practical needs are satisfied by kinfolk, whereas relations with friends satisfy their emotional needs.[18]

New friendships in later life appear to be less intense than earlier ones. This conforms to what we have seen in the Rossmoor community. Rossmoor social relationships tend to be somewhat superficial, perhaps because of sickness and the closeness of death of so many neighbors and friends. Maintaining emotional distance can be a way of protecting oneself from the distress of loss and death, which makes most relationships here seem tentative. We are, in effect, temporary residents, at most limited to a decade or two. One friend here said he never goes to funerals except, of course, his own.

If we consider the functional aspects of friendship—that is, what friendship does for each of us regardless of age—a number of themes have been suggested. They include, for example, the sharing of mutual interests and values and the capacity for fun, amusement, and recreation. Having someone we are able to trust and confide in and provide emotional support is another. Friends also offer a contrast with family and can sometimes even serve as a substitute.

Perhaps more important than any other function, and regardless of whether we are young or old, friendships provide feedback from other people about who we are on Spaceship Earth, which can help validate our value and identity in the world. Cultivating a career and raising children temporarily reduce the importance of this function, but the value of having feedback from others about who we are never disappears. The functions we have mentioned previously are provided on a highly individual basis. Thus, when a friend is lost, no other individual may be able to replace the function that person had served in the relationship.

The recent loss of a good friend who died of lung cancer created a void for Bernice, who saw this woman as the smartest of any of her friends. Throughout this woman's illness, Bernice kept in close contact with her. When her friend died, Bernice was certain that she could not be replaced by anyone else.

The way men and women manage friendships differs, on the average, though it is possible to overstate such differences and forget the great individual differences within each sex. These individual differences within each gender are probably even greater than the differences between genders. Often the differences between men and women are promoted and the similarities understated. Beware of sweeping generalizations about Mars and Venus.

In any case, women are said to emphasize what has been called emotion work, whereas men focus more on shared activities. Emotion work has to do with how one manages one's emotions intrapsychically and socially—for example, whether they are inhibited, shared openly, or employed to manipulate or control others.[19] Control, competition, and the avoidance of personal vulnerability appear to be more characteristic of male friendships than female ones, which is consistent with the traditional male macho role and the barriers to intimacy that it results in.

Friendships among the elderly are also influenced by the circumstances of life—for example, widowhood, illness, and infirmity—just as marriage and child rearing are major influences in youth and midlife. Women who are widowed or divorced discover that they tend to be dropped socially by couples with whom they were friendly earlier—couples usually seek other couples, not singles—though grieving over the loss of a spouse reflects a tragedy during which the need for social support is very great.

It is not clear why this happens, but one explanation is that the single woman can pose a threat to the surviving wife. She may view the single woman as a competitor for her husband's attention. Men are usually attentive to an attractive other woman, and the man's wife may mistake his attentions as sexual or even just a matter of mild interest. Usually there is a flurry of attention right after the death or divorce, but soon intact couples begin to maintain social distance. Another reason may be simply that couples engage in different activities than singles, and the previous good fit may no longer apply.

Retirement may result in a similar experience because working colleagues, to some degree, tend to be a bit wary of spending much time with retirees during working hours. The retiree's willingness to engage in extended conversation is too time-consuming for those still hard-pressed by career demands. And the retiree may no longer have as much authority or status as before.

Although colleagues are usually friendly toward retirees—after all, they will ultimately get there, too, if they are lucky—their body language often conveys the clear wish to keep the contact brief. They do not want talkative and circumstantial retirees who are, in a sense, on a permanent vacation, to govern their time before they, too, are ready to retire.

Both of us recall a prominent younger colleague who, when Richard was near retirement, enjoined him to please get out of the way and give the next generation a chance. We were taken aback by the frank, open competitiveness and ageism that were reflected in what was said. Competition is another issue that pertains to relationships between the old and the young. One way the young push the old out of the way is to draw on their work while failing to give any credit for it, thereby seeming to make it their own and removing a competitor.

Illness and infirmity can also lead to a degree of isolation from old friends. Not only must ailing persons curtail their social activity, but, for a number of reasons, healthy persons may be threatened by extensive contact with someone who is ailing. Some may think, for example, "There, but for the grace of God, go I." Friendship also involves mutual obligations and as a result of infirmity may become too demanding to be mutually rewarding.

People sometimes resist living in communities such as Rossmoor because of too frequent reminders of the painful nature of affliction, loss, infirmity, and death, which will ultimately catch up with them sooner or later, too. They may also be embarrassed or feel guilty about confronting affliction if their own health is robust. Or they may fear they will be asked to take on the demanding tasks of caregiving, the need for which seems to be unlimited in a community of elders.

Caregiving for the Ailing Aged

Given the problems of the elderly, and the growing number of old people who are alive and active today as a result of medical care, *caregiving* has become a tremendously important concern. As we noted in chapter 1, midlife individuals and couples feel the need to provide care for their ailing parents. Healthy spouses in danger of losing their beloved mate as a result of a terminal or handicapping illness usually feel this way, too, even though the task is apt to be onerous.

Increasingly, research articles and books document the unrelenting stresses of being a caregiver and how people cope with them.[20] The research of Susan Folkman and her colleagues deals with caregiving by partners of patients dying of AIDS rather than aging.[21] However, it turns out to be informative about caregiving problems that can arise with an aging spouse or parent, because in many ways they overlap.

Dorothy and Her Husband's Alzheimer's Disease

In keeping with this recent growth of interest, we now present a case history of a wife who cared for her husband after he developed Alzheimer's disease, one of the most stressful set of demands any caregiver can face. It also allows us to provide a not atypical description of Alzheimer's disease, which, along with stroke, is probably the disease of aging most feared by the public.

After thirty-three years of marriage with three children and an affluent husband who owned a successful manufacturing company, Dorothy found that her husband, Gardner, who was sixty-five years old, had begun to display odd behavior. Dorothy, at sixty, was healthy and vigorous. She knew nothing about Alzheimer's disease except for Ronald Reagan's public announcement that he suffered from it.

This announcement came after the end of Reagan's second term as president of the United States. His letter to the American public, written in his own hand, is deeply moving. In it, he said he was making this personal news public to raise awareness of the condition in hopes that by doing so, people afflicted with it, and families affected by it, would come to have a greater understanding of what he referred to as its "heavy burden."[22]

Dorothy soon learned that Alzheimer's disease is a slowly developing disorder of the brain in which dementia is the predominant symptom. Her husband was beginning literally to lose his mind. She had been a teacher, and up to this period in life things had gone smoothly in the main. Her two oldest children, a girl and boy, were in college, and the third was finishing high school. The family originally had lived in an upper-middle-class neighborhood, where the children had grown up. When Dorothy was sixty and

Gardner sixty-five, just before he began to show symptoms of dementia, the two of them had moved to a retirement community.

The odd behavior that Dorothy first noticed began one day soon after moving, when Gardner was making lunch for the two of them. This ordinarily competent and meticulous man did not seem to know what he was doing. He had said he would make scrambled eggs, bacon, and toast, but he hard-boiled two eggs and promptly put them into the refrigerator. Then he sat down on his living room chair to watch television and announced that he had enjoyed his lunch and hoped Dorothy had, too.

When Dorothy argued with him that they had not had lunch, he became greatly offended and accused her of making fun of him. She did not know what to do but proceeded to make the lunch herself. By that time Gardner had calmed down, and they ate silently, as if nothing had happened. Gardner seemed to be aware that something strange had occurred. He said he did not know what had just gone on but acknowledged that he was not his old self, adding that he was having difficulty remembering.

Dorothy was relieved that her husband had returned to reality. She was worried about the strange seizure he had experienced, but she was afraid to confront it, fearing it might have been a stroke. Then she remembered what she had heard about President Reagan. Could her husband be displaying some form of dementia? Dorothy secretly sought out information about dementia on the Internet and found a discussion written by someone from the Alzheimer's Association.[23]

She was not yet sure whether she and her husband should visit their primary care physician or leave things alone until the situation became clear. Gardner now seemed perfectly normal and in touch with what was going on. Their friends and people with whom they had business, such as shop clerks and waiters in restaurants, saw nothing amiss. Maybe what she had seen was just a transient episode that did not signify anything important. Or perhaps she had been mistaken about the whole event.

Neither of these latter possibilities seemed like the best guess. Still, if Gardner were now operating normally, the physician would be unable to see anything wrong. It would be like taking one's car to a mechanic when the glitch in its operation had disappeared. More can be learned when symptoms of the trouble are in evidence. So she waited.

As time wore on, Dorothy became increasingly convinced that her husband was very ill. He was more and more forgetful, even of the names of his children. He got lost a few times while driving home from work despite the fact that the route had been well practiced. Employees of his business were also becoming uneasy that Gardner was losing his marbles. At other times, however, he seemed perfectly normal.

From time to time Gardner had trouble following newspaper articles, which Dorothy could clearly see when they talked about what was going on in the news; he garbled the news stories. He would sometimes sit for hours in his chair without doing anything, something uncharacteristic of him. Though changes in his condition developed very slowly, it was increasingly obvious that Gardner was often disoriented and was occasionally aware of this himself. He could no longer calculate the tip at a restaurant, forgot to keep his accounts accurately, made checks out without keeping a record of them, often got the amounts wrong, and seemed withdrawn and depressed. He often was able to excuse himself in ways that suggested he was communicating that he was really okay.

At the table tennis club, players began to notice that Gardner was becoming quite erratic in his play and seemed increasingly unconnected with what was going on. Whereas before he was always pleasant and attentive, a man well liked by others, he would now interrupt play by taking a long time to hang up his outer garments. People tried to be patient with him.

Every case of Alzheimer's disease is different, and of course the severity depends on its stage. Some patients decline much faster than others. Their cognitive losses progress steadily while they are otherwise physically intact and seem healthy. Gardner still socialized a great deal and often seemed well oriented, but he was constantly intent on convincing others he was a person of importance, which he communicated to them in a somewhat agitated and repetitious fashion, as if he needed to deny that anything was wrong with him. Denial is common in cases of dementia, as is confabulation, in which the person makes up things to fill in gaps in his or her mind.

Gardner had become a nuisance and was making people uncomfortable. They began to avoid him, which only made him try harder. His actions conveyed the pathos of a vague understanding about what was happening to him and a desperate attempt to cover it up. Friends urged Dorothy to get him to a doctor.

It was then that Dorothy made an appointment with a family physician they usually visited once a year for a physical and who had known their medical history over a period of many years. Gardner made no protest, and after Dorothy told the doctor of her experiences with him, he sent them to a neurologist with some knowledge of dementia. The neurologist sought to make a diagnosis by ruling out, one by one, each of the other forms of dementia—he had already made an educated guess that Gardner was suffering from Alzheimer's disease, perhaps an early or middle stage. What he observed convinced him that his guess was correct.

Dorothy learned a great deal from Internet printouts and the simple, clear brochures she obtained from the Alzheimer's Association, especially one that dealt with how to communicate with a patient. The neurophysiological books she first looked at were largely scientific, some quite beyond her understanding, and not very relevant to the problem of relating to a patient on a daily basis.

While Gardner was temporarily in touch with things, he and Dorothy were able to talk about what they would do as the disease progressed, including the likelihood that he would ultimately need to be moved to a nursing home. He flirted with the idea of suicide but never acted on it. Dorothy tried to be open and supportive with her husband and their children and friends.

Among other things, Dorothy learned that Alzheimer's disease accounts for more than half of all forms of dementia and that its causes were not yet clear. Early onset—that is between age thirty and fifty—covers less than 10 percent of dementia, and most cases begin after age sixty-five. The Alzheimer's Association estimates that almost half of those over eighty-five develop it, and that four million people in the United States are victims of the disease. This figure is probably much too high—this association is an advocacy group—but an accurate figure is difficult to obtain. There is no treatment, though some new drugs, which are still being studied, may improve symptoms temporarily.

Among the most important things Dorothy learned was how to deal with her ill husband. Some of this information came from a brochure distributed by the Alzheimer's Association. By chance she came upon a useful book by Nancy Mace and Peter Rabins, which we have cited earlier. These sources were designed to improve communication with someone who has the disease. As the Mace and Rabins book makes very clear, it is important to be patient and supportive with anyone who has Alzheimer's disease.

One common problem is the Alzheimer's patient who wanders. Mace and Rabins point out that in most cases, these individuals were not really intending to wander but had decided to go somewhere, made a wrong turn, and gotten lost. These patients then became frightened and did not know what to do, so they wandered around hoping to find a clue about where they were.[24] Not infrequently at Rossmoor, someone will spot such a person walking around or sleeping on the ground and recognize that he or she is in trouble. If the patient does not resist, he or she can be brought home, to the great relief of the caregiver. If there is resistance, the security police will do this if they are notified by phone.

When episodes like this recur, it will probably be necessary to place the person in a nursing home, which is usually an agonizing decision. The worst agony for the close relative or spouse is to watch someone you love and once respected slowly decline and lose most of the vestiges of his or her intellectual integrity and distinctive identity. Though still looking more or less the same, the original person no longer exists. By the late stages of the disease, Dorothy's husband was no longer Gardner in any meaningful psychological sense. Though some days seemed better than others, he could no longer sign his name or carry on a sensible conversation, and he no longer knew who he was or what he once had been.

Family members or other caregivers need to approach such problems with empathy and understanding and learn what to do. Mace and Rabins describe scenarios in which they interpret what is really going on in the Alzheimer's patient's mind, which could be helpful to the stressed-out and befuddled caregiver. They also advise that caregivers can help themselves in little ways to keep from becoming exhausted. They cite the following example:

> Mrs. Levin says, "he gets up in the night and puts his hat on and sits on the sofa. I used to wear myself out trying to get him back into bed. Now I just let him sit there. If he wants to wear his hat with his pajamas, it's O.K. I don't worry about it. I used to think I had to do my windows twice a year and my kitchen floor every week. Now I don't. I have to spend my energy on other things."[25]

Many suggestions in Mace and Rabins's book are useful for the caregiver who needs to know how to deal with an Alzheimer's victim. For example, try to seem interested in the patient; avoid interrupting and give the patient plenty of time to communicate his or her desires; avoid criticizing, correcting, or arguing with the patient; if the patient cannot find the right word, it is OK to suggest one; try to focus more on the feelings being expressed rather than on the facts; encourage the use of pointing or gestures in order to communicate; and try to place the person with Alzheimer's disease in a part of the house that is quiet so he or she is less distracted when you are attempting to interact.

With respect to the advice not to argue with the patient, you may remember that after Gardner forgot he made lunch but had not eaten it, Dorothy tried to convince him he was wrong. You may remember, too, that this lapse was Dorothy's first clear intimation that something was very wrong with her husband. After she read about the disease, when Gardner would make a mistake by using the wrong word yet she understood what he meant, she did not correct him but let the matter pass.

Unlike those who are aging but not demented, typical Alzheimer's patients forget whole life experiences, not just a name or a word; but they rarely remember later what was forgotten. They gradually become unable to follow written or spoken directions or use notes to help them remember, and ultimately they are unable to care for themselves.

Dorothy's experience as caregiver for her husband was terribly frustrating, leading to a variety of emotional impulses, which she constantly struggled to control. These included annoyance (mild, controlled anger) when Gardner did something foolish, especially in the early stages, when she presumed he was more intact than he actually was. She usually felt guilty or ashamed afterward because her anger did not seem fair to this sick man.

She felt angry at the Fates when she thought about her plight, which, in turn, led to guilt feelings about being self-centered enough to feel sorry for herself. After all, it was Gardner who suffered the most. The high cost of the nursing home when she finally placed Gardner in one also angered her. This anger arose from her belief that families who were not wealthy should not have to squander their modest resources on long-term care, resources that should go to their progeny if possible. Such thoughts simply added to her feelings of guilt and shame.

When Gardner would unexpectedly wander away from home, Dorothy suffered from terrible anxiety, imagining the worst after she called the security police at her retirement community. The worst could include being hit by a car or run over, lying under a tree freezing or having died from the cold, being mistakenly jailed, taking the car without a license and running over someone else, and so on. She had read in the *Alzheimer's Association Newsletter* about others who had gotten lost: "Six out of ten dementia sufferers get lost during the course of the disease. Forty-four percent of drivers with dementia get lost routinely. Thankfully, most are found unharmed. Some of them end up as tragic headlines in the local news."[26]

Dorothy's worst emotional problem was a sense of despair that her misery would never end. She experienced recurrent anxiety, anger, guilt, and shame at the loss of her own life and freedom. When she finally placed Gardner in a nursing home, she struggled about how often to visit him and remained uncertain about whether he knew who she was. She kept thinking (perhaps hoping would be more accurate) even near the end of his life that he gave occasional signs of recognition. In any case, she was convinced that he was happier with her at his side even if he did not know who she was.

This is a frequent state of mind among caregivers of patients with dementia or those in a coma, especially intimates who need to believe they are recognized. They could be right because they know the person better than anyone else and are sensitive to signs that others might not notice. It is commonly very difficult to tell, however.

Dorothy's friends kept trying to tell her to write Gardner off emotionally and attend to her own needs, which she had great difficulty doing even when she tried. And then she would pay for the effort with guilt and shame, which only added to her despair. What made the problem worse was that Dorothy did not avail herself of help from people she could hire to give her some respite from the constant problem. She feared that anyone else would not know what to do or would fail to protect Gardner from himself.

Dorothy's family and friends during this long, trying period varied greatly in the extent to which they offered appropriate and significant support. Early on, some kept giving the same advice, whether or not Dorothy was willing to listen, namely, to put Gardner in a nursing home and to abandon him as a lost cause, a suggestion that still shocked Dorothy even after he had declined severely. If advice comes when a person is ready and able to listen to it, it can be useful, but often it is given when the recipient cannot even consider the message. Emotional support, which we discussed in chapter 3, can be a mixed blessing because it often fails to be truly supportive, and good intentions do not invariably lead to real help.

A few people, at different times during this long trial, were empathic and sensitive about what was happening, and their presence and understanding were helpful and welcome. They accepted Gardner without complaint, despite his irrational behavior, and they tried to understand how Dorothy must be feeling. Some were helpful simply because they listened and did not prescribe. They made it clear by their loyalty and thoughtfulness that they cared and would not be judgmental. They said more or less what they thought when asked but seldom or never gave unsolicited advice. Some gave material help such as food, provided a handy lift in their car, or, when Dorothy had to leave Gardner for a while, kept an eye on him lest he get into trouble without her knowledge. Still others showed little patience for her plight and soon disappeared from sight. Dorothy found that she could not have predicted which family members and friends would do one or the other.

At one point, Dorothy joined a support group for caregivers of Alzheimer's patients where people talked about their own experiences under the sympathetic eye and ear of the organizer and other members. She participated for several months, and two meeting sessions were devoted to her own experiences with her declining husband. At the meetings, she learned much about the varied experiences of other couples, some of which corresponded closely to her own. However, she found that the meetings were time-consuming and quickly reached a point at which the gain was minimal. Dorothy thought she already knew more than most of the other participants, who, it seemed to her, were not particularly informed or insightful about caregiver and patient problems and what might be done about them. She was also weary from the constant effort to be upbeat. It made her feel lonely and isolated from everyone. Needing more substance, she quit the group.

One must remember that Dorothy was a very independent soul. She had confidence mainly in herself, not others, and had a strong desire to take charge and be in control. Although Dorothy's experience with a support group was not positive, most others find such groups extremely helpful, even indispensable.

Dorothy tried to get her children to visit Gardner as often as possible, but they saw little evidence that he was responsive to them. They complained that the visits were futile and distressing, though visiting did salve their consciences a bit. One went more than the other two. They were already adults and had their own busy lives and children. It took nine years for this draining struggle to end with Gardner's death.

Now grieving would follow, but there was also some relief that the ordeal was finally over, which could be acknowledged more easily with the passage of time. Consistent with the type of person she was, Dorothy never considered or sought psychotherapy, though she had the financial means and might have done so to advantage.

We should end this case history by noting that a common problem of families of Alzheimer's patients is the recurrent, almost constant, emotional confusion, ambivalence, and distress that the disease provokes. It is very difficult to write off one's spouse, father, or mother, or even one's grandfather or grandmother. The struggle is about how to cope with the conflicting feelings the disease generates. Other common problems involve finances, the health of the caregiver, and decisions about what to do about such matters. Each individual must learn to cope in his or her way.

Within a year, faster than she would have thought, Dorothy had passed through the worst of her personal bereavement crisis, but she was also terribly lonely and lacked a close confidant with whom she could talk in a searching and honest way. The children could not help with this because their needs and experiences were so different, and they had distanced themselves from the problem by the time Gardner had been placed in a home. When Dorothy talked with other women who had gone through something similar, she sensed that they were different from her in so many ways that they could not serve as role models. She had to find her own way.

Occasionally, typically at anniversaries of wonderful times together with Gardner and the children, she experienced the wistful and comfortable sadness that indicated the worst of grieving was mostly over. The despair and hopelessness that had dogged her for so long began to be replaced with hope for the future. She felt she had to get away from the past, which had dragged her life down, and make a new life. But the past can never be completely ignored.

Even though Dorothy was now pointed toward the future, it did not beckon clearly, and she had no clear idea about what she would do. Everyone kept encouraging her, but few listened to her uncertainties. She still had a long way to go to revamp her life, but she was determined that she would find a way. She felt she must if her life was going to once again seem worthwhile. We are confident that, given her good sense and fortitude, she would get past this very low period of her life and emerge strong, resilient, and perhaps one day even happy.

With respect to successful aging, how do we judge the way Dorothy dealt with this life crisis? We believe that the sense of despair and the other emotions that were called forth in Dorothy, such as anxiety, anger, guilt, and shame, as well as her uncertainty about how she should handle things, are quite appropriate under the circumstances. Some friends stood by her, though they often offered poor social support and advice. Yet by dint of her own strengths and wisdom, she was able to get through this terrible period extremely well under the circumstances.

She retained decisional autonomy, stood by her husband loyally until it was no longer reasonable to do so, and made the sensible decision to put Gardner in a nursing home, which is normally traumatic no matter how appropriate or necessary. Our impression is that Dorothy was remarkably effective in holding together psychologically without displaying serious dysfunction during the long crisis.

After her husband died, Dorothy had to struggle with grief over the loss and reconcile her ambivalence about her role as caregiver with her needs as a person who still had her own life to live. One is always amazed at how resilient people can be in crisis situations like this, Dorothy among them.

Her life stress eased somewhat as her grief ended, but stress did not end. It continued with the realization that she had to find a way to live a new life without being smothered by old psychological baggage. Yet at the same time she needs to have some appreciation for the positive things she gained from her marriage to Gardner and by competently and diligently taking care of him when he needed it.

It should be evident from what we have said that in our view, Dorothy was a substantial success in her later life. She manifested a highly realistic appraisal of her own and her husband's tragic circumstances. Despite bad moments, she accepted what was happening and adopted a relatively positive stance in dealing with it. She never lost her verve for long. Nor was her positive self-regard weakened even during the period of grieving. She is now heading in the right direction toward a renewal of her life.

Coping with the Loss of Family or Friends

Dorothy's experience with the illness and loss of her husband prompts us to say something about the problems of coping with loss in this area of life. We have spoken about grieving in chapter 3 and in our discussion of Dorothy, but we need to address, even if only briefly, some of the experiences of loss from the standpoint of coping. They include becoming a widow, loneliness, missing intimacy and sex, and the struggle to find a new companion or group. Problems such as these are likely to be more common among the elderly, because of the likelihood of bereavement, than among any other age-group, and they should not be ignored. Divorce can bring them, too, but it is probably easier to consider a new relationship when one is relatively young.

Becoming a widow or a widower, like every other experience in life, is apt to vary greatly in its impact from one person to another. Probably the same could be said for divorce. Its emotional significance depends on how the loss is viewed. There may be deep resentment at being the victim, guilt about one's role in the loss, relief that a bad situation is finally over (as in Dorothy's case), and shame about wanting to start out on a new life. In effect, there may be all kinds of emotion based on the meanings a person gives to the loss. The bereaved elderly are also forced to make changes in their lives, sometimes dramatic changes, and to decide whether to seek a replacement or to give up on further intimacy.

What flows from the loss may be loneliness, which fuels the need for someone to share things with, to plan together, to find someone who provides help and comfort in dark moments, to spend time together. The desire is not merely for a distant acquaintance but for someone who cares and shares the most intimate thoughts. Some old people look for such a person, perhaps a new mate, not necessarily to live with but to be with much of the time without too much loss of autonomy. For some, marriage is important; for others, marriage is avoided, perhaps out of memory for the terrible period in which the spouse died. The solutions are as varied as the variations in the personalities of people.

Many seek but never find. In Rossmoor there is an unkind joke about the "casserole ladies" who, upon discovery of a recent widower, visit him with something to eat as part of their search. Some relish their autonomy and privacy. Some find another person quickly and join forces in a new start for the comparatively brief period remaining to them. Some find without really looking. A fair number of the couples we know in the building in which we live are products of such a late life change. How they deal with the property and funds they bring to the new relationship is not generally discussed with others.

There is also the question of physical intimacy and sex. Some want to have it—old people do not automatically lose their interest in sex, though many do. It should be remembered that a high proportion of the elderly who remain married have given up on sex for diverse reasons. Some have enjoyed it all their lives; others have little interest in it or prefer to avoid it. Many men at this stage of life are no longer capable of achieving an erection. Perhaps the nerves that make an erection possible were lost in prostate surgery, or other physical or psychological ailments make it difficult or impossible.

We know much about the efforts and motivation of youths to get together but little about how the elderly go about testing the grounds for sex in a new relationship. Although our culture seems obsessed with sex—it is used everywhere to sell all manner of goods and services—it is also too ambivalent to be open about it. For this reason, perhaps, systematic research on sex in old age, which might tell us how old people cope with the problem, is scarce.

Perhaps the most important lesson to consider from having read this chapter is that people, including caregivers, are remarkably resilient in dealing with terrible situations, and most manage to survive physically and psychologically even when the struggle is a very long one, as it was in Dorothy's situation. Another important lesson is that the roles of family and friends in one's life are complex, with great variation among different individuals, the family, friend, and the recipient of their services.

Family and friends can serve as very important resources for people in crisis, but one must be prepared to be frustrated at their occasional indifference, insensitivity, and lack of wisdom in the face of suffering, especially when it is drawn out. In our view, the critical issue is the coping process, which depends on a person's resources, willingness to seek information or help and to learn new things, courage, and perseverance, which are valuable assets in the best as well as the worst of times.

7

A Different Doctor for Every Organ

The slightly sardonic title of this chapter reflects the anomaly in modern American medicine of having separate specialists for the heart, lungs, gastrointestinal tract, genitourinary tract, cancer anywhere in the body, nerves, bones and muscles, blood, eyes, teeth, mind, having babies, and raising them. One specialist rarely knows what another is doing with the patient and has little time to be concerned about it.

There are great advantages to having such experts. However, this is not care for the total person but instead represents a narrow focus on particular diseases and parts of the body. If no single doctor is in charge, a large proportion of the elderly wind up ingesting drugs that enhance or cancel the effects of other drugs, and as a result they may suffer harmful drug interactions.[1] The primary care physician is the only professional who, at least in theory, has a full picture of the person's overall lifestyle and health. Although a single organ can kill as a result of cancer or some other disease, such as a heart attack, general health usually depends on the integrity of the whole bodily system and, of course, the mind. As patients, we must take charge of our health and use physicians as knowledgeable advisers, a pattern that has changed greatly since the time of our parents.

We should bring to the attention of our readers a chapter by Robert L. Kane in what appears to be a serious critique of our health care system. In deadpan fashion, he uses the explosive chapter title "Caution: Health Care Is Hazardous to the Aging Self." He says older people have a greater risk of psychological and physical harm because they are more likely to get sick or have chronic conditions requiring extensive care. They are also more likely to suffer from several problems, one exacerbating the other, and to be more disturbed than younger persons about how they are treated.[2]

We have several objectives in this chapter. One of our basic themes, as the reader knows, is to demonstrate the great variability in the physiological condition of aging people of dramatically different chronological ages. However, this is not enough to justify a series of health case histories. The causes of this variability are multiple, and if we leave it at that, it will seem like mere accidents of fate that one person is well at ninety compared with another person at fifty.

This in itself is not terribly interesting or revealing. Aside from being interesting stories, medical histories are worthwhile to read because they describe the psychological processes whereby people struggle to live with their ailments and still function. Some of the people we write about display remarkable resilience in dealing with medical ailments and crises. We want the reader to view some of the ways such people have coped—often quite successfully—with debilitating illnesses. Serious illness increases the demands inherent in managing one's life and also reduces the resources on which a person can draw.

We also want to reveal something about the emotions associated with serious illness. For example, anxiety, which expresses the mind-set of a person who feels threatened, is among the most common emotions in medical crises and handicapping chronic ailments. It is a mixed blessing: It helps mobilize efforts to cope, but when it gets too intense, it interferes with realistic thinking and problem solving. Anxiety also enervates the person who needs all the energy that can be mustered to cope. But many other emotions are typical of serious illness.

Shame is another important emotion that arises during illness because in the eyes of many people sickness is explained as God's punishment for having sinned. For example, Christian Scientists believe that bodily illness is a reflection of a person's sinful thoughts. Shame arises because symptoms of illness suggest a failure of faith; the person must blame him- or herself for being ill and is shamed in the presence of God and other people.

Other people experience guilt and shame for not having taken care of themselves—for example, for having smoked for many years—so that the cancer is viewed as a personal failure and a stigma on one's character. Most people want to believe that there is justice in life. Therefore, when someone is ill or experiences tragedy, the implication is that this punishment is deserved—the good are not punished in a just world, only the guilty, which is why victims are so often blamed for their misfortune.[3]

Our ultimate objective in this chapter is to describe and analyze people who are ill, what they are thinking and feeling about this situation, and, most important from the standpoint of coping, what they are doing about it. We shall say more about this from the standpoint of psychological treatment in chapter 9 and successful aging in chapter 10.

Physiological Changes in Aging

Before turning to our case histories of aging and illness, we offer a brief overview of the important physiological changes that are typical of aging, recognizing at the same time the existence of great variation from person to person. The physiological changes resulting from aging have been spelled out by Susan Krauss Whitbourne, on whose writings we draw here.[4] Whitbourne's discussion includes a number of vital bodily functions, for example, the cardiovascular system and respiratory system; regulatory systems, such as excretion, digestion, and the immune system; systems that serve reproduction and sexuality; the central and autonomic nervous systems; and the sensory systems that control vision, hearing, taste, smell, and equilibrium. We limit ourselves here to a modest number of physiological changes, particularly those that most of us recognize as important features of aging.

Most of us are aware that after roughly forty years of age, changes occur in muscles, bones, and joints that lead to more difficult movement and pain. Muscle strength is markedly reduced, especially after age seventy. We have already mentioned osteoporosis and broken hips. Functionally speaking, many older people have trouble lifting their arms above their heads or turning their heads when driving to see what is to their left or right. Balance is affected, and thus most of us fear standing near a precipice lest we fall. We also bump into things more readily and have an abundance of black-and-blue marks on our skin.

Most of us also know that heart attacks and respiratory diseases, such as emphysema and lung cancer, are increasingly common as we age, especially among smokers and people with poor diets. Vital lung capacity (the oxygen that is available for breathing) is progressively reduced as less oxygen reaches the bloodstream. This decreases stamina and increases fatigue.

Pulmonologists (lung specialists) use age-related charts that show the average lung capacity—that is, the oxygen that is available for breathing—characteristic of each chronological age. Training, exercise, and greater care in movement can reduce some of the effects of this loss in lung capacity and can help in general to keep us as fit as possible, given our overall health.

As we age, our kidneys also work less well in cleansing the blood of waste products, and the fluid capacity of the bladder is reduced. Sometimes the sphincter muscles that control urine flow are weakened by disease, which increases the danger of spillage and the need for collecting pads that can be used to soak up urine so that it does not soil one's clothes. An even more disruptive problem can be found in the loss of fecal control as a result of damage to the nerves that manage the anal sphincter.

Women, on the average, have more problems than men with *stress incontinence*, which refers to urine leakage with exertion, laughing, sneezing, lifting, or bending. Men, on the average, tend to have more problems with *urge incontinence*, or urine loss that occurs without warning. In addition to muscle weakness, prostate surgery, or radiation for cancer, these are common causes of such symptoms in men, resulting in fears of being embarrassed socially and making travel more difficult.

The immune system of aging persons also tends to lose effectiveness over the years, which increases proneness to infections. The elderly are encouraged to have an inoculation every year against flu viruses and every five years against pneumonia. More effective treatment of pneumonia keeps us alive longer, though this can sometimes be a mixed blessing. Social epidemiologists in the past have thought of pneumonia as "the old man's friend" because it resulted in death before the extended suffering and disability that can result from life-threatening ailments such as cancer, congestive heart failure, emphysema, diabetes, and dementia.

Most people also know that female reproductive capacity is reduced gradually after forty and usually ceases altogether by fifty or fifty-five years of age. The same hormonal changes also produce wrinkling and changes in body weight and fat distribution. Sexual enjoyment in women is reduced, and discomfort during sexual intercourse can be increased as a result of changes in the tissues of the genitals—for example, the reduction of fluid secretion.

Men, too, have a climacteric of sorts, though it is less abrupt. There is a reduction in viable sperm. Prostate changes reduce the volume and pressure of semen during ejaculation. Erections are slower to develop and less complete, and there is a longer period of latency between them. There are fewer penile erections in sleep, and orgasm is shorter and involves fewer contractions. Enlargement of the prostate and cancer of that gland are extremely common in later years, especially for men in their seventies and eighties and the surgical removal of the prostate eliminates semen altogether.

The effects of age on the nervous system are of great importance to the functioning of the elderly. As we have said previously, one of the most terrible brain disorders is Alzheimer's disease. This form of dementia progresses slowly, but the victim ultimately ceases to know who he is or was and no longer recognizes his family. The case history presented in chapter 6 describes a caregiver of an Alzheimer's patient.

Reduction of dopamine in the brain is common in normal aging, but a more severe version is found in Parkinson's disease. Strokes, in which blood pours out of ruptured arteries and directly damages brain tissues, or when the blood supply is blocked to some portions of the brain because of occluded arteries or blood clots, can also cause bodily paralysis, aphasia (poor meaning comprehension), and dementia.

Whitbourne points out that some cognitive abilities can actually improve with aging, such as higher order abstract thinking processes on which life decisions and judgment are based. Perhaps this is what happens when older people seem to gain wisdom. But as we said earlier, neither age, intelligence, nor knowledge provides any guarantee of wisdom. Nevertheless, the brain has considerable redundancy and plasticity, so it can compensate to some degree for some of the negative physiological consequences of aging. Too little is known about brain function to make assured statements in this area at this time.

Whitbourne also draws a number of interesting and encouraging conclusions about the normative biological changes involved in aging, some of which are worth quoting here to give a more positive slant to the negative realities of loss and deficit. For example:

> Older adults who overreact to physical changes may experience an unnecessary and potentially harmful sense of discouragement or despair. Conversely, those who deny or minimize the presence of age-related limitations in physical functioning may place themselves at risk due to overexertion or failure to take preventive actions. . . .
>
> It is important for clinicians or gerontologists to recognize the independence, autonomy, and vitality of spirit seen in many older persons, even those with severe losses or age related limitations. These persons are coping daily with physical changes that would daunt the younger professional or specialist. Gerontologists who condescend to older people or patronize them (perhaps as a result of their own fears of aging) are missing important opportunities for intervention as well as important opportunities to learn from the wisdom of their elders."[5]

Although we do not believe it has been documented or acknowledged, our own experience suggests that aging does not usually involve smooth transitions from a sound or youthful physical and mental condition to one that is clearly worse. Rather, the changes appear in periodic lurches or jumps; or, perhaps they are only noticed when they become pronounced as a result of a late-blooming disease. For a time there may seem to be no evident change; then, all of a sudden, within a year or two we look at the mirror and see a person who is noticeably older. What was once a straight posture has become stooped, a condition called osteoporosis. What was once a firm figure has now become flabby, with a noticeable protrusion around the midsection. We experience a more limited range of motion and must walk with greater care and uncertainty.

A disconnection also seems to occur between our superficial appearance and our physical well-being. People may comment, without intending to patronize, "You look great, much younger than your years." Some men or women respond to this with the contrarian statement, "Don't be fooled by my full head of hair [or still-feminine figure]. My insides know." Although compliments are usually welcome, the respondent is implying that there are physical limitations and ailments that did not exist earlier and may be hidden from view.

There is a good psychological reason for this awkwardness in communication. There are two ways of comparing another person or oneself with a standard of some sort. A standard is an average or norm, whether it is accurate or inaccurate, for most people or those of a given age. The person giving the compliment is usually making this kind of comparison.

But as we age, most of us compare ourselves with what we were in the past, and the difference clearly favors the past rather than the present. We know we are not what we once were. This explains why, when we are complimented on how well we are looking or doing, it does not always make us feel good, and why the person who gives the compliment may not understand the negative reaction.

Or we say something positive about how neighbors look, and they respond uncomfortably. Hemming and hawing, they may pour out a litany of personal troubles and ailments, as if they do not want us to think they are as well as we suppose. We recently asked a male neighbor about the health of another male neighbor, who for twelve years at least has been complaining he is about to die. We asked the first neighbor what was wrong with the other man, and the answer came back, "He has a very long list," which is an apt description of a hypochondriac or a person who does not want you to think he is really OK. As this is written, he is still vigorous, as far as we can tell.

Perhaps with a bit of tongue in cheek on our part, a suitable greeting for an elderly person from a proven friend would be: "You are not looking so well, but I'm impressed with your vitality and fortitude. I figure you must be doing something right." In saying this, you are complimenting him on coping well, not just looking well, so it is responsive to his implicit complaints. Chances are it would startle whomever we said it to, but it would be fun to try in any case.

We should also confront one of the problems of aging and disease that can be a source of much confusion. As we said in chapter 1, aging is not in itself a disease, but it can increase the risk of certain diseases. One of the main ways it does this is by a progressive weakening of the body's immune system.[6] Thus, although cancer is not at all uncommon in children, it is increasingly common in later life because the immune system may not be as vigorous and dependable in surveying the body for malignant cells. They grow out of control and destroy healthy tissue.

There is, however, another reason for considering diseases that are not caused specifically by old age. Many diseases affect how one lives as age progresses. For example, a back injury early in life has nothing causal to do with aging, but it can haunt a person late in life and lead to a dependency on anti-inflammatory drugs to avoid pain. It has to do with age in that sense. Prostate cancer, however, is age related in that its incidence rises directly with age and affects most men in their seventies and eighties.

Case Histories Showing Variations in Illness Patterns

In the remainder of this chapter, we illustrate individual differences in patterns of illness by presenting three cases, two men and one woman. Their stories suggest a complex portrait of health and illness as people age. In relating the case histories of illness, we first describe dispassionately the main features of each person's illness story, leaving out minor childhood diseases. Then we discuss the emotions and coping processes these major illness-related events have brought about.

Steve's Story

Now in his early eighties, Steve has survived almost ten years beyond the average for males. He considers himself fortunate and reasonably healthy because the life-threatening and potentially disabling diseases he has had were successfully treated, and he always managed to function well despite them.

Steve suffered a back injury in his teens when he was flying a kite. He fell backward into a large hole that contained a rock that jutted out and damaged several vertebrae. The injury required surgery, and his back has remained a source of trouble and pain throughout his life. This condition worsened as he got older, leading to substantial chronic pain. Like a large percentage of the elderly who have bad backs, knees, and hips, with chronic pain from osteoarthritis, he depended heavily on anti-inflammatory painkillers.

When Steve was seventy-three, he noticed blood in his urine, which turned out to be caused by an infected prostate gland. His urologist advised him to be examined for prostate cancer when the infection was over and the gland had returned to its normal condition. His blood PSA, which refers to a protein that is produced only by prostate cancer cells, was modest, about 4, normally not something to be worried about. Hand palpation, however, suggested the possibility of a malignancy on one side of the gland. A needle biopsy was then performed that clearly showed the existence of cancer.

The issue that Steve now had to confront was a very difficult one—that is, what treatment to choose: radical surgery, radiation, or a period of "wait and see." The latter is not infrequently suggested because this type of cancer typically grows slowly. Its aggressiveness can be estimated from the cancer cells extracted from the biopsy. If the man in question suffers from another life-threatening ailment, such as coronary artery disease, congestive heart failure, or emphysema, he probably will die of that condition before the prostate cancer does him in.

Surgery, which offers the best chance of a complete cure if the cancer is detected before it has spread, is not generally performed unless the patient has a good chance of living another ten years. Steve was a good prospect for surgery on this score. Both surgery and radiation can have negative side effects, such as sexual impotence and urinary incontinence. Radiation is the only option if the cancer has already spread. During Steve's surgery, it became clear that there had been no spread of the cancer into the local lymph glands. If it had spread, the operation would have been terminated, and radiation then would be the treatment of choice.

The difficult decision about treatment, which the patient must make, is complicated by the fact that there are usually conflicting opinions among urologists about the best course of action, a fact we noted in chapter 3. Little attention appears to be paid by physicians to patients' uncertainty about what decision they must make, despite its potential for being a life-or-death matter. Steve's father died of prostate cancer, which prompted him to choose surgery.

He was lucky. The preliminary evidence suggested that the cancer had remained within the gland, though this could not be certain without a direct examination during surgery of the local lymph nodes. A bone scan can help, but it does not yield dependable evidence unless the result is positive. Steve's bone scan was negative, which meant only that the cancer had not yet spread to his bones, though it still could have spread to his lymph nodes.

Steve's prostate surgery was for him a singularly unpleasant experience; the operation was lengthy, and on recovering from anesthesia he had to use a catheter to urinate during the two weeks following surgery. The catheter is inserted into the penile urethra and is attached to a plastic bag for collection. Such a bag can be attached to the leg; it fits under the trousers and enables the patient to get around during this period. Steve recovered quickly and came home after five days in the hospital. Being home was reassuring and supportive, but instead of having a hospital worker to remove and replace the bag, he had to manage this unfamiliar and undignified task himself, with the help of his wife. Loss of dignity can be expected as a condition of major illness.

Most prostate patients suffer from urinary incontinence for a while after surgery but can use commercial diapers and pads that keep clothing and bedding dry. The incontinence usually disappears, as it did in Steve's case, but not always. Steve has been seen regularly by his urologist every six months for more than six years. There has been no sign of cancer cells, and his PSA has been undetectable, which indicates that his surgery has probably resulted in a complete cure.

As in the case of a large percentage of elderly patients, Steve lost his ability to have an erection as a result of the surgery. There are options for preserving sexual activity, such as an implant, chemical injection, or chemical suppository. Steve tried the chemical treatment without good results and rejected the idea of an implant. He gave up on sex, which to him was a substantial assault on his gratification, sense of manhood, and feelings of adequacy. To some degree, it also interfered with the couple's physical intimacy, which neither partner appreciated after having had a long and satisfying love life.

It is estimated that more than thirty million American men suffer impotence, the problem having become common even among men in their forties. Most such cases are believed to have a physical cause, though the role of psychological factors remains unclear. Good data have not been made public about the prevalence of impotence among men whose prostate has been removed or radiated for cancer.

Steve's current health history also includes cancer of the bladder, which appeared a year later but was unrelated to the prostate cancer. It was discovered because blood had again appeared in his urine, which led to a systoscopic examination that revealed the cancer. Bladder cancer is a disease that increases in frequency as men and women grow older, which gives it a causal link with aging, possibly having to do with how long a person has been engaging in high-risk behavior, such as smoking. Steve had smoked from the age of eighteen. Then later, when the danger of smoking cigarettes became recognized, he turned to cigars in order to smoke less. His father, a heavy, lifelong smoker of cigars, never got bladder cancer—again, the luck of the draw! Here, too, however, age is not the proximate or immediate cause of this cancer, though it can augment it by contributing to a dose-illness relationship—a dose, in epidemiology, has to do with how long a person has engaged in some risk behavior. This could also apply to some genetic factors in disease, which may not emerge until the immune process has been weakened with age.

Again, Steve was fortunate that his bladder cancer was diagnosed when it was still at an early stage. A systoscopic exam showed several small, cancerous first-stage polyps that required surgical removal. If they were permitted to grow larger—for example, into third-stage tumors—they would penetrate the bladder muscle and metastasize into a deadly condition.

He must, therefore, be examined regularly every three months to check for new tumors, which must then be removed surgically if they recur. In the last four years, Steve has had three transurethral surgeries (through the urethra that extends from the tip of the penis to the bladder). They are performed under anesthesia, with a tube through which the surgeon can view the inside of the bladder with a light and use the scissors at the end of the tube to remove any small tumors.

Bladder cancer poses little threat to Steve's life so long as he continues to check on his bladder condition regularly and have the surgery performed whenever a tumor appears. For obscure reasons, Steve currently suffers from urinary incontinence. No one seems to know the exact reason for the incontinence, which has grown progressively more severe and has now affected his anal sphincter. He is undergoing diverse medical scans to try to pin down the cause. The incontinence imposes serious logistical problems, especially in social situations and while traveling, because of the danger that the pad will overflow, thereby wetting his pants, or that he will have a too-urgent bowel movement—with far greater embarrassment.

Steve also has a few other ailments that must be taken seriously if we are to adequately describe his health status. The most important is a form of arrhythmia, which is a disturbance in the timing of auricular muscle activity as it sends oxygenated blood (from the lungs) to the ventricle on its way to the rest of the body. This condition was diagnosed about six years ago. Arrhythmia is very common in later life and usually is not life-threatening. Steve plays vigorous table tennis with a considerable number of retirement community residents who have had electrical pacemakers installed to overcome an excessively slow heart rate. At this stage of the disorder it does not bother him, but eventually he, too, will probably need a pacemaker. His cardiologist has already tried a drug to control this condition, but its side effects forced him to abandon it.

One observation that might be made from Steve's medical history is that aging people must often take numerous tests to prevent life-threatening disorders, cancer and heart disease among them, or treat them at an early stage. As people grow old, they must take these tests with increasing frequency if they wish to avoid or ameliorate these disorders, especially if they have a relevant history or genetic disposition to them. Because Steve had a history of colon polyps—colon cancer is the second most frequent malignancy in men after lung cancer—he obtains a colonoscopic examination regularly every three to five years. This involves first cleaning out the large intestines by means of a strong laxative, followed by the direct inspection of the inside of the entire colon by a gastroenterologist. As in the case of bladder cancer, this permits the physician to remove polyps before any of them grow into a malignant tumor that would require major abdominal surgery. If a colon cancer is caught early enough, the removal of the part of the colon in which it is found provides a complete cure. That portion of the colon will usually not be missed.

All of this exemplifies the growing emphasis in modern medicine on what is called *secondary prevention*, which involves treatment of a known disease to keep it from becoming more serious or even deadly. Primary prevention, in contrast, is an effort to prevent a disease that has not yet occurred (see chapter 3). These treatments are, in effect, preventive and life-saving.

They may be one of the main reasons that, in advanced countries, people today live much longer than their parents and grandparents.

Steve's Emotions

Each of the diseases we have mentioned in Steve's medical history produced its own particular pattern of emotion. The primary emotion was anxiety over what his symptoms and diagnosed condition indicated for his overall well-being. When he was, for example, awaiting word about what was wrong with him in each case, anxiety was the prime and most frequent emotion. As a teenager, awaiting surgery for his back injury without knowing how serious his condition was, he felt extremely anxious about his fate. He worried he might be confined to a wheelchair. He felt lonely and scared.[7] But when he came out of surgery and the results were reassuring, he felt great relief.

As you have seen, Steve fared well in his medical crises, and one could argue that anxiety, which is a distressing state of mind, was probably also a factor in his decisions about coping with later medical problems. Anxiety is the natural consequence of recognizing a threat to one's physical and psychological integrity. Though often scared and feeling alone in his struggles with disease—illness is a personal struggle even if one obtains emotional support from others—he made sound decisions and had a certain amount of good as well as bad luck. He never fell apart but simply did what he had to.

Steve's middle years were relatively free of major illnesses. But he again suffered great anxiety when, at seventy-five, he awaited word about his prostate condition; he was reassured to learn that the cancer was not very aggressive and had probably not metastasized. Making a decision about which treatment he should select, radiation, surgery, or a wait-and-see strategy, resulted in recurrent anxiety. He was greatly annoyed, to say the least, to find that different physicians had strong but contradictory convictions about which treatment was best in his situation. These opinions seemed to depend on each physician's specialty. What is the poor patient to do? Somehow he must make up his own mind based on ambiguous information.

When he finally decided and chose a surgeon, Steve tried to convince himself that he had made the right decision and had chosen one of the better urology surgeons. There also may have been some denial in this state of mind. When there was an unexplained and long delay as he awaited surgery in the hospital's preparation room, he felt angry, yet helpless and unable to do anything about it while he and his wife waited for what seemed an interminable period. There was also dread, a form of anxiety, at the moments before he went under anesthesia, in the operating room, despite the sedatives given to ease his distress. This pattern was characteristic for him, as shown in part by a tremendously elevated blood pressure.

The struggle with the catheter was mostly just unpleasant, partly because he was clearly on the way to recovery. Anxiety, anger, and shame alternated during the period of incontinence, but he did experience some relief when he talked with others who had had a similar experience. Steve's present incontinence is a constant source of annoyance (anger) and sometimes depression as he realizes he probably must live with this problem for the rest of his life.

His self-confidence is threatened, and he anticipates feeling shame, which is even stronger than embarrassment, when he experiences a leak that wets his pants in public, though as a result of careful planning this is not very frequent. He carries extra underwear, pants, and pads to soak up and neutralize the urine smell, sometimes feeling that he has become like a small child wearing a diaper. Public toilets take on an importance they never had before, for the better when they are clean and accessible but for the worse when filthy or inaccessible.

It is interesting that Steve feels shame rather than anger about his urinary problems. Somehow we blame ourselves without our being really at fault, which suggests an oddity in our emotional outlook. Why should there be shame? Maybe the way we are taught as children about toilet training is a big factor. Children with enuresis—that is, the inability to control their urinary sphincters—feel great shame, too, perhaps because they are often teased, scolded, or punished for it. We do not know the solution to this problem, but it adds to the burden of many older people who suffer from such ailments and have to cope with them without adequate public assistance.

Recently, another potential cause for his incontinence, one that might be treatable, has emerged, giving Steve hope that it can be cured. A spinal tumor has been located, which could be affecting the nerves serving these urinary sphincters, though these nerves might also have been irreparably damaged. This problem has been most distressing for him, but he has somehow managed it reasonably well. When traveling, he takes along a large supply of pads, appropriate medicines, and extra underwear. For the most part he has been able to continue an active life, a pattern that illustrates well the resilience and good sense that people such as Steve display. The struggle drains energy, is hard work, and sometimes leads to moments of despair, but he tries not to complain and somehow manages.

In spite of his current ailments, Steve expresses few complaints, except sometimes to his wife. He occasionally rails angrily against the waste of his time and energy, as well as the discomfort of preventive medical procedures designed to keep him alive and well. He recognizes, however, that this is the price he must pay to stay alive and reasonably healthy.

Steve is also well aware that things could have been much worse as he looks around his retirement community and realizes he is lucky to still be alive and functioning pretty well in spite of his problems. As we pointed out in chapter 3, the realization that personal problems could be much worse and can be lived with is an important coping resource for the elderly who suffer losses and deficits. Even pessimists or chronic complainers can see the point if they take the time to evaluate what is happening.

Morris's Story

Morris's health history presents a dramatically different kind of health-related pattern. He is a man who claimed he never had a sick day in his life. If his children had been asked, they, too, would have said they never saw their father miss a day of work because of illness. In the late 1930s, he worked as a sales representative for a wholesale clothing company in a major eastern city. He was strong, energetic, and effective, a take-charge type of person who assumed the household duties from his incompetent and self-indulgent wife. He did all the shopping, washing, and cooking. He would walk many blocks to get home from the subway after work, rain or shine and sometimes in snow. Under each arm he carried a huge paper bag containing foods and staples for several days. He was always sanguine and boasted about his health and vigor.

His father and mother had been immigrants from Eastern Europe. Anti-Semitism and economic deprivation had driven them to immigrate to the United States. They had three children in the United States, first a girl named Minna, then Morris, then Arthur, the youngest. When Morris was ten, his father deserted the family and was never heard from again. As the oldest son, Morris was expected to leave school and get a job to provide for his mother, who barely spoke English, and his brother and sister. This he did willingly. Morris eventually married and had two children of his own.

In 1938, near the end of the Great Depression and just before World War II, he was unable to make a decent living. So Morris, his wife, and their two children moved to California. He knew only about the clothing industry and had to search a long time before he finally landed a job as a salesman. His sanguinity, outgoing personality, intelligence, and good humor won people over, and he began to do well in a ladies' dress store, eventually becoming sales manager. His children went to high school in the city, and his son entered college. Morris was still able to provide some modest funds for the East Coast segment of his family, which was needed less as the economy began to expand after the war.

In 1958, Morris celebrated his fiftieth birthday, still going strong as sales manager. By this time, he had divorced his wife and remarried but had no additional children. His son was studying mechanical engineering and after graduating went to work overseas, and he seldom saw his father or stepmother.

When Morris was sixty, he suffered a massive heart attack as he was dressing, minutes after he had gotten out of bed. He died before the ambulance team could resuscitate him. Everyone was shocked that this splendidly strong and healthy man, who seemed so vigorous, should die so young. They shook their heads in wonder and disbelief at the funeral.

Morris's daughter, Minna, who had taken the responsibility for dealing with his estate after his death, began to explore what had happened. For some reason she began to wonder whether her father had ever seen a doctor. She finally located one he had visited, quizzed him carefully, and learned the astonishing truth that her father had a long history of heart disease, though he had never told anyone or done anything about it. The doctor told her that Morris had several badly occluded coronary arteries and dangerously high blood pressure. No one among his family or coworkers had the slightest inkling of this.

Why had Morris cultivated the myth that he was strong and invincible when he was actually suffering from heart disease? The doctor did not know, nor does anyone else know for certain. Despite warnings that he needed to change his eating habits and take medication to lower his alarmingly high cholesterol and blood pressure, Morris did nothing about it and confided in no one. He must have known about his actual condition. His daughter's inquiry also revealed that he was often ill as a boy and later as a young man but not seriously enough to force him to stay home. He fought off illness rather than letting his family know about it.

Morris's Emotions

We know little about Morris's day-to-day emotional life because of his reluctance to share with anyone the truth of his outlook and medical condition. Minna began to piece together a picture of why her father preferred to have others believe he was strong and healthy. She came to the following conclusions, which consist of little more than a plausible speculation about how he might have felt.

First, he seems to have been ashamed to have anyone know he was not well, fearing that he would lose respect and admiration. He had come to believe that constant cheer and the image of strength and reliability made him effective in sales. From what people perceived and said about him, his daughter drew the inference that Morris was given to considerable anxiety and anger. He was often anxious about being effective at what he did, and early on he was angry about what he must accept in life, but he suppressed these emotions in his effort to portray himself as capable, in charge of things, and someone to be admired. He felt that no one should know the truth.

Second, and even more important, from the age of ten Morris believed that he was the only member of the family able to support his destitute brother, sister, and mother, and later his wife and children. He had become the surrogate father, and he dared not get sick, especially in economically precarious times. His claim that he had never had a sick day in his life, which he had made everyone believe, was fraudulent—no one else must know the truth—but it is possible that he managed to convince himself about it too. As time wore on, he began to be proud of the role he played in the family and undoubtedly obtained considerable satisfaction from it.

We would not want to suggest by this example that all persons who seem to be extraordinarily healthy throughout their lives are only fooling others or themselves about their condition. Many people live to a late age without serious illness, and some never have been in a hospital until near the end. Sometimes, though by no means always, they die suddenly of a stroke or heart attack or suffer for a relatively brief period very late in life during which they have a terminal illness. Still, a case like this illustrates an unusual pattern that is not often described or highlighted when the topic is examined—someone no one realizes is sick. It sounds like a put-down of good health that ended in disaster when, in reality, it was not good health at all.

Barbara's Story

Barbara had been an attractive, vigorous, and mostly healthy adolescent and a well-coordinated, graceful, and athletic young adult. Her main health problems were numerous allergies, but in her generation they were not well known or understood, especially by the public. When Barbara was in her fifties, her allergies markedly increased to include any kind of seafood and a large number of other food substances. Once she experienced an attack of anaphylactic shock from some crabmeat that was mixed into an egg roll in a Chinese restaurant.

This was about the time Barbara discovered that something much more serious was wrong with her. She and her husband had taken a trip, and they decided to rent bikes one day to tour a scenic area. Barbara was an experienced biker, but she found she could no longer stay up on the bike without falling. She seemed to have lost her balance. She realized, too, that for the last year she had been falling from time to time when she walked or played with the dog in the backyard at home. When they returned to the Bay Area, she visited an orthopedic specialist, who sent her to a neurologist to find out what was wrong with her.

Barbara turned out to be suffering from an autoimmune disease called *myasthenia gravis*, a Latin term that means severe muscle weakness. This was not inconsistent with the medical history of one of her relatives. The muscles of one leg were especially weak and prone to collapse, and she had the classic symptom of an eyelid that would periodically close. She also suffered occasionally from double vision when she was driving, which frightened her. If she pulled over to the side of the road, closed her eyes, and rested for a while, the problem would ease temporarily. She was always stronger in the morning, but as the day wore on she would become increasingly weak and vulnerable. It was estimated that she had had the disease for about twenty years.

There are a number of autoimmune diseases, each of which attacks a different body tissue. The immune system stands ready at all times to fight infectious diseases and foreign proteins by manufacturing antibodies. In this type of disease, the immune system mistakes the body's own tissues for substances that are foreign, such as viruses, bacteria, and cancerous growths.

Myasthenia gravis is a comparatively rare disease. Almost nothing is known about its causes, though it is thought to have a genetic basis. The incidence of myasthenia gravis in the United States is estimated to be approximately 36,000 cases. The average age of onset of the disease has increased, now being over fifty, with men affected more often than women.

The disease is centered at the synapse, the small space through which messages from the nerve must get to the muscle. The neural transmitter acetylcholine normally conveys the message. In myasthenia, however, this essential step fails to occur because many of the patient's muscle receptors have been impaired or destroyed by an overenthusiastic immune system.

Interestingly, the discovery of the drug Mestinon, which Barbara must take in order to restore the nerve-muscle connection, began with the recognition that the drug curare, widely used by the Indians of South America as a deadly poison, results in muscle paralysis.[8] In this research, in which the biochemical cause of the disease was established, several possible treatments were discovered that suppress the circulating antibodies that interfere with neuromuscular transmission, though there is no real cure.

Mestinon temporarily (for two or three hours or so) improves the transmission so that voluntary muscular activity can occur. In younger patients, removal of the thymus gland, which is involved in the immune process, is a second treatment that can often help to control the disease. Barbara developed the disease too late in life for this to work. She is totally dependent on the drug; without it, she becomes too weak to function. A third treatment is to supplement Mestinon with cortisone, a powerful hormone that has damaging side effects, such as the loss of calcium in the bones. Barbara refuses to take the cortisone because she suffers from severe osteoporosis. She must be vigilant about when she needs the drug. If she takes it without food, she overdoses and experiences severe cramps throughout her body. New drugs are also being developed that are less poisonous, such as Cellcept, which seems promising.

As Barbara has gotten older, the affected areas have extended to loss of speech, slurring of words as if she is drunk, and difficulty breathing and swallowing. As a result of the swallowing problem, she is in constant danger of having fluid and food leak into her trachea, which can produce aspiration pneumonia. This has happened at least once, and she must protect herself by trying to cough up this material before it results in the pneumonia. With the recent involvement of her diaphragm, her breathing is now often labored, and her vital capacity has been seriously reduced. This sometimes makes it difficult to tell whether she is suffering from heart failure or a consequence of myasthenia.

When she was about seventy-five years of age, the Mestinon alone was no longer capable of sustaining Barbara, and the drug is now no longer capable of permitting her to function effectively. Another treatment was instituted. At first, every four months she would spend four consecutive days as an outpatient receiving an intravenous infusion of immune globulin, which increases her strength considerably. With each passing year, the frequency of these infusions, which take about six hours each day, has had to be increased so that she now receives them every five weeks.

Her physicians are constantly exploring other treatments. They have sometimes tried plasma pheresis, in which her blood is removed and passed through special filters, much like kidney dialysis but designed to cleanse the blood of damaging antigens. This procedure, however, is far more invasive than the infusion, especially with her very small veins, and on one occasion she suffered a mild heart attack while undergoing it.

Recently, at seventy-nine, Barbara has been urged by some physicians to have chemotherapy, but she has resisted, not foolishly given her fragility. No one knows why some of these treatments help particular patients, but they are used because of empirical evidence of their utility. Her physicians are now trying a combination of regular plasma pheresis followed by infusions of immune globulin.

Barbara's Emotions

Barbara is generally cheerful and tries always to be independent. As she puts it, "I want to live until I die." Those who know her have much affection and admiration for her spirited approach to life in spite of her severe limitations.

She actively maintains her home and entertains her friends, children, and grandchildren, making dinner parties, cooking, and visiting with the grandchildren. The couple has taken many trips abroad. Sometimes Barbara has had a mild crisis during these trips. They are usually handled by increasing the Mestinon dose and obtaining more rest. At seventy-nine, she now realizes that long trips place too much demand on her to enjoy fully.

Although Barbara avoids freeways, she drives everywhere without accident. She refuses to give in to the disease and has learned to manage it without withdrawing from the world. When she overdoes her activity, she usually falls asleep on her chair while reading or watching television, but this kind of napping is hardly unusual in one her age. Her life during this twenty-year period is a testament to her ability to cope effectively, which draws on her personality traits of optimism, toughness, and resiliency.

Barbara's husband, being somewhat wary of idealized portraits of anyone, knows that she is capable of considerable anxiety, which she seldom shows. Because she is freer with him—or, as he says jokingly, she has much to complain about to him—he knows she has substantial anger but keeps it mostly under control. From time to time she lashes out at him, especially if he is at all critical of her. He believes this tendency comes to her from her mother, a matriarchal woman who, as a feisty old lady, said almost anything she thought but could also be nurturing.

Barbara's illness also has a strong emotional impact on her husband. Not infrequently at night he becomes alarmed when he hears her irregular and effortful breathing. He may awaken her to change her position in bed. He is aware of the dangers and tends to panic in bed lest this struggle suggests she is having a breathing crisis that will bring about the loss of his intimate companion of many years, a woman he still loves. When she is out shopping and is late in returning, he becomes very anxious lest her lateness mean she has been unable to control the car and has had an accident.

They now rely on their cellular phones to keep in touch with each other in the event of a problem. From time to time he gets edgy about the demands that an ailing spouse can make, but his genuine concerns about her well-being and his guilt at such feelings keep this emotional downside in check. Both of them know after so many years together that no one is so perfect that they experience only positive and sanguine feelings. It is the nature of life even at its best.

We end this chapter with some comments about lessons to be learned in considering these case histories. In recalling the stories of the illness patterns of these three persons, it is worth repeating how vigorously and resiliently Steve and Barbara managed their health crises. Steve was able to transcend his anxiety and shame by doing what was necessary in making the decision in favor of surgery for the prostate cancer. He sees the urologist dependably to check on his bladder, and several times when a growth was found, he needed to have transurethral surgery. He accepts this despite his dread of losing consciousness under anesthesia. He has also found ways of managing his incontinence and has modest hopes that this problem might be cured or eased. Barbara continues to cope effectively with her myasthenia gravis, living her life as normally as possible in spite of its ravages. In both cases, a realistic but hopeful attitude has facilitated their coping process and the compensations they make to overcome losses and deficits.

She is, in fact, more active than most victims of this illness of the same age. Her husband and children worry about this, but at the same time they do not want to infantilize her. She has learned how to time her medication so that she can usually function adequately, though she can only rise from the floor, and sometimes even from a chair, by pulling herself up with her arms, or getting an assist from someone else. She accepts the necessary help and her lot in life with grace.

Barbara manages to live fully despite serious physical adversity. Like most of us, she experiences a full quota of negative emotions, the most important of which are anxiety and anger. However, she controls them effectively and shows little, if any, dysfunction. She hopes she will be able to continue in this lifestyle for some time to come. Successful aging, in our estimation? Clearly yes on all counts.

Morris, in contrast, chose an unfortunate strategy of coping with his vulnerability to heart attack by concealing it and not doing anything preventive, and he probably paid the steep price of dying suddenly at a relatively young age. He did, however, make positive and unselfish contributions to his family, so we cannot fault him too much.

This chapter illustrates the highly variable pattern of health and illness among different people who are aging, despite the expectable physiological changes that characterize aging. There is no standard pattern. However, when old people do become sick, one again sees how resilient they can be. Seldom do they close down and await death; usually they work to stay alive and functional, and most succeed until their illness either disables them severely or kills them. Preventive medical treatment keeps many alive and functioning for a long time beyond what would have been possible without it.

What is more, there is no standard pattern of coping. Only in recent years have substantial numbers of research psychologists been studying the coping process with a view to finding out what works and what does not. We can see, too, that old people are usually capable of compensating for losses and deficits, which enables them to function, sometimes quite well (as in the case of Barbara) despite severe problems. This is a hopeful feature that those who suffer disabling or terminal illness can take to heart. All the cases presented in this chapter illustrate reasonably effective coping with serious ailments.

The individuals we have highlighted to illustrate different health histories could, with the possible exception of Morris, be regarded as good copers, depending on how one regards the conditions they faced and evaluates the functional and emotional outcomes of their coping patterns.

There are, of course, plenty of people who cope with their medical problems poorly, thereby shortening their lives unnecessarily and living unhappily. Some fail to seek medical help and allow cancers and other ailments to kill them prematurely. Others get discouraged over the constant struggle to stay alive and functioning. They give up early and turn inward, severely restricting their lives. Still others make both themselves and their friends and relatives miserable with their dour and complaining outlook. Reading about them without a trace of uplift would have been an exercise in misery for many readers.

As a final thought, we point out that in the process of struggling to cope with physical adversity, the people whose stories we have presented and who coped in favorable ways still experience all sorts of negatively toned emotions, such as anxiety, anger, guilt, and shame. Some religions, such as Christian Science, equate illness with sin, provoking guilt or shame over being sick. It is unfortunate that guilt and shame get connected with illness so often, as if people who suffer illness are to blame for it and should, therefore, suffer even more. Some have probably engaged in high-risk behavior, such as smoking, drinking excessively, and eating unwisely, earlier in their lives. But to blame themselves after it is too late does not do any good.

We have also known people to have lung cancer or emphysema who never smoked; high-risk behavior increases the probabilities of illness but may be irrelevant in any individual case, as we have already pointed out. To feel guilty or shamed by sickness is unfortunate because it is unproductive. These emotions failed to stop the dangerous behavior early on, when stopping might have done some good. Now it can have little positive value except to provide an explanation for one's bad luck or to promote wiser behavior in others who can see the negative result.

On the other hand, people who have serious illnesses to cope with also experience positively toned emotions such as hope love, joy, and relief. Emotions, both positive and negative, are an inevitable feature of life, as we pointed out in chapter 2. They are connected with the struggle to survive and flourish, and we must never regard them as evidence of a person's lack of psychological integrity. Only when an emotion is out of touch with reality should its appropriateness be questioned. When an emotion fits what is happening, it is psychobiologically natural to experience it. It communicates an important truth about how we construe important events in our lives, though we might sometimes prefer not to express it overtly.

8 ∷
Loss of a Useful Function in Life: Work

Throughout history, occupation has defined one's subjective identity and place in the world. Its loss can leave a person bereft. Doing useful work is a central value for most middle-class persons. We are convinced that this also applies to a substantial portion of the population and is especially important to the generation that today is aging or already old.

We remember the saying "Idleness is the Devil's playground."[1] It expresses the negative value our culture places on self-indulgent idleness. Our real message, however, is that it is usually risky and perhaps harmful not to have something interesting and, above all, useful to do—that is, something that makes a contribution to others, society, or the world, over and above any gain, monetary or otherwise. The danger from not having useful work can be boredom and a feeling of uselessness.

As with everything else people do, there is great individual variation in the goals that people fulfill with work. One, obviously, is to make money on which to live and to take care of others who are dependents. Work is also a way of occupying one's time; without it, life gets boring, and continuous recreational activities are seldom enough to lead to life satisfaction. Work also is a setting in which one can have social activity with people in the same class or circumstances; often it is not the job that is attractive but the relationships with others at work that provide the major source of satisfaction.

Then there is what sometimes is referred to as "having a calling"; some people are dedicated to doing certain things in the world—for example, to advance knowledge, to teach, to help people in trouble. Then there is the wish to be a celebrity at what one does, or to achieve fame or influence in the world, or to have power over others. The meaning of work to any individual includes one or more of these goals, sometimes several at the same time.

One of the most serious losses of aging is no longer to have a useful function in life, which means some kind of work, whether income producing or not. Consideration of this includes not just men but also women, whose major role in life traditionally has been raising children or taking care of the household and family economically, emotionally, or both. For those whose main role is raising children, a crisis often begins when the children leave home and it is necessary to face what has been described as the "empty nest." For those who provide the financial resources to support the family by work outside the home, a comparable crisis often begins with retirement even when it is voluntary, but especially when it is involuntary.

Here again, how well a person does in managing the loss of a work role in life depends on coping, which we discussed in considerable detail in chapter 3. There, the examples were mostly health related, and we said little about work. It would be helpful to remember the problem-focused and emotion-focused functions of coping and how they work.

We also spoke of compensation for deficits. In order to work at high-level activities, one must have one's wits and memory available. Therefore, some of what was said about memory, for example, applies after retirement or a lost job, whether voluntary or involuntary. An elderly person must be able to find ways of compensating for loss of strength, energy, stamina, memory, and so forth. Again and again we can see that coping is an important aspect of dealing with job loss and job change. It is not possible to talk about loss of a useful function in life without reference to the coping process. It is all intertwined.

There is an old joke about a Protestant minister, a Catholic priest, and a Jewish rabbi who are asked, "When does life begin?" The Protestant minister answers, "It begins at birth." The Catholic priest states, "It begins when a child has been conceived." The Jewish rabbi ponders the question a bit and responds, "Life begins when the children leave home and the dog dies." If we look at it from the rabbi's standpoint, a new freedom has been produced. The negative side is the need to replace a lost function with a new life role. One way or another, both perspectives have to do with changes that are inevitable for most people who are aging.

The moral of this joke is, of course, that not having to work is also a highly valued state of affairs. National studies suggest that retirement, including the empty nest, leads to improved life and marital satisfaction, so the sad story of loss of work must be balanced with this other message. Still, it must be compensated for by other activities that provide for satisfaction and one's identity.

Having work to do goes beyond having an ambitious career. We do not wish to make invidious comparisons among the many different things people do to make a contribution to themselves and others. This comment is addressed especially to older women who, in the past, performed work that was centered on the home.

However, the type of work performed by men and women has undergone a great social change in recent years. When we were married in 1945, men were usually the sole breadwinners, and their wives took care of the household and raised the children. When wives did work outside the home, it was usually to help their husband finish school or facilitate a new business, as was the case with Bernice. They expected to quit work as soon as the husband was financially on his feet. There have always been women who deviated from the norm of marriage and motherhood and became artists, musicians, literary figures, and scientists, but they did not represent the norm.

Today, in more than half of all marriages the wife works outside the home, sometimes just for income and sometimes to actualize the desire for a career in addition to marriage and children. Modern women who work outside the home still usually carry the brunt of household and child-rearing responsibilities. The single-income family, which once dominated the work scene, has now almost vanished.

Job loss can be voluntary if one is ready to retire and can manage it financially. It is involuntary when one has been discharged—we used to say fired—by an employer or when one faces the empty nest, but remember that this can be seen, either temporarily or permanently, as being a beneficiary rather than a victim. In any case, the absence of useful work can threaten a person's self-respect and involvement in life, though the involuntary loss is apt to be much more distressing.

In certain occupations more than others, aging persons invest in work commitments that extend well beyond retirement. A case in point consists of university professors who display a continuing involvement with their particular fields. Some might characterizes their retirement jokingly as, "how I retired without really retiring."[2] Many retirees who are financially comfortable are happy to dedicate themselves to volunteer work to help others or the community and to keep busy. At Rossmoor this pattern is widespread.

A survey of retirees from the University of California at Berkeley between 1997 and 1999 provides some remarkable statistics about their productivity. The 1,084 retirees from the faculty who responded to the survey (many of the most productive were unwilling or too busy to respond) state that in those two years they managed collectively to author 449 books, 2,114 articles, 477 book chapters, and 472 book reviews. In addition, they cited 284 abstracts, 331 professional reports, and 97 consulting reports. In the arts, these retirees claimed to have created 178 musical, dance, and theater performances, exhibited 130 artworks, and written 29 creative literary works. In addition, they indicated having secured 225 grants that supported 372 staff, which included graduate assistants and postdoctoral students. A goodly number also taught on the campus and served on numerous doctoral committees.[3] So much for retirement among academics; obviously, in what was once referred to as a "calling," it did not involve giving up their commitment to their work.

Why do retired academics so often continue to work? One reason is that they have long had the goal of advancing knowledge in the world, and many of them at institutions such as Berkeley have very unusual expertise in their field. It is not surprising that they want to apply this special knowledge even after retiring. This may be a very special population, and its pattern need not apply to others.

Second, what are they to do after retirement? Most of their lives have been spent pushing themselves in their fields and teaching students. Few of them can contemplate being satisfied spending their time on the golf course, playing bridge, watching television, or just socializing. They cannot be idle for long and have had a strong work commitment, which is what led them to the top of their fields in the first place.

Some of them also want to obtain additional income as inflation gradually eats away at their retirement pensions. Writing books is one way to do this, or serving as consultants. Still another reason is the desire to continue to receive the plaudits of others for their work. One gets little satisfaction in honors won many years earlier; one needs an encore. Their sense of self is still at stake, and they enjoy exercising their expertise.

This might seem strange to retirees in other occupations who were glad, at least initially, to end their working lives. Most engineers we have met at Rossmoor, for example, are in this category and seldom return after retirement to their profession, which does not mean that they are necessarily idle. Although they may have liked their work, for some reason it is not the stuff of which postretirement work commitment is made. Most blue-collar workers are happy to retire. Work for them has been mostly for income, and in many cases it was viewed as drudgery. It is not that they do not wish to remain active, but their jobs have never been attractive enough to continue that sort of work late in life. The physical demands of the job might also have become excessive with age.

Many older retirees ultimately reach the point at which they are in danger of being bored by not having to work. Retirement ends their job or career, and they must find something else they can still do. Even though they were initially glad to quit work, and because idleness creates a distressing amount of boredom, many opt to make useful contributions to others as volunteers. In effect, they go back to work without pay to preserve their engagement in life.

About the importance of work in our lives, a distinguished sociologist wrote:

> People at all ages engage in many types of unpaid work, or, as I and my colleagues have termed them in our research, productive activities,

> including household work, child care, voluntary organizational activities, and informal assistance to family and friends. Among all forms of work and productivity, only paid work and child-care decline sharply with age. Failure to consider other activities grossly under-represents the work or productive activity of many individuals and groups, most notably of women, whose total level of work and productive activity equals or exceeds that of men at all ages, and especially at older ages. The relative well-being of "non-working" people of all ages, including retired older persons, may in part reflect that most of them are still working, though not for pay, and very likely to be doing amounts and types of work that they have voluntarily chosen and that hence are more likely to be characterized by the conditions of work that . . . are supportive of well-being.[4]

In light of what we have been saying, it is not unreasonable to suggest that the loss of the opportunity to work presents a widespread, if not universal, aging crisis that must be coped with even if we do not need to work for income. In this statement we are presuming that the most dependable way to remain contented, happy, and vital in old age is to be active and engaged, and this may require an effort to compensate for the loss of personal resources on which this engagement might depend.[5] The nature of these resources and deficits will make a major difference in what can be done. The particulars of this choice are one of the most significant ways elderly individuals differ from each other.

Without some outside commitment, there is a danger that women might compensate for their empty nest by interfering with their children in their own child rearing. Sometimes this focus, which is a way of trying to remain useful, gets them into trouble by provoking a negative backlash and even rejection by their children. This may lead them to be lonelier than ever. We know such a woman who says she forcibly shuts her mouth and bites her tongue every time she has the impulse to give advice to her children.

Men, too, when they retire, can get into trouble with their wives if they expect them to change their lifestyle just to cater to them. They often interfere with the running of the household by being home under foot with nothing else to do, and they get in the way when the "girls" get together for lunch or bridge. Under these circumstances, their wives wish their work-deprived husbands would find something to do and leave them alone during the day. Neither the women nor the men are malicious or looking for trouble. They just need to find ways of filling their time and being active. The women make their children feel guilty, and the men do the same to their wives. When George Weiss, the highly successful general manager of the New York Yankees baseball team, was forced into retirement after the 1960 season, his wife was quoted as saying, "I married him for better or worse, but not for lunch."[6]

Weiss returned to baseball about a year later to fill the same position with the newly formed, less prestigious New York Mets.

The involuntary loss of a job in midlife or later is especially traumatizing. A special issue of the official publication of the Society for Stress and Anxiety Research (STAR) devoted to the psychological problems of industrial downsizing (in which people lose jobs) noted that people gain self-esteem and a sense of mastery and accomplishment through their jobs. They also make meaningful social contacts with others, including sharing camaraderie with fellow workers.[7] The effects of job loss can be extremely distressing, though not always, as we shall see in one of our case histories. The result is often a loss of self-esteem and a sense of control over one's life. Job loss is anxiety provoking and can also lead to depression if another acceptable job cannot be found.[8]

Case Histories of Loss of Work

In the rest of this chapter we present four brief case histories to illustrate some of the things we have been saying. The first two individuals are men who lost their jobs in late midlife. One considers this a disaster, the other a great boon because he was very dissatisfied with the work he chose in order to make a good living. The second two are women who became dissatisfied with their lives in late midlife after functioning as mothers and homemakers and who cope with this quite differently.

Harry's Story

At fifty-five years of age, Harry was a successful midlevel manager for a major American manufacturing company. He was comfortable but not wealthy and looked on his job favorably, though without much enthusiasm. He had risen in company rank and salary from a primarily technical role as engineer to the head of a significant department. His managerial responsibilities were largely centered on personnel, and he dealt with procedures that were essential to the efficient flow of various phases of production. He would seem to be a counterexample of the assumption that work is a positive psychological force. It turns out, however, that the loss of a job, even one that was not terribly satisfying, was a disaster for Harry and led to depression and alcoholism; even when he managed to pull himself together, he was just a shell of the man he had once been.

Harry's managerial role was a major source of stress. To advance he needed to become a manager, which meant dealing with people. He could, with effort, handle this requirement. Harry was technically oriented and competent but socially awkward and uncomfortable. He would much rather struggle with an engineering question than deal with people and their emotional problems. Yet, as is often the case with major companies that make a product, he was initially hired as an engineer, then was promoted, and his career with the company had been stable for more than thirty years.

Along with many Americans after World War II, Harry assumed he would remain with the same company until it was time to retire. Although his work did not thrill him, he felt secure in his family life and about his future and comfortable with his life situation. But, as we shall see, this was not enough. Without warning—perhaps he should have seen it coming—the widespread expectation about a lifelong career with the same company suddenly ended during the 1980s with a rash of job terminations that became known, euphemistically, as downsizing.

Companies began to discharge large numbers of long-term employees, sometimes as a consequence of corporate mergers and sometimes because of economic slowdowns suggesting a need to cut costs and increase efficiency. Many midlife career employees were discharged, and Harry, at fifty-five years of age, was one of them. He was one of the lucky ones; at least he was offered a pension commensurate with his position.

From a practical standpoint, Harry's dilemma was what to do at this point in his life. He was much too young to retire. However, after searching for another job for a while, he learned that any job he would be offered involved greatly reduced responsibility, status, and pay. He finally chose to end his job search and be a full-time retiree.

His wife, not unusual for even this in-between generation, was not employed outside the home. There were two young adult offspring who still needed attention and financial help. One was a son, who had been disabled; he lived at home and considered himself unable to work. The other was a daughter who was living unmarried with a man Harry and his wife distrusted, which resulted in a great deal of family conflict and distress.

Harry's family understood his distress but thought he was making too much of it and believed he should get over being fired and get on with his life. They did not seem to realize how essential Harry's job was to him. It was the main way of defining himself, on which he depended heavily.

They also did not want him to take his troubles out on them. When loved ones are blamed, even if only implicitly, for something they are not responsible for, they are likely to fight back. Being blamed made Harry's family members feel unloved because they recognized the presence of another agenda—in a sense he was criticizing them for being an unnecessary burden. They turned away from him, and this only created additional psychic damage for Harry.

As a result, Harry became increasingly estranged from his family. In his misery, he turned inward. He refused to let anyone help him with the stressful situation in which he had become enmeshed. He grew depressed, began to drink heavily, and soon became an alcoholic. Few people are more psychologically destitute than a man or woman who no longer has a place or function in the world and drinks to obtain psychological relief. Alcohol abuse is common in the elderly, especially those who lack satisfying relationships with others and enjoyable things to do. Harry had no adequate coping resources for fighting what had happened to him.

We should note in passing that depression is not a single emotion but a combination of several—for example, anxiety, anger, guilt, and shame. In clinical work, depression is too often viewed as a pathology, a form of mental illness. But emotions should not be regarded as pathological unless they are inappropriate to one's circumstances or lead to serious dysfunction. Many depressions are mild, and most people sometimes feel blue or down in response to losses or disappointments in their lives. We would regard this as normal and sometimes even adaptive when it leads people to review what is going on in their lives and consider more effective ways of coping.[9]

The criteria for deciding whether depression is a psychopathology—we tend to avoid the term *illness* here because depression is most commonly the result of problems of living rather than a biochemical anomaly—should be its severity, duration, and the harm it does. Experienced professionals distinguish a clinical depression from reasonable mood swings. Alcoholism, as distinguished from merely moderate or sometimes even heavy drinking, can be a disaster for both the alcoholic and his loved ones. Harry's drinking frightened and depressed his wife and children. At first they felt sorry for him (and for themselves), but in dealing with an alcoholic, one's patience eventually wears thin. His family began to experience considerable anger over the way he was dealing with his problem, further isolating him.

What we just said about the legitimacy of feeling depressed does not really apply in Harry's case. He was in serious trouble and needed professional help. However, allow us to digress a moment about the danger of thinking positively as we try to cope with the disagreeable features of life. Because it is important to recognize and accept painful realities, we must sometimes permit ourselves to feel bad when there are good reasons for this. These days, clinical psychology and medicine, including psychiatry, have an unfortunate tendency to regard as pathological any sign of distress, especially depression.

When we refuse to allow people to think negatively about their condition of life, we also trivialize their suffering. Without thinking much about the consequences, those who care about someone who is sick or dying may apply subtle pressure on that person to think positively and maintain a happy demeanor. This often requires that the patient deny what is evident—for example, that he or she is critically ill, dying, or has lost the will to live. Physicians, too, are offended by illnesses they cannot control or cure—it is their mission to prevent or cure, and they often feel uncomfortable about this helplessness. The solution is to prescribe a pill, but much of the time the real problem does not go away.

The result of this well-meaning but often harmful pressure is that those who are suffering legitimate distress cannot feel authentic about their feelings. They not only must face the loss of their lives but also are made to fear the loss of their loved ones, who are clearly troubled by what is happening and may be showing signs of distancing from the dying patient to protect themselves. Patients in this situation fear that they will lose contact with their loved ones who cannot cope adequately with the imminent loss. So they may go along with the cheerful charade despite their distressing plight.[10]

But to return to Harry and his family, his wife suffered guilt feelings because she believed she had not been as attentive and sympathetic about her husband's troubles as she should have been. As is usually the case with the spouse of an alcoholic, what begins with empathy for her husband, as well as anxiety about what was happening to their family and hope that things would change for the better, soon turns to resentment. This was true in the case of Harry's wife as he continued to fail as a husband and father and could not respond to entreaties that he give up drinking and turn his life around.

Harry's disabled and indigent son received much abuse from his father during this period, and early on retaliatory anger was the son's most important emotion. At length, he turned away from his father, distancing himself as much as possible and expressing empathy for his mother. He believed she was severely victimized by what had happened. Having become contemptuous of men, including her father, whom she now regarded as inadequate, Harry's daughter broke up with her live-in companion and returned home. This provided some household help and companionship for her mother. The daughter was determined to revamp her own life and found a job that allowed her to contribute to the family's well-being.

After five years of destitution and at the constant urging of his family to get professional help, as well as threats that they would leave him if he did not, Harry agreed to see a psychotherapist. Opposed to religious observance, he refused to try Alcoholics Anonymous. He remained in therapy for six months and began to understand the parental pressures on him when he was a child that made him prone to shame and guilt. He also gained insight about how he had alienated his wife and children.

Harry began to pull himself together. He stopped drinking on and off but eventually stayed off alcohol completely. He remained prone to depression, but for the most part he was not as clinically depressed—that is, seriously dysfunctional—as he had been earlier. For the first time, he began to cook gourmet food and to garden, which helped him regain some of his former self-respect. However, he rarely left home, a fact that was deeply frustrating to his wife, who wanted to travel and do other things she had been deprived of, such as theater and vacation cruises. She found women friends for company, mostly widows and divorcees.

Harry now goes to movies or the theater occasionally and seems reasonably content, but he remains a shell of his former self. Even though he keeps busy cooking and gardening, he has occasional bouts of depression. But with more peace within himself, he has grown closer to his children, giving evidence of interest in them that he had not shown before. He has also become more of a source of strength to them, and they now regard him with sympathy and even affection. As he ages, he struggles with serious cardiovascular medical problems that will ultimately do him in.

Harry's Emotions

Thus far, though we mentioned his wife's and children's emotions, which are part of Harry's story, we have presented only the bare facts of what happened without pointing to the main emotions he experienced at different periods of his personal crisis. As with all of us, these emotions came and went as Harry's thoughts were directed to this or that interpersonal and intrapsychic feature of his plight.

One of the main emotions Harry's loss of job aroused in him was anxiety. Harry had been anxiety-prone most of his life, but the anxiety became acute immediately after he was informed about his discharge. Anxiety is a universal and important emotion. At bottom it has to do with threats to what we want to be or believe we are in the world and where we are heading in life. Its relational meaning is *facing an uncertain, existential threat*.

Harry's anxiety was centered not only on conflicts about who he was but also on uncertainty about his future. A solid pension helped assuage any concern about his family's financial situation, but it did not help him deal personally with the loss of a respectable place in the world and something useful to do each day. His life seemed suddenly to be cut off and in limbo.

Another major emotional consequence of Harry's firing—one that he could not readily admit or talk about—was a deep sense of shame about what he took to be his own personal failure. This made him feel woefully inadequate. Shame is one of the most terrible states of mind a person can experience because it usually arises in connection with the implied self-accusation that one has a bad character. Its relational meaning is *having failed to live up to an ego ideal*, which is a powerful personal standard that helps direct one's life.

What do you do about shame? There are only two good alternatives. One is to externalize the blame for what has happened; the other is to hide from everyone so your defect cannot be seen. Harry seemed to have no defense except to hide.

For shame to occur, there must be more than an observation by others of this failure. People who feel shame must have also internalized a social standard of conduct that is esteemed by themselves, family, and usually their society. The term *internalization* is employed to point to the developmental process by means of which such standards are acquired and become an integral feature of one's personality.[11] This means that people who feel shame have accepted a standard as part of their innermost selves and have acknowledged to themselves that they have failed to live up to it.

The personal standard leading to shame need have nothing to do with public morality. One can feel ashamed even about not being a successful thief or con man. Harry believed he had failed to live up to his obligations as a husband, father, and, indeed, a man to be respected. When he was alive, Harry's father had been a stern, demanding figure who would have been openly disgusted with Harry and ashamed if he had observed his son's failure. Even when a parental figure is no longer present or alive, the expectation of disapproval can still rule from the grave. Those who are perfectionists about themselves are apt to be prone to shame or what is sometimes referred to as being shame-ridden.

A third major emotion emerged in Harry after he gave up looking for another job. Harry felt guilty about not having tried hard enough. This was for him a moral lapse; the relational meaning of guilt is having transgressed a moral imperative. In Harry's eyes, the prime source of his guilt feelings was, as he saw it, his arrogant unwillingness to accept any reasonable job he was offered. Like shame, guilt requires that we blame ourselves for our moral shortcoming, especially if it has unjustly harmed others. It had harmed Harry's family, both the one he grew up with and his present wife and children.

Unlike with shame, when we feel the pangs of a guilty conscience, we want to undo the damage, to do penance, to seek forgiveness rather than hide it from others. It does not matter whether we are really guilty of anything in an objective or legal sense, only that we view ourselves as having behaved immorally. People who try to maintain an impossibly high moral standard are especially prone to feel guilty. The emotion of guilt seems to control their lives, and we speak of them as guilt-ridden. How could Harry atone for his arrogance in not accepting a lesser job? Not only would that further demean him, but things had gone far past the point at which anyone would hire him for an industrial job.

Guilt-ridden people are probably raised with considerable moral pressure, and certain ethnic groups seem to cultivate guilt in their children. Jews have often been said to foment guilt in their children, although they are by no means the only ones—Chinese are often spoken of in this respect, and Japanese are known for their shame-inducing child-rearing practices.[12]

Harry also felt a great deal of anger about what had happened to him, especially when he was reminded of the injustice he had experienced at the hands of the company officials who had deserted him without just cause. The anger was also directed more vaguely at the society that cared so little for anyone in trouble. Anger even burst forth periodically in the presence of his family, whose three other members had never accepted responsibility for Harry's plight. However, when he expressed this anger, it made him feel added guilt because it was so unjustified.

The anger felt by Harry was actually useful to him psychologically because it allowed him to shift some of the blame he had accepted for his debacle from himself to others. It helped ease some of his shame and guilt, and it reduced his feeling of helplessness. In a highly competitive society, most people feel more significant and effective when they lash out at others rather than meekly accepting being slighted or demeaned. When anger is repeatedly directed toward loved ones, however, as it was in Harry's case, it can be very destructive to these relationships.

Some Comments about Existential Neuroses

We close Harry's story by suggesting that the near-universal need to be engaged in useful work is why so many elderly men and women, still reasonably vigorous, engage in volunteer work. Even though Harry was not thrilled with his job, to be happy or contented, we think that most of us need to feel useful in the world. One cannot enjoy a vacation when one is already on a permanent one, which is probably why so many of the scions of wealth have, at least in the past, committed themselves to productive work. One thinks of the Roosevelt family, the Rockefellers, and the Kennedys, among others, whose lives were devoted to the political arena when their wealth would have allowed them to be totally idle and self-indulgent.

Harry's state of mind is not very different from what is sometimes referred to as an *existential neurosis*, in which a person cannot find something in life that he or she wants to do.[13] This almost goalless state of mind also occurs in young people who may seek help through psychotherapy or from others. Some explore eastern religious philosophy, such as Buddhism, or are attracted to the writings of individuals such as the Dalai Lama.

Often they will ask plaintively how they might find themselves, which is a plight similar to that of Willy Loman's son Biff in Arthur Miller's *Death of a Salesman*. Because of inner conflicts over having seen his father involved in an affair with a woman other than his wife, and having a low opinion of himself, Biff is demoralized. His father, himself a failure as a salesman, constantly exaggerates his son's resources, foolishly repeating accounts of the boy's success as a high school football hero, though Biff understands all too well that being a football star was no longer relevant to his future. In the face of this inappropriate enthusiasm about the young man's promise, Biff cries out to his father, expressing the pathos of his situation in the line, "I'm one dollar an hour, Willy." His ambition and self-esteem have been thoroughly undermined.

Geriatric therapists usually struggle to help elderly persons with an existential neurosis get more out of life. Their counterparts, young people struggling with the same syndrome, are also usually frustrating to treat, so this is not just a problem of age or work status, but it is a common problem of many elderly persons. The inability to become committed to something is just as incapacitating and depressing for elderly persons as for others. They wish to be motivated to engage in some productive activity yet are unable to do so. This motivation can only arise from within, not from the urgings of others. Many continue to remain unengaged and live a marginal, unhappy existence waiting, as it were, for death.

The stories of many other elderly persons are far more encouraging. Elderly volunteers work for the public good without compensation, often doing things similar to what they were once paid for before retirement. This might include lecturing, teaching, or writing books. Volunteers often provide modest services that fall below their previous standards of skill and complexity—for example, helping patients and visitors in local hospitals or providing home care. Volunteer work, whatever it is, gives them something to do that helps them feel useful. It is also a reason to get up in the morning and to shave and dress.

Many Rossmoor residents are reasonably and sometimes spectacularly successful in finding satisfying things to do. For example, they focus on previously uncultivated talents in music, painting, sculpture, and other creative activities that, early on, were subordinated to the practical demands of working life. One of our neighbors learned how to make professional-caliber movies of his travels to give to his grown children when they visit. Some make jewelry and occasionally become quite skilled, displaying and selling their work. Still others explore new technologies in the local computer club. Quite a few Rossmoor residents belong to one of the many social groups, such as the Kiwanis or Lions, whose members are devoted to raising money for particular charities.

Some residents serve as administrators for Rossmoor itself or enter local politics. Many play bridge, tennis, and table tennis or participate in competitive bowling (called bowls) on grass courts. Golf is one of the main attractions in this community, and, as is common with golfing enthusiasts, some residents are out on the course rain or shine, even when the cold or heat is daunting. Our list is, of course, incomplete and merely illustrative, since the variations in the ways in which older people cope with retirement and aging are great.

Psychotherapy appears to have helped Harry substantially. Somehow he began to shape up. He stopped drinking and stayed sober during the therapy, lapsed when he quit therapy, then once again took hold and stopped permanently. He never completely lost his tendency to depression, but he began to relate better to his wife and children and got interested in cooking and gardening, which improved his morale.

You may recall that Harry had remained housebound for a long time, but now he occasionally goes out with his wife. The last time they did so was to visit his daughter and son-in-law fifty miles away when they had their first grandchild. As mentioned in the case history, he gets along better now with his family and is less withdrawn.

Harry is more successful now with respect to his aging than during the terrible period following the loss of his job. He now enjoys cooking and gardening and only occasionally shows any significant depression. However, as we said, he is a shell of his former self, lacking in self-regard, withdrawn from most of life, narrowly committed to wife and family, and mostly housebound. His functioning as he ages is marginal at best, though it could have been much worse.

Fred's Story

Like Harry, our second male example, Fred, was not fulfilled by his work and also lost his job at age fifty-five, but with results that were very different from those of Harry. An early decision about making a good living locked Fred into a job that was a serious mismatch with his personal needs. He worked for many years for a large accounting firm. He had always been a highly sociable, outgoing fellow, but being an accountant forced him into solitary work that he did not find rewarding. He remained in this occupation because it earned him a good living and he could think of nothing else that was a practical source of income for him and his growing family.

Early in his career as an accountant, Fred had begun to feel unhappy with his work, and by his fifties his lack of enthusiasm began to be reflected in his performance at the job. After a number of warnings from management, he was finally let go. Now he was without a job and did not know what to do. It seemed too late in life to cultivate another career, and, besides, who would give him the opportunity? Luckily, Fred's wife was a well-paid dress designer, and the children were mostly grown and successful. The family could manage adequately even if he did not work for pay, but he could not conceive of being idle at this relatively young age.

One of the things he had been doing on the side for the previous five years was part-time acting. From time to time he played minor parts in dramas and musicals that were being presented in a nearby community theater. He enjoyed doing this, but because of his regular job, and despite encouragement from actors and directors that he had talent, he could not commit himself to acting beyond an occasional small part. Now he began to wonder whether he should seek a career as an actor, an idea that nearly all his friends and wife considered crazy.

Despite this negative feedback, Fred decided he would try, and he joined a local actor's workshop to obtain professional training. The workshop had attracted about fifty students seeking to become actors, directors, or playwrights. It was not large or famous but was considered quite good and would serve his current need to learn the acting trade.

Fred recognized that he was entering a competitive field, with so many actors competing for roles that his chances of attaining fame, or even a modest degree of prominence, were exceedingly slim. He knew it would also take time to demonstrate whether or not he had talent, but he was determined to make a go of it and was having fun. He experienced none of the feelings of loss or damage to his self-esteem that Harry had suffered in losing his job. Fred viewed what was happening to him not as a failure, a loss, or even a new high-risk venture but as having made a late course correction in his working life. In effect, he had a unique opportunity to obtain the first real satisfaction in life and work that he had ever had.

Within a few years, Fred was getting some substantial parts, gaining an appreciative local public, and earning some income. He had learned the craft of acting and had a sound intuitive sense about how to play the parts to which he was assigned. He often had to travel some distance for this purpose, but this posed little problem for his marriage because his wife had a professional life of her own and his children were no longer living at home. For the first time in his life he was having a rewarding work experience. It seemed like a dream come true.

He could tell from the warm reaction that the audience frequently appreciated what he was doing, though he was still something of an amateur. Like all actors, he needed enthusiastic applause, and he shrank defensively when an audience failed to respond or showed indifference to or impatience with his acting. It was always challenging to experiment with small changes in the way he played the same role from one performance to another.

Acting proved to be hard but rewarding work, though he never earned much income from it because most of the plays in which he performed were local and suburban, not big-time. But he had finally been freed from the confines of his accounting job and had found a way of life that matched his talents, needs, and personality. The change had been a wonderful piece of good luck. Oddly, it also brought about an improved relationship with his wife, with whom he previously lived in an emotionally distant fashion. He was more animated, attentive, and confident with her, and she appreciated the change and reciprocated. Approaching sixty, Fred was a new man who had found himself at last.

Fred's Emotions

At the outset of his story, we find Fred disappointed with his work situation, and because he thought nothing could be done to change it, his dominant emotion was to be chronically without enthusiasm and somewhat sad. The relational meaning of sadness is having experienced an irrevocable loss. His loss was not to be doing something stimulating. The management at his company did him a favor by discharging him. Instead of experiencing anger or anxiety over the blow to his self-esteem, as happened with Harry, Fred reacted with cool detachment as he tried to decide what to do. Because his children were now successfully on their own and his wife had a substantial job, the loss of income seemed of no great importance. He felt free to do as he pleased.

As he moved gradually toward an acting career, his main emotions were anxiety about how he was doing in his acting, relief that he was free of an unsatisfactory job, and joy that he had found a good fit late in life between his outgoing personality and his work. When a performance led to substantial applause or recognition, his joy was explosive.

The relational meaning of joy (or happiness) is *making reasonable progress toward the realization of an important goal*, but this does not reflect the excited state of mind that comes from a peak experience.[14] Joy generally is an acute, temporary emotion because one must usually get on with the next step in life. Ironically, getting what one wants is not what is important; rather, being able to work toward it is—that is, doing something one cares about. Happiness is, in effect, a process, not a result. It is doing, and a by-product of what one does, not something for which we can strive.

Fred does not aspire to fame as an actor, so great disappointment or distress does not characterize his present life pattern. He is mostly challenged and exhilarated rather than threatened in his work, though, like most actors, he expands psychologically when the audience loves him and contracts when it is indifferent or impatient with him. He also feels grateful for his good luck in escaping a job of drudgery. The relational meaning of gratitude is to *appreciate an altruistic gift that provides a personal benefit*. Fred regards having been discharged from his old job as such a gift.

Instead of becoming depressed, anxious, and ashamed as Harry had following the loss of his job, for the first time in his adult life Fred was really enjoying himself. This was first as a student in a local actor's studio, then in the acting parts he was being invited to take increasingly often. It was at times anxiety producing, but quite often thrilling, especially when he could sense the audience's approval. Even his marriage improved as a result of his generally positive mood and his greater attentions to his wife. What had started out as a loss of work got transformed into an epiphany. There is no need for psychological treatment here. Fred is a successful old man and constantly improving. He ended up better than he began and is coping well.

Joan's Story

Right after completing her bachelor's degree, Joan, an attractive but flighty twenty-two-year-old, married David, a twenty-eight-year-old physician who had just completed medical school and an internship at a well-respected medical school. He had accepted a residency in neurology and seemed headed for a highly successful medical career. They both came from upper-middle-class families, so money was no serious problem.

Joan had been mildly interested in history and literature. These academic subjects did not seem to offer strong career possibilities, so she decided against going on to further study. She had some vague thoughts about writing, but marriage and family seemed more attractive. Besides, she could be a writer while being a wife and mother; writers can do their thing at home.

During David's residency, the couple rented an apartment that was not far from the medical school. Their money came mostly from Joan's parents. Having two sets of affluent parents who were ready to help and could easily supplement David's as yet meager income, Joan was ready to start a family. David agreed, though it was understood that he would be too pressured by his residency and the ultimate need to establish a medical practice to contribute much to the household or child rearing. This was an arrangement Joan would come to regret.

By the time David had finished his residency and had begun to establish a practice, they had four children, three girls and a boy. David spent four days a week at a county hospital and one day at a retirement community dealing with the neurological problems of the elderly residents. With help from both sets of in-laws, he and Joan bought a modest home, which was convenient to both places where David worked.

David was heavily occupied with his practice. Joan was busier with the household and four young children than she had ever anticipated and had no time to write. During her early years of marriage, she was rather isolated from her husband, who came home too tired to be much of a husband, lover, or father. Nevertheless, she found her interaction with the children and other young mothers who lived in the neighborhood pleasing, and her position as a doctor's wife gave her built-in positive status. Always busy, with relatively little interaction with her husband or other married couples, Joan gave little attention to where her life was heading.

The years went by quickly in this domestic pattern until, lo and behold, she suddenly found herself entering middle age. Sooner than she could have imagined, the children were in high school and college, and Joan began to sense that she was soon to face the moment when they would no longer need her as, one by one, they went off on their own. What had been at first a dim, inchoate sense of being cheated, but had remained in the back of her mind, now became a gnawing sense of lack and was finding a place front and center in her consciousness.

As a result of the type of life Joan had slipped into without any real planning, she told herself, she had not been able to pursue further study or do any writing. With a husband who had little time for her, the couple had grown apart. The children were soon to be gone, so there would be little to engage her at home. As the women's movement gained attention in the media and she saw many younger women aiming for careers, she became increasingly disgruntled with her life, but she could find nothing obvious in the way of a solution.

"What's the hurry?" she asked herself a bit defensively. It would take several more years before the arrival of the empty nest, when she would be free to do her own thing. Her son was already distancing himself, as young men will do as they gain maturity and establish their independence, but the girls still needed her. The children had problems common to their age, socially, at school, and in their relationships with each other, which were competitive and often hostile. Ominously, however, they too were showing signs of resisting parental control, which sometimes made Joan feel unloved. The problem of what she would do continued to fester, and there was increasing family tension, but Joan kept drifting and took no steps to deal with the inevitable.

It was at this point that Joan, at the suggestion of another woman she knew, sought psychotherapy, hoping that it would help her redirect her life. She spent eight months in therapy, during which she listlessly reviewed her privileged life with no clear direction. She enjoyed the visits to the therapist—it was one of the few times in her life that she could revel in narcissism—but never gave the task her central attention. Nor did she seek an understanding of why she was in the position she was in and what was the basis of her dissatisfaction with her life. After six months of therapy, lonely and bereft, she began to have an affair with a married man, though she never spoke about it to the therapist.

The man was a teacher and was younger than Joan. She met him at a PTA meeting at the high school where both had children attending. She was still a very attractive woman, and after the standard approach and an invitation to lunch, they ended up in bed in a rented room in a location where they were unlikely to bump into anyone they knew. Suddenly, the inattention and sexual indifference she had always known changed into a torrid relationship. Her counterpart, too, was disenchanted with his marriage, and the two heartily made up for what they had been missing. They met more and more frequently, typically getting together about three times a week. Because of her husband's commitments, Joan was quite free to adapt to her lover's teaching schedule and home obligations.

Not thrilled with hotel rooms for their liaisons, on some of their meetings they drove into the countryside, where they found a secluded grassy spot, and made love on a blanket. At other times, they rented a boat and had fun exploring, usually finding a quiet spot along the shore where they could make love in private. On one thrilling occasion, with no one around, they skinny-dipped and ended up making love uninhibitedly. It all seemed idyllic.

The affair continued for a little more than a year, but as they became increasingly secure and careless, a friend of her paramour's wife finally saw them in a compromising action as they were having dinner at a restaurant. When the irate wife learned the details of the infidelity and sued for divorce, the affair was exposed publicly, and Joan and David now had to face their own marital problems. Joan learned from her husband that he had been having an affair, and there had been a succession of previous liaisons of this type.

Two poor marriages were about to break up, but Joan's affair also had to be abandoned amid bitter recriminations. When the dust settled, Joan found herself mostly alone at fifty-two, which seemed to her like a late midlife gateway to old age. The idea of writing, which had been lost early in the demands of marriage and child rearing, had been totally abandoned with the passage of time.

Joan eventually remarried and settled in a retirement community, spending her time on the golf course and playing bridge, which never seemed to satisfy her but was at least a way to fill time. There was little sexual excitement or gratification in this second marriage, and at this point she abandoned any interest in sex.

She lost her second husband to a deadly heart attack and very quickly married again. This marriage was more a matter of social access and position than any significant affection. This man developed Parkinson's disease two years after the marriage, became an invalid five years later, and died of pneumonia a short time after that. Joan was determined never again to get involved with a man. It was a bore and a drag, especially when they had the poor taste to get sick and die.

The three husbands, all well-to-do, netted her a great deal of money, which she boasted about constantly, looking down her nose competitively at women who were less well off. She did this to compensate for her underlying feelings of failure and inadequacy. Her hostile self-promotion earned her the resentment of most of the other women she met, which further isolated her.

Joan is still alive at eighty-two but now suffers from macular degeneration and is almost blind, about which she complains bitterly, for good reason. She pays excessive fees to a constantly changing collection of immigrant caretakers, each of whom, she thinks, are ripping her off. They take care of her, drive her where she wants to go, and clean her condominium. Her children, who are married and live their own lives, with only one in the area, show little interest in their mother. An exception, perhaps, was their attempt for their own personal gain to manage their mother's large estate and some country property she had inherited from the last husband, who loved to hunt.

In many ways, Joan's life was wasted, built on shallowness and self-indulgence. It is difficult for us not to feel some sadness about Joan's story for this waste. It did not have to be, and at the outset she had so much in her favor. This reaction arises from knowing her. Although her outlook was shallow, she did not seem to us to be malicious, and in our eyes she was an unnecessary victim of circumstance, a person who never caught on to what a good life should be about.

Joan's Emotions

Joan seems always to have been uninvolved with anyone other than herself. It is difficult to say whether she started out on her marriage in this way or evolved into a narcissistic person as a result of an unsatisfactory marriage to someone who gave her little attention.

At first she seemed pleased with her life situation, and like most young married women with children, her major emotional ups and downs, perhaps reflecting a rose-colored view of her distant past, included situational joys, anxiety, love, anger, and sadness, which reflected events in her daily life. Increasingly she was faced with disappointment, but she never reflected much on her life or made any plans to change things as she became increasingly disenchanted. She felt increasingly lonely, unappreciated, and angry, leading to an affair that provided her with attention, infatuation rather than love, and plenty of sexual passion, which she had been mostly deprived of with her husband.

When the affair was discovered, and she learned her husband had also been fooling around, Joan felt betrayed and furious (despite the fact that she was also a betrayer). The capacity for feeling guilt was not one of her major suits. Both her affair and her original marriage had collapsed, and this physically attractive but self-centered woman spent much of her elderly years in superficial marriages of convenience. She had become increasingly competitive, angry, and isolated from other women and even her children, who evidently recognized her self-centered outlook and paid her no mind.

Joan must be cared for constantly toward the end of a self-indulgent, wasted life. Psychotherapy might well have helped her had she given it half a chance, and it might do so now, but she is very unlikely to try it at this stage of her life.

Joan has been a failure in later life, though she did not do particularly well early on either. In spite of all her early advantages—beauty, wealthy family, and intelligence—she turned into a narcissistic person who never got much out of life, never did the writing she had planned, and is likely to die lonely, unmissed, and unmourned. It is a sad life story.

Martha's Story

Our second example of a dissatisfied middle-aged woman presents important contrasts to Joan. Martha had been a bright sociology student in college and had begun a Ph.D. program in the South. She married while a graduate student and in the course of the next six years had three children, two girls and a boy.

Her husband eventually became an executive of a large corporation. He ultimately moved to the West Coast after accepting a top executive position in the corporation. This meant that Martha, by then thirty-five, was affluent but forced to abandon her studies. In keeping with major differences in emphasis at distinctive American universities, if she transferred to another sociology program, she would have to begin her studies all over again from scratch.

Martha had begun to have serious doubts that it was practical for a woman to raise a family and simultaneously achieve an impressive career. After some reflection, she concluded that, with three young children, it might be more sensible to wait until they were older before trying to go back to school. When her children were at last reasonably well along in their development, it seemed time for Martha to return to graduate school and proceed with her career ambitions.

Marriage and family had never provided gratification enough for her, and she was dissatisfied with the limits the traditional feminine role imposed on her life. Her husband, who was heavily involved in his own career, accepted and supported her decision and was actually relieved not to have to cater emotionally to his wife. On the other hand, she was still quite inexperienced and unsure of herself and had a great deal to learn.

Martha applied to the sociology departments at two nearby universities but was rejected by both, which only added to existing doubts about her prospects. She persevered, however, and was eventually accepted as a graduate student in a highly regarded program.

At first Martha was unable to find anyone on the faculty who would give her significant attention or provide research opportunities for her to do a dissertation. Eventually, she found a female professor who recognized her worth and became her mentor. Martha was able to obtain a doctorate in three years. This was just a start, but a vital step toward achieving a successful career.

Martha was first appointed by her mentor to manage a substantial research project. After five years in this research management role, she had published a number of articles with her mentor, who on several occasions, in order to advance her promising student's career, gave Martha first authorship, which ultimately provided important academic visibility. Having learned from her mentor how to obtain research funding, it now seemed the better part of wisdom for Martha to go out on her own, to which her mentor agreed. Martha found a research position at a nearby university and within a few years established her own research program.

Her research, which was timely and effective, made her visible in public health circles, and over the next several years she received numerous invitations to speak about it, both within the country and abroad. In these forays into the outside research world, Martha initially felt inadequate and obsessed constantly about what she was going to say. However, she gradually learned how to project herself confidently and effectively and became a widely sought speaker.

Now in her seventies, though aging, Martha is a significant research and administrative force within the university and serves usefully in professional organizations—a successful role model for women who believe it is possible after child rearing to have a significant work career. When people asked her how she did it, she would answer, "I'm a tough old broad."

Martha's Emotions

Early on, Martha's predominant emotional state was anger as a result of not being able to complete her doctorate in the South, which she considered unfair. But she lived up to her family obligations conscientiously, deferring any return to graduate school until the children were well on their way. And she was circumspect in verbalizing these appraisals and mostly private feelings.

Martha's ambition then took over. Despite rejection by some graduate schools, as a result of her determination and persistence she ultimately succeeded in establishing a research career against the odds. She had struggled with periods of despair and depression but also was sustained by hope and gratification as she overcame adversity and gained successes in her chosen field.

Her most important and recurrent emotion was anxiety as she faced strong competition and the need to display ability to get ahead. Her anxiety was illustrated, for example, on occasions when she had to professionally present her work and thinking. As a beginner, she was uncertain and inexperienced at doing this. She worried constantly about what to say and how to say it, often getting little sleep the night before a presentation. Eventually she became an effective speaker and a well-known researcher. She had always recognized the importance of controlling her doubts, anxieties, and anger, however, in an effort to win a place in her field. Her persistence paid off, and she succeeded against the odds.

In these four case histories, we see how strong goals, persistence, ability to cope effectively, and a favorable match between the person and the environmental circumstances that must be faced play important roles in a person's work life. These desirable personal qualities, and many others, too, influence how someone who has been thwarted in work by being fired or by not being able to get started can find a suitable career niche.

Again, we see how important individual differences are in shaping the response to a major loss, in this case that of work. The personal meaning a person derives from this loss is of major importance in how he or she will react. But to a considerable extent, we think that the work a person does or, to put it more broadly, the way people live day in and day out, defines them socially and in their own minds. This is one of the main reasons why loss of job can be so disastrous.

Harry did not have the resources to cope and ended up a shell of his former self.

Fred had an epiphany in getting out of a job he never should have been in (except for its financial rewards) and finding a new career that actualized his potential.

Joan made fatal mistakes early on and never learned how to grow up and establish favorable values on which a suitable life could be built. Hers was the biggest tragedy of these four persons.

Martha, by dint of effort, perseverance, and competence, was able to establish a successful career against the odds.

Recognizing that human goals and values differ greatly, what can be said about the emotional impact of loss of a useful function in life? Large numbers of people react to this as a disaster, especially when it comes relatively early in life but too late to allow one to readily reinvent oneself, say, when a person is in his or her fifties. Others, maybe most, look forward to retiring and do well with it, though there is a danger of boredom unless other activities replace lost work. We presented examples of these alternatives displayed at Rossmoor in earlier chapters.

Some persons actually gain from an involuntary loss of job, as was the case with Fred, who never should have become an accountant. But he does illustrate how gratifying it can be to be committed to some activity that is self-actualizing and pleasing to others. Premature job loss, however, can be a very serious harm and threat, especially when a suitable alternative is not available.

As always, how a person copes with such a major change in one's life, even if it does not represent a career commitment or a calling—after all, work occupies a lion's share of our time—is of the utmost importance. To the extent this is true, loss of job, whether within the home or outside in career terms, must lead to a significant reformulation of one's life pattern. Again, how people do in this context is a product of individual variation in the coping process.

The cases we have presented are not about the oldest of people. Some of them could even be thought of as middle-aged, yet we observed them at a crucial time in their transition to old age. On the way to becoming old, each faced a potential crisis that influenced where he or she was heading.

In our view, what is most important in our discussions of aging and its emotions, which includes the coping process, is our theme that people are very different from each other. A science of human mind and behavior that is based solely on the search for broad generalizations that simplify—we would say oversimplify—the extremely complex creatures that we are and the world we must face cannot provide an understanding of aging. This is all the more true if this understanding is based solely on human norms or averages and lacks careful description of individual variations. This is why we have chosen to include case histories as a way of presenting brief portraits of people struggling with the aging process.

Most of the people we have described in our case histories did not seek professional help. Some might have gained from it and had very different degrees of success in coping with the problems of living, both early and late. In the two instances in which treatment was undertaken, both psychotherapeutic in outlook, the outcomes were quite different.

The same applies to psychological treatment. We have raised the question of whether professional treatment is desirable or necessary for any particular aging person. We have also addressed the question of whether and what kind of psychological treatment should be considered for those who suffer problems of aging that they cannot cope with adequately. Should it be standard counseling, advice, teaching, or psychotherapy, which is designed to help clients make discoveries about inner conflicts and defenses that might lead to personality changes and help them acquire more effective ways of coping? This subject is taken up in the next chapter.

V ∷

PRACTICAL APPLICATIONS

9 ∷

Psychological Treatment

This chapter is mainly about psychological treatment for elderly people who might be in trouble functionally and emotionally. It also includes modest attention to the period usually referred to as the end of life. The term *psychological treatment* is employed because not all treatment is designed to be psychotherapeutic, which calls for change in one's understanding of oneself and one's coping pattern. Psychotherapy is usually centered on neurotic conflicts and defenses that have been getting in the way of effective coping and mental comfort. Other approaches to treatment consist of providing emotional support in a crisis, overcoming misconceptions, advice or counseling, and teaching. Often these objectives are combined.

If one explores the many books on psychotherapy, which is a large, diverse, and interdisciplinary enterprise, one rarely finds references to aging. Few writers on this topic have addressed the question of whether psychological treatment is useful for older adults. Inger Hilde Nordhus, Giertlostmark Nielsen, and Gerd Kvale answer from a psychotherapeutic standpoint with a robust yes. They describe a relatively rare outpatient clinic for people over age sixty at the University of Bergen in Norway and illustrate their psychotherapeutic work with three case vignettes. One involves the threat of a significant loss, another is centered on coping with loneliness, and still another has to do with nonassertiveness.[1]

There are a number of reasons for this lack of attention to the elderly. One is that emotional problems are often subordinated to the increasing incidence of medical problems. The elderly generally go for diagnosis and treatment to physicians who deal with bodily ailments. Because the oldest current generation is less likely to admit to having psychiatric symptoms, it places a greater emphasis than a younger population would on general physical decline. This does not mean, however, that older people have fewer or less compelling emotional problems for which psychological assessment would be appropriate.[2]

A second reason is that many people, especially those over sixty-five, are ashamed to ask for help with emotional problems, among the most common of which are anxiety and depression. It is easier for them to explain their emotional distress on the basis of physical losses, deficits, and evidence of aging than to face the idea of mental distress, however mild it might be.

A third reason is that much of psychiatry, though not clinical psychology or social work, has been biologized, and pills to change mood are among the most common treatments. Our view is that, frequently, drugs to deal with anxiety or depression can often prevent a person from recognizing and confronting their problems of living, which the person must learn to cope with more effectively. Such drugs are apt to be prescribed too freely.

There is growing evidence and professional conviction among psychologists, as well as some psychiatrists, that psychotherapy competes favorably with drugs, though many clinicians believe a combination of medication and psychotherapy may offer an advantage. We still do not know if this belief is correct because of the methodological and practical difficulties of evaluating the outcomes of treatment.[3] Besides, with the expansion of private medical insurance and health maintenance organizations (HMOs) in the United States, there is strong pressure to hold down the costs of treatment. This favors pills over extended psychotherapy and short-term over long-term treatment regardless of the needs of the client. (This is not to say, however, that there are not people whose situations do dictate treatment through such drugs. Telling such a person, as used to be common, that his or her problems are "all in your head" is nonproductive and possibly harmful. As we have said throughout this book, there is great variety among people, elderly or not, and careful case-by-case evaluation is advisable.)

Finally, because of the elderly person's focus on current problems, gaining insight about neurotic problems from the past often seems less salient. Therefore, psychotherapy with older adults tends to be shorter in length and flexibly interactive—that is, there are more interchanges between client and therapist and more advice and information offered by the therapist.

Because of the mix of emotional and physical health problems in older people, psychological assessment is often employed with these clients, as well as neuropsychological evaluation for diagnostic purposes, especially when the issues being dealt with involve cognitive deficits or dementia.[4] These assessments require care lest cohort effects lead to misleading diagnoses if the diagnostician uses age norms derived from cross-sectional data for evaluating the functioning of a patient.

The Prevalence of Emotional Problems in the Elderly

Major epidemiological studies have provided data on the most common emotional problems of later life, but they are difficult to interpret. Among the most common emotional problems are specific anxiety disorders, such as phobias, with a prevalence rate of 4.8 percent among those over age sixty-five. The prevalence of mood disorders such as chronic depression is estimated at 1.8 percent; major depression is diagnosed in less than 1 percent of the elderly.[5] These figures seem low and are, in any case, much lower than those reported by younger people from eighteen to forty-four years of age, yet a number of epidemiologists think that anxiety and depression are significant problems among the elderly.

Bad moods appear to be reported more frequently in old age. But older adults focus more on the symptoms of depression while not actually complaining about being depressed. This may be because sleep and appetite disturbances are regarded as signs of depression yet may reflect physical conditions as well as emotional disturbances.

Various estimates of the combined prevalence of three common emotional disturbances—panic disturbances, obsessive-compulsive symptoms, and phobias—range from 5.7 to 33 percent. This huge range leaves the true prevalence in considerable doubt. Phobias are reported to be more common in older women and the second most common emotional problem in older men.

There could be underreporting here; a dysfunction has to become severe for the current generation of older persons to seek help. Baby boomers, on the other hand, have relatively high self-reported rates of depression, anxiety, and substance abuse. One wonders, therefore, whether the younger generation really has higher rates of emotional distress or is simply more open to reporting it, which would be a cohort effect. It is evident that data on the emotional problems of old people are currently a scientific mess because accurate estimates of the prevalence of such problems among the elderly are so difficult to arrive at.

There is a tendency today among physicians to be very sensitive, perhaps even overly so, to any sign of depression in their patients because they believe that depression is generally underdiagnosed. This contributes to the tendency, noted earlier, to overprescribe antidepression medications. Troublingly, these drugs are used not just for depression but for almost anything that ails patients, which sounds a bit like the snake oil remedies of a hundred years ago.

We also need to know more about how older people cope with anxiety and depression and the life conditions that bring them about. Individual appraisal and coping processes make an important difference in the distress that is experienced. But attention to coping is inconsistent and often negligible. Nordhus et al. echo our view of the importance of individual differences in coping: "How each person adapts in response to changes and losses is a critical therapeutic factor. This factor is more a matter of individual variability than how older people as a group adapt."[6]

Making the Decision about Psychological Treatment

As in the case of clinical medicine, psychological treatment is more of an art than a science. To some extent the treatment plan needs to be tailored to each particular individual. It depends on the presenting problem, client characteristics, and the approach of the therapist.

A question that should be addressed early in treatment is why the client is unable to function adequately without help from a therapist. Usually the professional person who treats clients begins with an intake interview to learn about the problem that brings the person to treatment. The answer to this question about the provocation for seeking treatment could contribute to understanding the client and planning the treatment. If the therapist works in a clinic, the first interview is apt to be followed by a staff conference to discuss the treatment strategy.

There are two ways of thinking about why a prospective client is having trouble in managing life, which includes aging. The first and most common way of looking at treatment for the troubled elderly person is that the failure to cope effectively with problems of living is the result of neuroticism of some sort. Indeed, it often is, in which case psychotherapy to change faulty ways of thinking and coping patterns is appropriate.

There may, indeed, be a long-standing neurosis in which reality-distorting defenses make it difficult to cope effectively with aging.[7] Most of what has been written about psychotherapy with the elderly—and as we have said before, there is not much—tends to assume this. Training in psychiatry and clinical psychology has tended traditionally to center on this assumption.

The second way of looking at treatment is that there is an acute problem of living in an otherwise sound person. When we try to understand why a client is having difficulty handling the problems of aging, it may turn out that this person is experiencing a novel crisis and is, in effect, unprepared for what has happened. The client mainly needs guidance about tackling it. There might, for example, be an intractable family conflict, a physical illness, disability, signs of a mental deficit, a devastating loss of social role or job, grief over the loss of a loved one, severe loneliness as a result of this loss, the emergence of a previously suppressed dread about death and dying, and so forth.

Therefore, to put the onus on neuroticism is not always appropriate.

Even sound people falter when facing a severe life crisis, which is why crisis intervention evolved (see chapter 3). Emotional crises are not unusual with advancing age, and some clients primarily need to learn how to manage them. Besides, not all problems—such as terminal illness, disability, and death itself—are solvable.

Perhaps the troubled person has to learn to accept the way things are. On the other hand, it is not neurotic or inappropriate to "rage against the dying of the light," to cite Dylan Thomas's wonderful line from his 1952 poem, which begins, "Do not go gentle into that good night." In any case, many individuals who are aging and face distressing but common life conditions could benefit from short-term, superficial psychological treatment, advice, or education. But if we treat the problem as if it were the result of psychopathology, we will be missing the chance to provide sensible counseling and advice that might help greatly to resolve an emotional crisis. The person being dealt with clinically needs help, but not necessarily major personality change. Whether it is one or the other, or a bit of both, must be resolved early in treatment.

Here are some examples of problems that may not be the result of neurotic defenses. Elderly persons, like younger ones, have misconceptions about many things. They may believe that mild memory deficits suggest an early stage of senility or dementia in the form of Alzheimer's disease. Some are vulnerable to falling or have other physical limitations—for example, having trouble getting to the phone to call for help. They need to learn about electronic communication devices that can be purchased and worn around the neck or carried in a pocket. The cell phone is a recent alternative, but many elderly persons have difficulty using them. Information about this sort of thing could be helpful, and adequate knowledge about such matters can provide the power to be effective in an emergency rather than helpless.

Old persons may also be too embarrassed to ask about how to deal with urinary incontinence, sexual dysfunction, and sensory losses such as impaired eyesight or hearing, all of which are common in later life. Professional persons can offer substantial help by dispelling misconceptions and providing information. The importance of such information and misinformation in the life of the elderly should not be discounted.

If psychotherapy is required, the elderly often need advice about how to locate a suitable psychotherapist and how to make the right choice, issues that most people, young and old alike, may know little or nothing about. An experienced counselor will often have lists of qualified professionals. For those who do not have access to such a person, many university psychology departments, especially those with clinical psychology training programs, maintain such lists or have someone on the faculty who will know how to find a therapist.

There are also important differences between qualified, ethical therapists and poorly trained or exploitative ones. We are inundated nowadays by radio and television psychologists who speak with telephone callers who are seeking help and advice. Often after a few moments of conversation, they will offer opinions or advice, sometimes haranguing the person who has asked for help without sufficient knowledge about the person in need. Some of them have little or no training in clinical work, even if they have a doctorate from a reputable educational institution in a field other than psychology or are smart (or articulate) enough to sound credible. Nor are all psychologists qualified by training and experience to do psychotherapy. The role these radio or TV therapists play is largely that of an entertainer who exploits needy people for their commercial value.

The mess some people make of their lives, which they seem all too willing these days to talk about to anyone who will listen, is fascinating to most listeners or viewers. This is the reason human foibles are exploited by the media as entertainment. Listening to them may also create a feeling of superiority or reassure audience members about themselves. Other listeners hope to get tips on how to manage their own lives. This cynical commercialism is a public disgrace that demeans all responsible professionals, the media as well as those who worship the almighty dollar.

What should a person expect when going to an experienced and responsible therapist? A therapist should be someone who can be trusted by others in his or her field on the basis of adequate training and a commitment to professionalism. Though making a living doing therapy, the qualified therapist is also concerned with the well-being of the client. If the therapy does not help, the client should be able to leave without discomfort and try someone else. Who would want to go to a surgeon who was unqualified any more than to someone who claims without justification to be a psychotherapist? Before choosing a therapist, one should try to find out about his or her professional qualifications and integrity (of course, the latter can be more difficult to evaluate).

You may have noticed that we never refer to a "patient," but rather to a person or client seeking help. The reason lies partly in the previously mentioned alternative ways of thinking about treatment. Someone who has emotional problems of living is not necessarily sick in the sense of having a brain or biochemical abnormality. The problem should not automatically be turned into a medical one, as if an operation or a drug offers a simple cure. We should not pathologize every human problem of living.

There is also something impersonal and technical about the word *patient* that seems inappropriate for all variants of common psychological problems of living. A patient is always a *person,* and we prefer to use that word; or, if we want to emphasize the professional relationship with a therapist, the word *client* is appropriate. We can be clients of a lawyer, a businessman, or a psychologist without being sick in a medical sense.

Individual Psychotherapy

Let us now examine psychotherapy with older persons whose problems are diagnosed as being based on neurotic factors and whose treatment aims at personality change. We have no doubt that many aging persons could benefit from psychotherapy. Nordhus et al. present a very simple-to-understand account of their form of psychotherapy. It builds on the premise that the clients' difficulties arise from vicious circles they themselves have created in their lives.[8]

These clients have, in effect, locked themselves into patterns of thought, feeling, and action that repeatedly harm them and others, and they cannot seem to avoid doing so. In trying to establish satisfying relationships with others, achieve a goal, or satisfy a need, these clients engage in recurrent self-defeating behaviors that unwittingly re-create past conflicts, traumatic experiences, and disappointments.

When pathogenic beliefs and defenses from the past are central to a current coping failure, clients are vulnerable to feelings of guilt, shame, anxiety, anger, and depression, which are often integral features of their present suffering and dysfunction. The distortions of reality that their defenses create result in chronic or recurrent distress and other troubles and lead them to get help. In psychotherapy, the client must be helped to break the vicious circle and learn more flexible and effective ways of getting along with others who are important in their lives. Safe, respectful, and private therapeutic sessions with a skilled psychotherapist can help the troubled person understand what has gone wrong and learn new ways of coping.

Psychotherapy is often referred to as the "talking cure," but, most important, it is a learning experience—clients learn about themselves and their relationships with others, especially what they are doing wrong and how this might be changed. This takes time. The therapy is designed to reduce suffering and dysfunction and increase the effectiveness with which aging clients cope with their problems. Both the client and the therapist are active participants in a complex interpersonal process in which the client-therapist relationship is an important feature.

For the aging person who does not want or cannot afford to spend years engaged in this process, what is being described by Nordhus et al. is somewhat different from the traditional Freudian psychoanalytic therapy session in which the therapist minimizes active intervention for long periods of time. In psychotherapy with the elderly, the therapist focuses more on the present and deals with the therapist-client relationship flexibly; when indicated, he or she shows empathy, gives support, offers direct advice, and even teaches.[9]

Family-Oriented Psychotherapy

Bob Knight and T. J. McCallum provide another important and interesting version of psychotherapy with older persons that is centered on the family. Although most others who deal therapeutically with the elderly take the family into account, therapy sessions with clients are usually limited to a single individual. Family therapists try to bring together as much of the family as possible to participate in the sessions. The account of these authors adds substantially to what we have already said because they offer a distinctive perspective and procedure for family-oriented therapy.[10]

Knight and McCallum point out that families are multigenerational. Typically, they include minor children, parents with children, and late-life members, such as grandparents and great-grandparents. Younger family members sometimes blame family crises on the elderly, though it may be the younger ones who are causing the most serious problems. By projecting their own problems onto their elders, the youngsters are refusing to acknowledge these problems and their own role in family conflicts. So family therapists must be skillful in trying to understand the family dynamics and the defensive games each family member from a different generation may be playing.

These authors also make much of cohort differences, which we have discussed extensively already. In chapter 2, we described the confusion the cohort problem creates for research about whether age or generational outlook is the cause of differences in stress, emotion, and coping. The family-centered therapeutic focus, however, transforms the cohort problem into a very rich clinical account of generation-linked conflicts and misunderstandings that can occur within the same family. In other words, for Knight and McCallum the cohort problem becomes an interpersonal and clinical issue as well as a methodological one.

For these family therapists, it is important that younger and older generations within the same family understand each other; as a member of a 1960s cohort might say, they need to grasp where each other is coming from. Generation-based views of life and the world are "expressed in the cry of children everywhere to parents that 'you can't understand me, you grew up in the ——s.' "[11]

This suggests that younger persons often have some awareness that the generations differ. Marriage and divorce, for example, meant something quite different in the 1930s than they do today. If children realize the origins of the cohort-based perspective of their parents, and vice versa, it could improve their relationships. They must learn how the period in which each generation was raised is reflected in their respective ways of thinking, values and goals, and feelings. The participants in therapy can discover how these differences lead to generational conflicts within their family.

It may take some added maturity on the part of the youngest generation to appreciate this fully, but the exploration of generational differences could synergistically augment the growth of genuine friendship between parent and child. Many younger family members have not examined with any care the perspectives of their older relatives, and vice versa. This knowledge can be provided in one or two therapeutic sessions. Knight and McCallum are quite willing to arrange for intergenerational discussions expressly devoted to the mutual discovery of generational differences that family members need to be aware of to relate successfully to each other.

These authors also point out that certain values are maintained by the younger generation's parents—for example, the idea of showing respect for them by doing as they say—even though the cultural outlook has changed markedly in the interim. The parents' own adherence to these values when young may have been inconsistent, but they may still press them on their children.

For example, when the parents were growing up, they may have struggled to get away from their own parents—that is, their children's grandparents—and establish their own home. But they may now be pressing the next generation to live up to an older tradition of staying respectfully close to their parents even though they did not follow that tradition themselves. Discovering contradictions like this in family therapy could go a long way toward softening opposing positions, possibly leading to reconciliation between the generations and lessening conflict.

These authors also discuss some of the specific challenges of later life. The purpose is to suggest that it is not chronological age per se that is so important in intrafamilial conflict as much as the specific stresses with which old people must cope—for example, chronic illness and disability, grieving, and caregiving. Families must often care for chronically ill or disabled older relatives, or both, and they struggle to manage this while pursuing their own agendas.

Certain kinds of illness can readily become a taboo topic within a family; everyone is aware of the illness, but it cannot be openly discussed. One of the most important social compacts that civilized people make is not to press issues openly if one knows they will needlessly distress another person. The same rule applies to family and friends who are aware of secrets that everyone would want to keep private. A good example is a life-threatening illness or dementia. Another consists of a tendency toward sexual peccadilloes. Still another is incontinence.

Knight and McCallum point out that this kind of social compact leads to a family environment that seems to be shrouded in secrets despite the fact that they are not secret at all. Bernice remembers that when her mother was dying of stomach cancer, no one could mention the word *cancer*, especially to her mother, though she clearly knew what was happening, as do most of those who are dying. An older relative's disability is often in the consciousness of everyone in the family, yet there is guilt and blaming about it that may date back many years. The guilt and blame may never be explored because any change in this is resisted.

The authors illustrate this idea with a personal example about grieving that suggests the messy emotional problems created in the context of special late-life challenges, which can be understood fully only in the context of a particular family and the way it handles stress. The "one of us" referred to in the following quotation is not identified but is either Knight or McCallum.

> One of us . . . once saw a middle-aged son for a consultation regarding how best to encourage his father to seek counseling for unresolved grief. During the interview, the son repeatedly referred to the father being unable to get over the death of "his wife." Toward the end of the hour, the therapist inquired if the father's wife was the son's mother. The son nodded and then cried throughout the remainder of that visit.[12]

The family, as these authors point out, is a complex system of relationships in which decisions are made in the same way as in any other group—for example, by means of communication, persuasion, and power. As a partial summary, Knight and McCallum offer the following important comment:

> As we have noted throughout the chapter, real and strategic considerations may limit the opportunities to actually have an entire family meet together for multiple sessions. However, it is often possible to "think family" even when one cannot "do family". . . . We would argue that it is virtually always beneficial to think family, even when involved in individual interventions with older adults or with younger adults who are caring for older ones.[13]

Before we leave this topic of generational misunderstanding and conflict, let us mention a remarkable experimental program to educate ten-year-old Austrians about the problems faced by their elderly grandparents. We learned of it from Christa and Peter Erhart, whom we recently visited when we traveled to Austria to give some lectures on our work.

Peter is the medical director of a large, publicly supported geriatric clinic in Salzburg, Austria, the name of which, translated from German, is Geriatric Division, Neurological Long-Term Therapy. The clinic assists people with all sorts of ailments common to the elderly (for example, Alzheimer's disease and Parkinson's disease), housing them at the clinic for a time as part of the effort to facilitate the patients' ability to function.

Christa, his wife, is a gerontologist who manages this program. What is unusual about it is the premise that young children recognize but do not understand the struggles of their elderly forebears, and old people in general, in dealing with physical handicaps. The purpose is to teach children about this with a set of clever devices that create experiential analogues of loss of sensation, visual problems, and unresponsiveness of their bodies.

In one such device, the ten-year-old puts on thin latex rubber gloves and must try to remove particular coins of different values from a purse, mimicking in this way the loss of tactile sensitivity. In another device, they put on eyeglasses that are made cloudy to represent fuzzy sight. To illustrate the unresponsive heaviness of an old person's limbs, weights are placed in their shoes. Here we have an educational program designed to increase the youngest generation's understanding of and empathy for the oldest members of their families and the elderly in general.

The Life Review as Psychotherapy

Writing about individual psychotherapy with the elderly, Meyer D. Glantz has pointed out that most therapeutic techniques that are used with older persons are also used with younger adults.[14] However, one useful technique that is specifically directed at the elderly is a *life review* procedure, which was originally suggested by Robert Butler, the first director of the U.S. National Institute of Aging.[15]

Butler's idea for the life review arose from his observation that as death approaches, there is often a tendency to think about the past, especially its emotional conflicts, and to seek psychologically useful meanings about one's life from that past. Butler proposed that reminiscences of this kind constitute a healthy way to resolve previous problems. It is an opportunity to reorganize how we view our personal history and reconcile it with the present, which can lead to a sense of accomplishment for ourselves and help create a legacy for our progeny.

The idea of life review overlaps the way we previously described the process of grieving (see chapter 3) over the loss of a loved one, which usually includes efforts to reconcile past, present, and future. However, it is usually an emotionally more positive experience than that of grief.

The procedure for an elderly life review in the psychotherapeutic context is to ask the client to write an autobiography. The task can be made easier through the use of scrapbooks, photo albums, saved letters, family histories, and genealogies. Other members of the family and friends can be contacted, and the client can even travel to places that had been important in the past.

If the client is willing, the experience of writing the autobiography and what it produces can serve as a basis of conversations with the therapist that could help resolve present dilemmas and conflicts. The life review can also provide pleasure derived from interactions with family and friends. Whether it is done formally, as proposed by Butler and Lewis, or in informal oral conversation between client and therapist, the procedure can be a valuable way to get at personal struggles having to do with aging.

The Period of the End of Life

An important topic that we have not yet dealt with directly in this book is life's end. In most of what we have said, we were concerned with those who were still living actively. The topic of the end of life carries weighty existential and spiritual issues and is too emotional for many old people and their family to want to deal with. For this reason, it is just hinted at rather than faced openly, and most people detour around it. We should address it here.

Ernest Becker, as we noted earlier, won a Pulitzer Prize for his book *The Denial of Death*, in which he argued persuasively that much of what humans have accomplished—including the monuments they built to themselves—constitute, at bottom, attempted denials of the end of life. The religions of the world facilitate this denial by holding to the reassuring tenet that there is life after death.[16]

In some religious denominations, we are said to meet God and either end up in hell, suffering eternal fire and damnation, or be reunited with our loved ones, even our pets, in heaven. Fantasies about heaven are common, some of them almost childlike if taken literally, as in Marc Connelly's 1930s movie *The Green Pastures*, which is basically the Old Testament story retold with God and his archangels personified.

For multitudes of people, religion supplies emotional support for the problem of facing death, as well as other personal disasters. No one who believes in resurrection can say what it would really be like. Many, including those who have strong religious faith, reject the idea of life after death as literally true and view it in more symbolic or metaphoric terms, as a kind of spiritual survival in the memories of those we leave behind. Who would want openly to challenge another's faith about this or be themselves thus challenged? Perhaps if we hold the belief strongly enough, the dread of death as an anonymous void—that is, oblivion, in which we no longer have any conscious existence—may be considerably eased.

There has been little research on how serviceable this belief is for most people who are near death. Presumably, this depends on the extent to which the belief is merely pro forma—that is, held only superficially—or is a deeply held article of faith that engages the person fully. It is easier, however, just to affirm such a belief publicly—it is often the way we were taught. This is why agnosticism is commonly expressed more openly than atheism, especially given the obvious public distaste for avowed atheists. This is certainly a difficult topic in which to engage in research, given that it is so touchy and emotional.

Earlier in this book, when we were discussing coping, we pointed out that it is often difficult to tell whether a reaction that seems like denial is a disavowal of reality or merely an attempt to avoid thinking or speaking about something that is threatening. When we distance ourselves emotionally from the idea of our death, it may not be a denial at all but an avoidance. In other words, we prefer not to think about it because we do not know exactly what to expect and we cannot change what is.

In his published autobiography, Richard's final chapter is entitled "Retirement Years: Musings about Life and Death." He writes that he can find no satisfactory way of preparing for his own death psychologically—aside from the legal questions of will and funeral.[17] Both of us realize that the end of our life as we know it is inevitable and increasingly imminent, but neither of us sees any gain in ruminating about it. We are both saddened by and perhaps fearful of death, but there is nothing to be done about it. We both hope it will not be too terrible an experience and that we will deal with it in a way that is considerate of our family and others. This is one of many ways of treating the inevitability of death, but it is more like avoidance than denial.

Richard also muses about why he continues to work and be productive when he does not expect to be in a position to care about the significance of his work after he is gone. He says, however, that it is important to him now while he is still alive, and that it is the process of working that is vital, regardless of the ultimate reception of this work. Besides, continuing to produce creditable works as long as possible sustains his interest and enthusiasm about life in general.

Bernice is more reserved about communicating her inmost thoughts and feelings about this sort of thing. Others deal with this issue differently, and we would not want to second-guess them in this respect. Considering one's own fate should be a private matter for most people unless one is willing to talk about it publicly. Given our physical conditions, we have the feeling that it is a race against time to complete our book before we cease to be able to work on it effectively. But we recognize, given our current ailments, that it is not far from the end for us.

E. H. Bradley et al. point to three main clinical trajectories through which a person could pass at the end of life.[18] These trajectories, described briefly here, are published in an Institute of Medicine report on the decline of health near the end of a person's life. One trajectory is sudden death from an unexpected cause, such as a heart attack or an accident. This has the virtue of a quick end without much suffering. A second trajectory is a steady decline in health as a result of a predictable disease, such as cancer. This can involve suffering and the terrible decision of deciding whether it is worthwhile to prolong life when there is little or no hope for a reasonable quality of life. A third trajectory is a gradual decline as a result of diseases such as chronic obstructive pulmonary disease (e.g., emphysema) and congestive heart failure. These diseases involve periodic crises, one of which ultimately results in death. The person usually knows what is to be faced and most often can do little about it, short of suicide. The problem for professional caregivers is to identify the biological and clinical signs of approaching death, which could be helpful in providing suitable palliative care, as in the hospice movement.

As the authors point out, dying takes place over time, and, in addition to its clinical aspects, it is a complex and sometimes an extended *social process* rather than a single event. Medicine tends to treat dying as a biological event, which it is, too. The end of life is difficult to predict with precision. Patient and family usually recognize that there is no available treatment that could reverse the process and that death is imminent, though it is not uncommon for there to be a surprise about how long it takes to die. But the impact of such awareness on the emotional state of patient and family is not clear. Nor has an adequate examination been made of the things that are important to the people involved in the dying process, both the patient and family and friends.

What we have said here seems calculating and cold in light of the horrors we have seen in neighbors who appear to be on the way out. Within a month after one neighboring couple had moved to Rossmoor, the husband, who was a sociable man but had a long history of diabetes, lost his leg to gangrene. It was not possible, apparently, to replace it with a suitable prosthesis. The problem of what to do dragged on and on, to the distress of the wife as well as the son, who came from time to time to help. The husband was seen outside in a wheelchair only once after that. Then he lost his other leg and had to be placed in a nursing home. We have learned that he stopped eating, hoping to die, and that his mind seemed to be going.

We recently came upon his wife in tears over what she had seen at a reputable hospital while her husband was recovering from the surgery. He was unattended, half covered, and lying on his bed in his own feces. For several years, during which the couple struggled with the husband's declining condition, we have been aware about how much they suffered. Much of this time the wife has appeared stoical, but privately we know that it has been a terrible ordeal. One of the most difficult decisions for those who have little quality of life remaining is whether it makes sense to try to stay alive with heroic treatments. As we all know, this is especially apt to be the case with some stroke victims and terminal cancer patients, in whom the period of the end of life can be prolonged and without relief from misery.

Quality of life during this period involves many psychological considerations, though physical functioning and symptomatology are the ones most commonly explored in research. For example, pain, which is most often studied, is inadequately treated in a large proportion of dying patients. Distress and depression are common, involving as they do more than a third of dying patients, though physicians have become more concerned with this problem in recent years. As we saw earlier, however, the precise incidence of depression, even among elderly persons who are not close to death, is difficult to estimate with any accuracy. Suicide rates are higher in terminally ill adults than in healthy adults of similar ages, but this act is still relatively infrequent.

Few studies of social support for the terminally ill have been reported, despite the importance of this topic. Complaints that patients have unmet emotional needs, such as someone to talk to, vary from very few to about a third of such persons. Despite the importance of religion in the United States, relatively few studies have focused on the role of religion or spirituality in the period of the end of life; most of them remain superficial and scientifically inadequate. This may be changing.

It has been pointed out many times that communication between patient and physician, including at the end of life, is traditionally poor, and this applies in spades to the elderly. Such communication is bound to be a complex problem for which physicians are not commonly trained and in which they do not appear to be very interested, given the economics of modern medicine. Most patients say they want the physician to be honest with them about their disease, but they also hope the doctor will be optimistic, which sounds contradictory. It probably means that patients need empathy and reassurance as well as a dose of reality. Few of us, in fact, know how to relate to those who are terminally ill, including our loved ones.[19] It is clear that to be effective, communication must contain a delicate balance between compassion and truth telling.

Quality of life also varies over time during the year before death, and, not surprisingly, its direction is downward as the patient's condition worsens. Sometimes a person said to be dying makes a dramatic turnaround and recovers. Only one month prior to death, more than half of patients are said to have a positive attitude overall, which is as confusing as the findings on life satisfaction or well-being in general (see chapter 3). It is difficult to know what was really going on psychologically before the patient died, and few observers can throw much light on it retrospectively.

Still, for some patients, social or spiritual health is said to compensate for the deterioration of physical health, and they continue to report a positive quality of life even as they die, however difficult it is to guess what this means. Maybe such patients are referring to satisfaction with the past life. Perhaps they have distanced themselves from what is happening at the moment. Another possibility is that they are glad their suffering is about to end or hoping it will not be drawn out. Still another possibility is that for many dying persons psychological numbness may have set in. Answers referring to these alternative ideas about the outlook of dying persons are not well grounded empirically or theoretically at the present time.

Few studies have looked in detail at the patterns involved as the individual moves inexorably toward the end of life. They are probably variable and depend on what patients consider particularly important to them as they die. Difficulties of communication are probably the most important obstacle to valid knowledge. Considering the importance of death in human existence, and the vacuity of so much research, our ignorance about it is remarkable, yet somehow not so surprising. Anyone need a dissertation topic?

It becomes clear from this review by Bradley et al. that there is a great need for in-depth research on the period of the end of life and that little has been learned of great importance.[20] We need to know what is truly in the minds of the participants—that is, the patient as well as family and friends—including the emotions they feel as they are dying. For this we have to rely on what the dying person reports before death, which may be unreliable, and the observations of those close to the dying person, who have their own emotional agendas.

Given the social constraints, complexities, and situational intentions of the parties to the death, we may never really know, even if we wish to use our knowledge to minimize suffering. The same applies to how patients and their families cope with their plight (there is almost no mention of coping). We must remember, however, how touchy the subject of death is to deal with in our society, which is probably why we know so little about the psychology of the process.

In this chapter, there are two major concerns in treatment. The first has to do with one of two ways of thinking of treatment—namely, whether it should be directed at an otherwise sound person who is having an unusual crisis, which calls for counseling, advice, and a certain amount of education of how to deal with the crisis. Often the life review procedure, which is an exploration of meanings in the life situation of elderly people, is an effective way to help in the late stages of life.

The other way of thinking is based on the presumption that the person in trouble is suffering from a neurosis. This means that such persons, as a result of defenses and a failure to understand what is happening to them, have become locked in a vicious cycle. Although seeking to achieve personal goals and create satisfying relationships with others, they are actually engaged in self-defeating behaviors. They are, in effect, stuck in past conflicts, traumas, and personal disappointments that produce the opposite of what they want. A choice between these two outlooks is required before therapy can begin. The therapist, in collaboration with the client, generally makes it.

Psychotherapy's purpose is helping clients achieve insight into what has been causing dysfunction and distress in their lives. The presumption is that a better understanding of their self-defeating behavior would allow them to improve the way they are coping with life and their problems. Thus psychotherapy is, above all, a learning experience.

However, as we said earlier, change is usually threatening and apt to be resisted as people become set in their ways, especially as they grow old. The client must struggle to take advantage of what has been learned; insight is not enough. It must be applied and tested for success diligently. This means being willing to do the difficult psychological work required to deal with situations that were handled poorly in the past.

A special approach that is particularly appropriate when more than one generation is involved within a family in trouble is family-oriented psychotherapy. It is characterized by bringing together in the therapy sessions the different generations: children, parents, and grandparents. An effort is made to help each of them discover the conditions of life and outlooks that characterize each generation-based cohort. Some of their conflicts and misunderstandings could be eliminated in this way, which could also lead to a reduction in conflict and a greater appreciation of the multiple generations within a family.

Nevertheless, in either case, psychological treatment is quite appropriate for elderly people who are having troubles with aging. This includes the end-of-life condition, in which it is clear a person is dying and could benefit from all manner of professional assistance, along with his or her loved ones. Despite old age and generation-based prejudices about psychological treatment, the thrust of the chapter is that many elderly persons who are experiencing distress and dysfunction in the course of aging could profit from professional help.

10 ∷ Principles of Successful Aging

Who among us wants to grow old? Because it is natural to cling to life short of deep despair and suicide, the answer is, no doubt, all or most of us. After all, we have to consider the alternative.

As a result of our advanced brain and mind, it is probable that only humans, and maybe to a lesser extent a few other primates, are able to recognize clearly that we have a past, present, and future. This makes it possible both to anticipate and to dread death. Still, even more than death, most of us dread being demented, helpless, utterly dependent, in constant pain, and unable to function with reasonable adequacy.

At this point, we approach the pièce de résistance of our book by moving toward what it means to speak of successful aging. To do so, we must first confront the philosophical enigma of what is meant by health, well-being, and the good life. Despite the traps that lie in wait for anyone who takes on this issue, ultimately we arrive at eight elementary principles of successful aging that make sense to us and emerge from what we have been saying in this book.

Here, then, are a few questions that need to be addressed before we offer these principles. What, for example, do we mean by health, not just physical health, but mental health too? Should mental and physical health be conjoined or kept separate—that is, can we have mental health without physical health and vice versa? In future discussions, however, we avoid the term *mental health* because of its medical connotations and use *well-being* in its place though, given what most readers expect, it is a bit more awkward to take this terminological detour.

There are good reasons why physical health and mental well-being should not be separated completely but must overlap to a modest degree. The overlap is necessary because to retain psychological integrity, vitality, and engagement in living in old age requires a minimum of physical strength and energy. Some illnesses and what is required to keep them at bay can sap these necessary resources. Besides, an elderly person who suffers from dementia and is physically healthy can hardly be said to experience the good life. And, if we cannot be mobile even with the help of mechanical devices, we are quite limited with respect to productive work or social interaction. We have seen neighbors decline and all but disappear from sight within their residence except now and then on a warm day in a wheelchair being pushed by a spouse or a hired helper.

It is also important to keep some separation between well-being and physical health. The best reason for this is to be found in some of the case histories in chapter 7, in which physical ailments were to some extent transcended as a result of a person's determination or will. People recover from severe strokes by a major effort to relearn lost mental functions. Old people (along with some young) must cope with a wide range of debilitating and embarrassing ailments, compensating for them in order to engage in social activity or productive work. Obviously, then, though there is some interdependence between well-being and physical health, there must also be a degree of separation between them so as not to patronize those who manage well despite the losses and deficits of aging.

There is a widespread belief among psychologists who have thought and written about this topic that health must include both the mental and the physical. In the discussions that follow, you will see that often the word *health* is used without specifying whether well-being or physical health is being referred to or both, perhaps because of this belief.

Psychologists have had the temerity to take positions on all this, despite realizing that speculation about the good life is more philosophy than science. We are, in a sense, forced to do so as a result of the concerns of the mental health professions—namely, medical psychiatry, clinical psychology, and social work—all of which deal with psychological dysfunction. If we are willing to talk about this, however imprecise the concept of mental well-being, we must also address the problem of what should be meant by it.

It is not just the talk about mental health that forces us to examine this issue. Societies put people away in institutions, mental hospitals, clinics, and prisons and make it their business to provide advice and treatment, whether based on religion or simply the way they understand personal and social problems. Our concern with successful aging falls within this mandate.

A related issue is often raised about whether well-being—physical, mental, or both—should be defined merely as the absence of illness or is best thought of as something more. Should we say that people are not physically healthy merely because their bodies' organs do not function ideally? Or should we enlarge our consideration of health to positive health or wellness?

Should we say that people are mentally sound merely because they are not having psychological troubles of one sort or another, or is mental well-being also more than the absence of dysfunction or distress? For example, are people for whom positive emotions dominate negative emotions psychologically better off than people whose state of mind is largely negative? Do optimists have a more positive well-being and physical health than pessimists? We really do not know the answer to these questions and many others like them.

Carol Ryff and Burton Singer have been among the most recent writers to argue in favor of an enlarged concept of health or wellness and against the traditional medical concept of health as the absence of disease. They still use medical terms like *health* because it fits our traditional vocabulary. Echoing other psychologists, they take the position that positive health is more than the absence of illness and speak of health in the broadest sense of the word, which includes both the physical and the mental.[1] But what it is remains forever ill defined and vague.

There is a serious danger in requiring that the mental and physical be conjoined. If they are tied together too closely, we do a disservice to the elderly, or even a young person who is not well physically. By failing to recognize that considerable psychological integrity is required to transcend many physical ailments and live effectively in spite of them, health then becomes an ideal that is seldom to be found, certainly less among the elderly.

Ryff and Singer go on to make an important point, however, which is consistent with what we have been saying but seems to contradict their main thesis. They argue that difficulties and traumas of living can often facilitate finding deeper life meanings.[2] People often extract positive growth from negative life experiences. In grief over a major loss, for example, we often eventually acquire new psychological strength and meaning in our lives after a considerable struggle. In short, we can gain from and transcend losses and deficits, both physical and mental.

We must, therefore, take a position of relativity. Wellness of mind should be defined as how well we do given our physical and mental deficits and limitations. There can be no uniform or universal standard of successful aging. Successful aging depends on what we have to compensate for—that is, losses, deficits, and limitations, the opportunities to be selective, and the resources available. These resources include those provided by the society, which can be crucial for how well people do when they get old. If what we have to deal with is daunting in relation to our resources, less should be expected of us, though old people and many of the young who are handicapped often exceed expectations about what they can do.

The World Health Organization defined health as a "state of complete physical, mental, and social well-being and not merely the absence of disease or infirmity."[3] This, too, is an inclusive concept of health, though what is meant by well-being remains vague and a source of conceptual confusion.

Such a stance sounds as though the definition of health is that old aphorism "a sound mind in a sound body," which many of us have heard all our lives.

Some people are luckier than others with respect to physical health and mental resources. This is why we must apply a relative or variable standard for what constitutes successful aging rather than a universal or absolute one. The bottom line of this argument is that many elderly persons who are quite disabled physically may still be managing their lives very successfully and should be admired, considering the bodies they have to work with.

We have met people in Rossmoor who would dislike our emphasis on illness and disability in aging. They insist, sincerely, that they have never had it so good. These people are often in their early seventies or younger. As Meyer Glantz, who does psychotherapy with the elderly professionally, put it, "Old age can be and very frequently is a very fulfilling and satisfying period of life. In many cases, older adults have overcome or left behind the problems that plagued their earlier years, making their elder years the most enjoyable."[4] But by the chronological age of the late seventies or early eighties, this may have all changed, and mental depression appears to become more common. The opportunities for outstanding or even just successful aging vary from person to person and stage of life. Successful aging cannot be defined merely by averages based on each chronological age. Giuseppe Verdi wrote one of his most magnificent operas, *Falstaff*, when he was eighty-eight years old.

The good life has been characterized as consisting of three kinds of engagement: first, *purposeful living*, which centers on meaningful goals, objectives, and pursuits; second, *close ties to others*; and, third, a sense of *positive self-regard and mastery*.[5] Each of these criteria provides a substantial part of the total potential for a good life, both for the young and for the old. It also helps us to define the essence of successful aging but represents only part of the story. Successful aging also depends, as we have argued, on how a person copes, which includes accepting as well as *compensating* for losses, deficits, and adversity, which is an essential form of coping in old age. In our view, a few additional criteria are also important, as will be seen shortly.

Principles of Aging Successfully

We must now bring together what it is that elderly persons must do to manage aging successfully. Fundamentally, a certain set of outlooks and actions is needed to permit elderly persons to remain independent, productive, and socially active as long as possible despite increasing deficits or the threat of them.

We offer eight principles that define what it takes to be successful in aging. These principles are derived from what we have said thus far in this book. Some are more important than others, but together they represent what is more or less necessary for producing a range of success that goes from just successful to outstandingly so without trying to quantify this precisely. We must also understand that how successful an elderly person is in dealing with aging will probably vary as the conditions of life change.

First we list the principles, then discuss each in greater detail as necessary. Sometimes we add somewhat lengthy accounts of research and theory that support a given principle with an empirical basis—in effect, providing some chapter and verse of what aging researchers and theorists have been exploring in recent years.

Our list of principles is as follows:

1. To be clear about the realities of one's situation
2. To accept those realities and view them in the best light possible
3. To be able to cope effectively with those realities
4. To be able to compensate for losses and deficits
5. To be actively engaged in purposeful striving
6. To be wisely selective about what one takes on
7. To maintain close ties with others
8. To retain positive self-regard despite losses and deficits

Principles 1 and 2

To be clear about the realities of one's situation and *To accept those realities and view them in the best light possible*. We discuss principles 1 and 2 together here because they both follow from what we said in chapter 2 about the process of appraising and relational meaning. We said it always involved a *negotiation* between wanting to know the truth about one's situation and wanting to put a favorable spin on it. Our circumstances could always be worse, as can be seen daily in the fate of others. Many of the harsh realities we face cannot be changed, so we must learn to live with them and make the best of our situation.

If we view what is happening as a version of doom and gloom, we shall be in danger of arriving at a state of despair and depression. Despair undermines efforts to be actively engaged in living. Being able to psych oneself up in order to deal with adversity, which is about coping (addressed shortly in principle 3), provides motivational support for attacking a loss or deficit head-on and finding a way to improve our circumstances.

People who are prone to depression are said to catastrophize about what is happening. They view the situation as much worse than it actually is, unlike others who adopt a wait-and-see or positive attitude about what is happening. In effect, both sides of the negotiation involved in appraising—that is, a focus on reality and maintaining a positive attitude in spite of this reality—are equally important.

We might also refer to the second principle as being able to *think positively*, an overused aphorism that is often pooh-poohed. Yet there is evidence that being capable of doing so is a powerful resource, a position with which increasing numbers of psychologists agree.[6] We need to find out whether and how this outlook can be achieved.

Although it sounds a bit Pollyannaish, how about putting it as follows: "When life isn't the way you like it, like it the way it is." Anyone, including the authors, who must deal with adversity knows full well that this principle is much easier said than done. Following it requires determination and hard work, and few of us come through without moments of discouragement and even despair. But it is the long haul that counts, not just the bad moments.

To be successful at the psychological tasks of aging, we need to be capable of enjoying positive gains or outcomes, though this is not so easy when we feel blue. This is when friends or family may say to a depressed old person, "Why can't you appreciate the good things in your life, and there are plenty of them, and stop whining about the bad?" Wallowing in our troubles indefinitely is not very productive, and soon the sympathy we seek wears thin. We can easily get the feeling that no one knows or cares about how tough it is, but we cannot afford to overdo telling others about our troubles because they do not want to hear about them—they usually have their own.

We might consider positive thinking as an ability not everyone has. It seems difficult to convince dour people to adopt this attitude. Some people are described as pessimists because they maintain a negative stance about how things are with both themselves and humans in general. Injustice, corruption, and cruelty in the world offend them. However, we need such people to express outrage at human depravity, which is rampant and should offend us all. Given the way things are in the world, maybe we need pessimists as much as or more than optimists.

In writing this, both of us agree that Bernice is an optimist, whereas Richard is a pessimist who never stops hoping. We joke about the fact that, like most accused of pessimism, Richard responds by saying he is not a pessimist but a realist.[7] This sort of interchange usually produces some hearty laughter at parties.

But even pessimists can age successfully. We may believe we are in terrible shape, but we can also recognize that it could be worse. As we rue what are called the golden years, we say half in jest, "But we must consider the alternative." This frequent bit of sardonic humor among the elderly, like humor in general, helps us distance ourselves emotionally from our troubles and makes them easier to bear. Many elderly people feel reassured if they can believe they can terminate their life if they so choose when its quality becomes too poor. Most will never do so, but they want to believe they exercise control over their own life and death, which is why the Hemlock Society flourishes.

A potentially negative feature of positive thinking is that it is risky to view our circumstances unrealistically. Positive thinking can often mimic denial of the realities of life. If we misread reality, we may fail to do what is necessary to alter damaging conditions of life when we have the power to do so.

Yet people who can hope, or even be optimistic, are more likely to make an effort to improve their circumstances, which can make a major difference in their actual circumstances and morale.[8] So positive thinking that involves denial is a mixed blessing, as we demonstrated in chapter 3. Sometimes it is beneficial, sometimes harmful.

Principles 3 and 4

To be able to cope effectively with those realities and *To be able to compensate for losses and deficits*. Principles 3 and 4 should also be considered together.

For those in the authors' generation, the principle of compensation immediately brings to mind Franklin Delano Roosevelt, our four-term president from 1932 to 1945, who died just before the end of World War II. We all knew he was a victim of polio, unable to use his lower limbs, before becoming president. He had to be helped to the platforms from which he would speak with great vitality and verve to nominating conventions, the public, and Congress.

What was remarkable in those more civil and less angry days of our society was the respect, forbearance, and understanding the press and public alike had for a handicapped man elected four times during some of our country's most trying days. Here was a man who was able to combine great dignity and cheerfulness in the role of the country's leader. Even in cartoons, he was usually portrayed bearing a broad grin and jauntily sporting a cigarette in a rakish holder.

More recently, there was a fuss about whether a new statue of Roosevelt in a Washington, D.C., memorial park should show him in his wheelchair, which would symbolize his well-known handicap—in effect, as a cripple, which is a harsh old word for being disabled that today has been discarded—or have him standing upright. What is interesting about this episode is the notion that it would demean Roosevelt to portray his handicap. In our opinion, the truth is decidedly otherwise. The wheelchair symbolizes for us his great courage and commitment. It should remind us that a person capable of greatness can successfully compensate for an ailing body, all the more so with the support and sufferance of others. Elderly readers might experience some nostalgia in thinking about this man and those times.

Notice that we speak of principles 3 and 4 in terms of the ability of persons to cope effectively and compensate for losses and deficits. In recent years there has been extensive research and theory about *competence* or *functional ability* among elderly persons, which we should take into account in these principles before moving on. We draw on a recent book edited by Sherry Willis, K. Warner Schaie, and Mark Hayward, which concentrates on competence among the elderly from both a sociological and a psychological perspective.[9]

Competence overlaps coping effectiveness, both of which center on individual variations in the ability of people to manage demands that tax or exceed a person's resources. Maintaining social relationships and engaging in constructive work are, to a high degree, outcomes of effective coping skills. Above all, the most important task of research on competence is to discover which forms of coping lead to good functioning and emotional satisfaction.

Functional ability is the term employed by Eileen M. Crimmins and Mark Hayward for competence in the elderly from a demographic (sociological) perspective. Their research is designed to determine to what extent older persons are able to carry out their normal or usual activity, such as working, keeping house, shopping, and taking care of themselves so they can live independently.[10] Competence and functional ability are, therefore, overlapping ideas.

These researchers present fascinating international data about the number of years of active life expectancy and inactive life expectancy people of a given age have remaining. The former is defined as being able to engage in independent living; the latter is being unable to live independently. This, of course, is a minimal standard of successful aging.

Unlike what most of us would ordinarily think of as functional ability or competence—that is, as a property of persons—Crimmins and Hayward wisely treat it as a result of both the person and the environment; in effect, their approach is relational (see chapter 2). They regard functional ability or active life expectancy as a result not only of what the individual person is able to do, but also of the social conditions that make it easier or harder to do it.

How long a person is able to function independently varies from country to country among ten advanced societies of Europe and North America. In Crimmins and Hayward's data, it is highest in Switzerland and lowest in the United States. If we are old, it is easier to get along independently in some advanced countries than others because of the availability of social programs devoted to the aged. These programs lengthen the number of years of active life expectancy compared with inactive life expectancy. Indeed, the United

States appears to lag behind most other industrialized countries in programs that help the elderly get along. Shame on us, the richest and most powerful nation on earth, for the harshness with which we address the oldest segment of the population! (The same can be said about our treatment of children.)

There is, nevertheless, a current impression that the elderly do better in living independently these days than in the past. In effect, they are said to be aging better. This has been confirmed by the research of Burton H. Singer and Kenneth G. Manton at the Duke University Center for Demographic Studies. They report a substantial and continuing increase since 1982 in the ability of those over sixty-five to take care of themselves in the routine activities of living. This change is attributed to improved education, medical care, diet, and exercise.[11]

It is well known that women live longer than men, but Crimmins and Hayward's data also show that women are more subject to deteriorating functioning because their health grows worse during the extra years that they live beyond men. On the average, men die before they reach the point of no longer being able to care for themselves, but women live well beyond this point.

The approach of Crimmins and Hayward to competence or functional ability in the elderly is useful in projecting population trends. However, as in the concept of social network, its sociological or demographic focus does not advance our understanding of what constitutes competence or functional ability in individuals and how it should be measured. So we must now turn to a psychological approach to competence, which is represented in the writings of Timothy A. Salthouse in the same volume. He writes: "It is apparent . . . that [competence] often refers to minimal levels of proficiency, as opposed to high levels of excellence. Indeed, it would be considered very faint praise to characterize an artist or a professional as merely competent, rather than with a more laudatory adjective."[12]

Salthouse offers a definition of competence that includes four important ideas:

> First, competence is specific to a particular activity and is not universal or general.
>
> Second, competence is usually multidimensional in that it is based on several aspects or dimensions rather than a single critical dimension, . . . a skill, or possibly an ability.
>
> Third, competence implies some type of assessment or evaluation.
>
> Finally, competence involves a judgment. The resulting classification may be a dichotomy, such as competent or incompetent, or it may reflect a continuum corresponding to degrees of competence.[13]

The author points out that the usual approach to independent living fails to consider the different demands made by the diverse activities that might be involved in self-care. Here, too, the approach is relational. For example, at a basic level it would be feeding, bathing, toileting, and basic mobility. More complex activities could involve managing medications, shopping for necessities, managing finances, using transportation, using the telephone, maintaining one's household, and preparing meals. Each of these activities can be assessed at three levels: can do without help, can do with help, or cannot do.[14] One can evaluate the proportion of people at different age levels who fall into one or another of these three levels.

Salthouse refers to a number of test procedures that address different domains of competence. In one such procedure designed for direct observations of elderly persons (in contrast with questionnaires), the activities include time orientation, communication, finances, shopping, eating, and dressing. Still another observational test procedure focuses on food preparation, medication intake, and telephone use.

Elsewhere, Sherry Willis has suggested that cognitive or intellectual abilities may be differentially important in various tasks of independent living, which argues for their assessment as a predictor of competence for independent living.[15] With respect to some daily activities that are relevant to independent living, the cognitive demands are modest, but for others they are more substantial. Denise C. Park (1997) classifies the requirements of various demands of daily living on the basis of a person's sensory, cognitive (thinking), and physical capabilities. According to Park, a growing number of studies demonstrate that most age-related variations are the result of two kinds of cognitive activity that decline with age—namely, working memory and speed of processing. This puts older persons at a disadvantage not only in tests of these cognitive activities but, presumably, in their daily functioning.[16]

The connections between cognitive competence as a general concept—that is, working memory and processing speed—and the ordinary practical tasks of living and relating to other people remain obscure. It will probably be necessary to differentiate among a number of cognitive abilities to make more precise predictions and to incorporate individual differences in goals and goal priorities, which also probably play a role in the practical tasks of living.

If we are right about the importance of coping with cognitive deficits (see chapter 3), the psychology of coping also should not be overlooked when social and work effectiveness or the competence of the elderly is being considered. Older persons are often able to compensate quite successfully for any measured deficits they display, as long as they do not suffer from dementia. Compensatory coping could limit the relationship between measures of cognitive competence and the ability of old people to function.

If the definition of competence is kept at the minimal level needed to live independently, it neglects all the complex tasks and skills that many of the elderly draw on in what they do to be useful. In Rossmoor there are highly trained and extremely skilled old people who would not be happy to settle for merely being able to live independently. They assess themselves quite differently and want to be able to continue at what they do until very close to the end of their lives.

What we are saying about cognitive abilities and the daily tasks of living, incidentally, is reminiscent of the earlier history of intelligence testing and the practical measurement of achievement. This testing was ultimately designed to predict how well students could handle educational tasks in school. In an effort to study the cognitive abilities underlying competence, researchers might end up reliving many of the theoretical and practical struggles in the intelligence and achievement testing movement. We recognize now, for example, that intelligence is only one of many attributes facilitating success in school and in life. Wisdom, motivation, organized habits, and knowledge are all factors in what old people can still accomplish.

Having digressed from some of the details of the measurement of competence or functional ability, it is time to return to the principles of successful aging.

Principle 5

To be actively engaged in purposeful striving. You may recall that purposeful living was also one of three main criteria cited by Ryff and Singer in their treatment of positive health.[17] And in one of the case histories in chapter 8, we wrote about Harry, who, at fifty-five years of age, lost his managerial job to downsizing. Harry became severely depressed and alcoholic for quite a few years. He withdrew from the world and for a long time took no interest in anything.

In our discussion of Harry, we pointed out that this state of mind is sometimes referred to clinically as an *existential neurosis*, a condition that disables some young people, too. It is one of the most pernicious states to take over a person's mind, and it is fairly common in old people. Existential neuroses are among the most difficult clinical problems to treat. Clients who suffer from it say that they know they ought to be interested in some kind of activity or striving, but nothing seems to interest them, and they just cannot seem to get started.

Often such persons look for someone else, including the psychotherapist, to show them how to get mobilized. But a goal cannot come from the outside; it must arise from within. Nothing is so sad as to see an old person who is still able to function but who cannot seem to become engaged in a purposeful activity.

This activity could also be attempting something creative, versions of which we also discussed briefly in chapter 8 to illustrate the wide variety of activities engaged in by residents of Rossmoor. However, purposeful activity does not have to be anything impressive but should reflect verve for living rather than withdrawal into a safe, vegetative shell to await death. Such a withdrawal would by no stretch of the imagination be thought of as successful aging.

Principle 6

To be wisely selective about what one takes on. This means that the elderly may need to limit their efforts to attain goals and engage in social activities they consider personally important enough to warrant making demands on their already limited resources.[18] Selectivity could help them avoid overcommitment.

We need not add to what we have already said about this here and in chapter 6, which deals with family and friends. The principle of selectivity applies not only to socializing with family and/or friends but also to any kind of useful work. Illness, reduced energy, and loss of stamina require cutting down somewhat on the ambitiousness with which we strive purposefully, regardless of the type of commitments we choose. Individual differences always apply, however, and aging persons must make their own decisions that are appropriate to their circumstances and tastes.

Principle 7

To maintain close ties with others.[19] In the social sciences in the 1970s, there was great interest in what came to be referred to as a person's *social network.* As we pointed out in chapter 3, social isolation—for example, losing social ties, being unmarried, or having inadequate social relationships—has been found to be associated with a number of negative life outcomes such as poor health, longevity, and well-being.[20]

One of the problems in this research is its exclusively sociological perspective—that is, the term *social network* represents *membership* in a group but does not reflect the *emotional involvement* in and *quality* of relationships with network members. A social network only reflects how many social connections one has, not what these connections are like as sources of psychological satisfaction. One might have many such connections that are mainly acquaintances rather than friends, and there are many families whose members hate each other (see chapter 6).

Principle 8

To retain positive self-regard despite losses and deficits. This principle repeats one of Ryff and Singer's criteria of positive health. Alternative terms to self-regard are *self-esteem, self-respect,* and *self-confidence.* These authors speak of mastery as well, though we are not altogether clear about what they mean by it. Not all problems in life can be mastered, so we tend to assimilate mastery within coping; we would rather refer to managing stress, which includes accepting the reality of one's situation and learning to live with it.

It is difficult to think of successful aging without there also being positive self-regard. This means not feeling ashamed of deficits, which in most instances are neither blameworthy nor matters one can do anything about. One reason self-regard is so important is that a person who has little confidence in his or her ability to deal with life and its many demands is far less likely than those with positive self-regard to make efforts to actualize their life potentials. Even when such people are competent, they are apt to project a lack of competence, which appears to others as a handicap even when this impression is inaccurate.

Self-regard has been shown to be a problem for children as well as the elderly, but those interested in aging could learn much from the naive efforts to promote self-regard in elementary and secondary schools. Much of this effort was directed at rejected minorities and focused on improving school performance. The naïveté of this approach is the tendency to give praise whether or not it was earned or deserved. When it is not earned, praise eventually fails and may well do harm. It has no credibility. Youngsters who have not been successful in reaching the classroom performance norm can readily see that they have not done well; they gain little or nothing from being told lies about how wonderful they are. Praise must be convincing to be useful—that is, it must be contingent on effective functioning.

It is no easy matter to build positive self-regard from the outside. Any hypocrisy in such an effort is likely to be even worse than useless because it is easy to see through. Children as well as the elderly need to believe that they are valuable as persons, deserve respect from others as individuals, and should also respect themselves without being fooled about what they are able and unable to do and be.

Even though we are no longer what we once were, old people should expect—perhaps even demand—respect, consideration, and care from others. Age discrimination and indifference would be greatly attenuated if the elderly, even the unaccomplished elderly, expected proper treatment from others and acted as if they deserved it. Though it is a worthy objective, how to increase self-regard among the elderly when needed would be as complex and uncertain a task as it is with children. As the population of the old increases, we must insist on being treated with respect. This also means voting accordingly in political elections and supporting organizations that lobby for the elderly.

Before we close this chapter on successful aging, we should point out that general principles like those presented here about how to think, feel, and act are usually oversimple because what can be done and their consequences vary with the physical and social circumstances of the individual. Nevertheless, we stand by these principles as useful ways of thinking that need to be cultivated, if possible, even if we also fully understand their limitations.

Living up to these ideals requires much psychological work. We, the authors, can attest to this as we ourselves decline physically and must struggle to drive a car and manage our writing. Not infrequently we feel like getting off the treadmill of life, but somehow it seems better to remain active and engaged. The alternative—namely, giving up—is usually worse, though not always.

No person can teach another how to live up to these principles. It takes determination (will, if you like). From time to time, most of us feel like giving up when the struggle seems too much and leaves us discouraged. Some people seem to be better at this than others, for reasons no one fully understands. Many of us have been doing something like this, without realizing it, for most of our lives. Deciding to do it as a conscious effort could bring it under more volitional control and also provide the basis for continuing vitality.

NOTES

When Richard Lazarus died, his wife and coauthor, Bernice, was left with three different versions of *Coping with Aging*: one complete book and two partial revisions. Grieving and herself ill, she sent this material to Oxford University Press to be compiled into a final version. We have no reservations about the body of the book as it now stands, but the notes and references (the latter existing only from the first version) had some problems. After our best efforts, a few notes still lack page numbers or other elements, but we believe these missing data do not seriously compromise the quality of the book. And although some entries in the reference section are not connected to the notes below, we have preserved all entries on the theory that inclusiveness is the safer path in terms of giving credit where due. Ultimately, our feeling is that so much good can come from people having access to *Coping with Aging*'s insights that it would have been a shame to withhold it solely because of these small flaws.

INTRODUCTION

1. Lazarus & Lazarus (1994).
2. Lazarus (1998c).
3. Gergen & Gergen (2000).
4. Krause (2000).

CHAPTER 1

1. Nuland (1994).
2. Pope (2002).
3. Shneidman (1989).
4. Adams (1918).
5. Shneidman (1989), p. 693.

CHAPTER 2

1. See, for example, Somerfield & McCrae (2000), as well as Lazarus & commentators (2003).

2. Aristotle (1941 trans.); Fortenbaugh (1975).
3. Kaplan (1961).
4. For a review of recent work on the immune system, see Kiecolt-Glaser & Glaser (2001).
5. De Kruif (1926).
6. Lazarus & Lazarus (1994).
7. Scherer, Schorr, & Johnstone (2001).
8. Examples of this focus on narrative psychology include Bruner (1999); Gergen & Gergen (1986); Josselson & Lieblich (1993); and McAdams (1996).
9. Lerner (1980).
10. Lazarus (2000).
11. Schaie (1994).
12. Cohen, Tyrrell, & Smith (1991).
13. Lazarus (1998b).
14. *New York Times*, July 15, 2002, pages unavailable; *New York Times*, July 16, 2002, pages unavailable.
15. Grossack & Gardner (1970), p. 115.
16. Knight & McCallum (1998), page number unavailable.
17. Magai & Passman (1997), p. 129.
18. Elder (1974).
19. Clausen (1993).
20. Folkman, Lazarus, Pimley, & Novacek (1987).
21. For reviews, see Salthouse (1998) and Strongman (1996).
22. Gross et al. (1997).
23. A senior research analyst from United Behavioral Health, Loren M. McCarter, Ph.D., helped greatly in the development of this method of portraying these overlaps. The final result in figure 2.1 was the work of Dr. McCarter, who created it. We thank him for his efforts. We also thank Professor Emeritus Bill Meredith. Consultation with him about the statistical merits of this kind of analysis encouraged us to use it here.
24. Spiegel (1997).

CHAPTER 3

1. Lazarus (1996, 1998b, 1999b).
2. Freud (1946).
3. Erdelyi (2000).
4. See Shapiro (1965) and Cramer (1991) for useful guides to the Freudian defenses.
5. See also Lazarus (1966, 1993b, 1999b).
6. Notable examples include Aldwin (1994); Gottlieb (1997); Lazarus (2000); Lazarus & Folkman (1984); Snyder (1999); and Zeidner & Endler (1996).
7. Zeidner & Endler (1996).
8. J. L. Levenson, Kay, Monteferrante, & Herman (1984); Levine et al. (1987); for a review of this kind of research, see Maes, Leventhal, & de Ridder (1996).
9. F. Cohen & Lazarus (1973).
10. Krohne, Slangen, & Kleeman (1996).
11. Staudenmeyer, Kinsman, Dirks, Spector, & Wangaard (1979).
12. LaMontagne, Hepworth, Johnson, & Cohen (1996).

13. LaMontagne, Hepworth, & Cohen (2000).
14. Lazarus (1983).
15. Heller (1986); Suls (1982).
16. Mechanic (1962).
17. James (1902).
18. McFadden & Levin (1996); see also Burgess, Schmeeckle, & Bengtson (1998).
19. Folkman & Lazarus (1988).
20. Holmes & Rahe (1967); see also Dohrenwend & Dohrenwend (1974).
21. Kanner, Coyne, Schaefer, & Lazarus (1981); DeLongis, Coyne, Dakof, Folkman, & Lazarus (1982).
22. Bradburn (1969).
23. Radloff (1977).
24. Diener (1984).
25. Diener & Suh (1998).
26. Lazarus & Lazarus (1994); Gatchel & Baum (1983); Feist & Brannon (1988); Rice (1998); Taylor (1986).
27. S. Cohen et al. (1991).
28. George, Scott, Turner, & Gregg (1980).
29. Marucha, Kiecolt-Glaser, & Favagehi (1998).
30. F. Cohen, Kearney, et al. (1999).
31. Kiecolt-Glaser & Glaser (2001).
32. Schulz, (2000).
33. Skinner, source unavailable.
34. Mace & Rabins (1991).

CHAPTER 4

1. T. S. Friedman, *New York Times*, January 30, 2001, p. A27.
2. Lazarus (1999b).
3. Lawton (1980). See also Schaie & Peitrucha (2000).
4. Regnier (1997). See also comments by Charness (1997).
5. Bryer (2000).
6. R. Herbert, *New York Times*, January 29, 2001, p. A27.
7. Benedict (1934).
8. See also Maslow (1964), p. 155.
9. Bond & Smith (1998), p. 227.
10. See Bandura, Ross, & Ross (1963).
11. See Kim, Triandis, Kâgitcibasi, Choi, & Yoon (1994) for sophisticated discussions of this.
12. See Kelman (1961) for a brief statement of the contrast between compliance and internalization, and House (1981) for a highly sophisticated treatment of this process.
13. See, for example, Ehrlich (1968); Hardin (1969).
14. See More (1995).

CHAPTER 5

1. Novacek & Lazarus (1990).
2. Caspi & Roberts (2001) have briefly described most of the longitudinal studies in their recent discussion of stability and change.
3. Elder (1974); Clausen (1993).
4. Allport (1942).
5. Allport (1965).
6. T. Wolff, *New York Times*, April 28, 2001, p. A23.
7. Caspi & Roberts (2001).
8. M. Lewis (2001).
9. Costa & McCrae (1996), p. 379; emphasis added.
10. Ibid., pp. 369–370.
11. M. Lewis (2001).
12. Schaie & Lawton (1998).
13. See Folkman et al. (1987); Labouvie-Vief (1997); Vaillant (1977); Vaillant, Bond, & Vaillant (1986).
14. See, for example, Bugental (1990); Freeman, Simon, Beutler, & Arkowitz (1989); Mahoney (1991); Safran & Greenberg (1991).
15. Guidano in Safran & Greenberg (1991).
16. Lazarus (1991).
17. Rice & Greenberg in Safran & Greenberg (1991), p. 207.
18. As an example of a source, a book by K. C. Peterson, Prout, and Schwarz (1991) could be cited, but there are also many others.
19. Lindemann (1944).
20. Slaikeu (1984), p. ix.
21. Lazarus (1999b).
22. Cf. Marris (1975).
23. See VandenBos (1996).
24. Paloutzian, Richardson, & Rambo (1999), p. 1048.
25. Ibid., p. 1065.

CHAPTER 6

1. For example, Carstensen, Gross, & Fung (1997); Carstensen, Graff, Levenson, & Gottman (1996).
2. Carstensen et al. (1996), p. 229.
3. Cowan & Cowan (1992).
4. Ibid., p. 230.
5. Ibid., p. 231.
6. Lazarus (1984); Folkman et al. (1987).
7. Jung (1933); Guttmann (1974).
8. Gottman (1994).
9. Carstensen et al. (1996), citing the U.S. Bureau of the Census (1992).
10. Carstensen et al. (1996).
11. Ibid.
12. Antonucci (1985).
13. See a review of this area by de Vries (1996).

14. Carstensen (1992).
15. Johnson (1983).
16. Averill (1983).
17. Blau (1973).
18. Felton & Berry (1992).
19. Hochschild (1979).
20. See, for example, Cantor & Brennan (2000); Cavanaugh (1998); Mace & Rabins (1991); Schulz (2000); Zarit, Johansson, & Jarrott (1998).
21. Folkman (1997); Folkman, Chesney, & Christopher-Richards (1994).
22. Ronald W. Reagan Presidential Library, Simi Valley, California.
23. For additional sources about Alzheimer's disease, see Albert & Logsdon (2000); Kumar & Eisdorfer (1998); Lawton & Rubinstein (2000); and Mace & Rabins (1991).
24. Mace & Rabins (1991).
25. Ibid., p. 214.
26. *Alzheimer's Association Newsletter*, Winter 2001, p. 6.

CHAPTER 7

1. Folkman, Bernstein, & Lazarus (1987).
2. Kane (2000).
3. See Lerner (1980); Lazarus (1985).
4. Whitbourne (1998); see also Whitbourne (1996).
5. Whitbourne (1996), p. 101.
6. Kiecolt-Glaser & Glaser (2001).
7. See Janis (1958) for a pioneering psychological study of the stresses of surgery.
8. See Horowitz (1986), a molecular biophysicist who has described the fascinating story of the multidisciplinary research that led to the discovery in some detail; see also Keesey & Sonshine (1998).

CHAPTER 8

1. There is no proper source for this quotation. It is generic in that some version of it appears in various places, and there are many versions of the same idea. In Benjamin Franklin's *Poor Richard's Almanac* (1757), the aphorism reads, "The idle man is the devil's hireling," which is pretty close to our version. In Thomas Fuller's *Gnomologie*, No. 3054, it goes, "Idle fellows are the devil's playfellows." We like the version we used, but it has no specific reference.
2. Lazarus (1998c).
3. Berst (2000).
4. House (1998), p. 301.
5. M. M. Baltes & Carstensen (1996); Lazarus (1996).
6. Dickson (1991) p. 467.
7. Greenglass & Burke (2001).
8. See Rosow (1976); Schooler, Caplan, & Oates (1998); Warr (1998); Westerhof & Dittmann-Kohli (2000).
9. Klinger (1971).
10. For an in-depth discussion of the trivialization of distress and its psychological causes and effects, see Lazarus (1985).

11. House (1981); see also Kelman (1961).
12. See, for example, Kitayama, Markus, & Matsumoto (1995).
13. May (1950).
14. Csikszentmihalyi (1975) [reference unavailable].

CHAPTER 9

1. Nordhus, Nielsen, & Kvale (1998).
2. See Tweed, Blazer, & Ciarlo (1992).
3. See VandenBos (1996).
4. Segal, Coolidge, & Hersen (1998); Hestad, Ellertsen, & Kløve (1998).
5. Gatz & Smyer (1992); also Nordhus et al. (1998).
6. Nordhus et al. (1998).
7. Ibid.
8. Ibid.
9. Ibid.
10. Knight & McCallum (1998).
11. Ibid., p. 315.
12. Ibid., page unavailable.
13. Ibid., p. 325.
14. Glantz (1989).
15. Butler (1974); M. I. Lewis & Butler (1974).
16. Becker (1973).
17. Lazarus (1998c).
18. Bradley, Fried, Kasl, & Idler (2000).
19. Lazarus (1985).
20. Bradley et al. (2000).

CHAPTER 10

1. Ryff, Singer, & commentators (1998).
2. See also Stoebe, Hansson, Stroebe, & Schut (2001).
3. World Health Organization (1948), p. 28.
4. Glantz (1989), p. 471.
5. Ryff et al. (1998).
6. See, for example, Folkman & Moskowitz (2000); Lazarus (1999a); Snyder (1999); Taylor (1989).
7. See C. Peterson (2000) for an interesting and sophisticated discussion of optimism and, by implication, pessimism.
8. Lazarus (1999a); Snyder (1999).
9. Willis, Schaie, & Hayward (1997).
10. Crimmins & Hayward (1997).
11. Singer & Manton (1998).
12. Salthouse (1997), p. 51.
13. Ibid., p. 52.
14. Ibid., p. 57.
15. Willis (1991).

16. Park (1997), p. 73.
17. Ryff et al. (1998).
18. See also Carstensen (1992).
19. See also Ryff et al. (1998).
20. Berkman & Syme (1979). The pioneers in this field include Cassel (1976); Cobb (1976); and others too numerous to mention here.

References

Adams, H. B. (1918). *The education of Henry Adams*. Boston: Houghton Mifflin.

Albert, S. M., & Logsdon, R. G. (2000). *Assessing quality of life in Alzheimer's disease*. New York: Springer.

Aldwin, C. M. (1994). *Stress, coping, and development: An integrative perspective*. New York: Guilford.

Allport, G. W. (1942). *The use of personal documents in psychological science*. New York: Social Science Research Council.

Allport, G. W. (1965). *Letters from Jenny*. New York: Harcourt, Brace and World.

Antonucci, T. C. (1985). Personal characteristics, social support, and social behavior. In R. H. Binstock & E. Shanas (Eds.), *Handbook of aging and the social sciences* (2nd ed., pp. 94–128). New York: Reinhold.

Aristotle. (1941). *The basic works of Aristotle* (R. McKeon, Ed.). New York: Random House.

Averill, J. R. (1983). Studies on anger and aggression: Implications for a theory of emotion. *American Psychologist, 38*, 1145–1160.

Baltes, M. M., & Carstensen, L. L. (1996). The process of successful aging. *Aging and Society, 16*, 397–422.

Baltes, P. B., & Baltes, M. M. (1999). Psychological perspectives on successful aging: The model of selective optimization with compensation. In P. B. Baltes & M. M. Baltes (Eds.), *Successful aging: Perspectives from the biological sciences* (pp. 1–34). New York: Cambridge University Press.

Bandura, A. (1997). *Self-efficacy: The exercise of control*. New York: Freeman.

Bandura, A., Ross, D., & Ross, S. A. (1963). A comparative test of the status envy, social power, and secondary reinforcement theories of identification learning. *Journal of Abnormal and Social Psychology, 67*, 527–534.

Bargh, J. A., & Barndollar, K. (1996). Automaticity in action: The unconscious as repository of chronic goals and motives. In P. M. Gollwitzer & J. A. Bargh (Eds.), *The psychology of action* (pp. 457–481). New York: Guilford.

Becker, E. (1973). *The denial of death*. New York: Free Press.

Benedict, R. (1934). *Patterns of culture*. Boston: Houghton Mifflin.

Berkman, L., & Syme, S. L. (1979). Social networks, host resistance, and mortality: a nine-year follow-up study of Alameda County residences. *American Journal of Epidemiology, 109*, 186–204.

Berst, C. (2000). Summary of the 1997–1999 Emeriti Bibliography Survey. *Berkeley Emeriti Times*, pp. 2–5.

Blanchard-Fields, F. (1997). The role of emotion in social cognition across the adult life span. In K. W. Schaie & M. P. Lawton (Eds.), *Annual review of gerontology and geriatrics: Vol. 17. Focus on emotion and development* (pp. 238–265). New York: Springer.

Blau, Z. S. (1973). *Old age in a changing society*. New York: New Viewpoints.

Bond, M. H., & Smith, P. B. (1998). *Social psychology across cultures*. Upper Saddle River, NJ: Pearson Allyn and Bacon.

Bradburn, N. M. (1969). *The structure of well-being*. Chicago: Aldine.

Bradley, E. H., Fried, T. R., Kasl, S. V., & Idler, E. (2000). Quality of life trajectories of elders in the end of life. In M. P. Lawton (Ed.), *Annual review of gerontology and geriatrics: Vol. 20. Focus on the end of life: Scientific and social issues* (pp. 64–96). New York: Springer.

Breger, L., Hunter, I., & Lane, R. W. (1971). *The effects of stress on dreams*. New York: International Universities Press.

Bruner, J. S. (1999). *Acts of meaning*. Cambridge, MA: Harvard University Press.

Bryer, T. (2000). Characteristics of motor vehicle crashes related to aging. In K. W. Schaie & M. Pietrucha (Eds.), *Mobility and transportation in the elderly* (pp. 157–211). New York: Springer.

Bugental, J. F. T. (1990). *Intimate journeys: Stories from life-changing therapy*. San Francisco: Jossey-Bass.

Burgess, E. O., Schmeeckle, M., & Bengtson, V. L. (1998). Aging individuals and societal contexts. In I. H. Nordhus, G. R. VandenBos, S. Berg, & P. Fromholt (Eds.), *Clinical geropsychology* (pp. 15–31). Washington, DC: American Psychological Association.

Butler, R. (1974). Successful aging and the role of the life review. *Journal of the American Geriatrics Society, 22*, 529–535.

Cacioppo, J. T., Berntson, G. G., Larsen, J. T., Poehlmann, K. M., & Ito, T. A. (2000). The psychophysiology of emotion. In M. Lewis & J. M. Haviland-Jones (Eds.), *Handbook of emotions* (2nd ed., pp. 173–191). New York: Guilford.

Campos, J. J., Campos, R. G., & Barrett, K. C. (1989). Emergent themes in the study of emotional development and emotion regulation. *Developmental Psychology, 25*, 394–402.

Campos, J. J. Mumme, D. L., Kermoian, R., & Campos, R. G. (1994). A functionalist perspective on the nature of emotion. In N. Fox (Ed.), *The development of emotion regulation: Biological and behavioral considerations* (pp. 284–306). *Society for Research in Child Development, 59*.

Cantor, M. H., & Brennan, M. (2000). *Social care of the elderly: The effects of ethnicity, class, and culture*. New York: Springer.

Carstensen, L. L. (1992). Social and emotional patterns in adulthood: Support for socioemotional selectivity theory. *Psychology and Aging, 7*, 331–338.

Carstensen, L. L. (1995). Evidence for a life-span theory of socioemotional selectivity. *Current Directions in Psychological Science, 4*, 151–156.

Carstensen, L. L., Graff, J., Levenson, R. W., & Gottman, J. M. (1996). Affect in intimate relationships: The developmental course of marriage. In C. Magai & S. H. McFadden (Eds.), *Handbook of emotion, adult development, and aging* (pp. 227–247). San Diego, CA: Academic Press.

Carstensen, L. L., Gross, J. J., & Fung, H. H. (1997). The social context of emotional experience. In K. W. Schaie & M. P. Lawton (Eds.), *Annual review of gerontology and geriatrics* (Vol. 17, pp. 325–352). New York: Springer.

Carver, C. S. (1996). Foreword. In M. Zeidner & N. S. Endler (Eds.), *Handbook of coping: Theory, research, applications* (pp. xi–xiii). New York: Wiley.

Caspi, A., & Roberts, B. W. (2001). Personality development across the life course: The argument for change and continuity. *Psychological Inquiry, 12,* 49–66.

Cassel, J. (1976). The contribution of the social environment to host resistance. *American Journal of Epidemiology, 10,* 107–123.

Cavanaugh, J. C. (1998). Caregiving to adults: A life event challenge. In I. H. Nordhus, G. R. VandenBos, S. Berg, & P. Fromholt (Eds.), *Clinical geropsychology* (pp. 131–135). Washington, DC: American Psychological Association.

Charness, N. (1997). Commentary: The FSU approach to design: Feedback from senior users. In S. L. Willis, K. W. Schaie, & M. Hayward (Eds.), *Societal mechanisms for maintaining competence in old age* (pp. 251–265). New York: Springer.

Clausen, J. A. (1993). *American lives: Looking back at the children of the Great Depression.* New York: Free Press.

Cobb, S. (1976). Social support as a moderator of life stress. *Psychosomatic Medicine, 38,* 300–314.

Coelho, G. V., Hamburg, D. A., & Adams, J. E. (Eds.). (1974). *Coping and adaptation.* New York: Basic Books.

Cohen, F., & Lazarus, R. S. (1973). Active coping processes, coping dispositions, and recovery from surgery. *Psychosomatic Medicine, 63,* 375–398.

Cohen, F., Kearney, K. A., Zegans, L. S., Kemeny, M. E., Neuhaus, J. M., & Stites, D. P. (1999). Differential immune system changes with acute and persistent stress for optimists vs. pessimists. *Brain, Behavior, and Immunity, 13,* 155–174.

Cohen, F., Kemeny, M. E., Kearney, K. A., Zegans, L. S., Neuhaus, J. M., & Conant, M. A. (1999). Persistent stress as a predictor of genital herpes recurrence. *Archives of Internal Medicine, 159,* 2430–2436.

Cohen, S., Miller, G. E., & Rabin, B. S. (2001). Psychological stress and antibody response to immunization: A critical review of the human literature. *Psychosomatic Medicine, 63,* 7–18.

Cohen, S., Tyrrell, D. A., & Smith, A. P. (1991). Psychological stress and susceptibility to the common cold. *New England Journal of Medicine, 325,* 606–612.

Conquest, R. (2000). *Reflections on a ravaged century.* New York: Norton.

Costa, P. T., Jr., & McCrae, R. R. (1994). Set like plaster? Evidence for the stability of adult personality. In T. F. Heatherton & J. L. Weinberger (Eds.), *Can personality change?* (pp. 21–40). Washington, DC: American Psychological Association.

Costa, P. T., Jr., & McCrae, R. R. (1996). Mood and personality in adulthood. In C. Magai & S. H. McFadden (Eds.), *Handbook of emotion, adult development, and aging* (pp. 369–383). San Diego, CA: Academic Press.

Costa, P. T., Somerfield, M. R., & McCrae, R. R. (1996). In M. Zeidner & N. S. Endler

(Eds.), *Handbook of coping: Theory, research, applications* (pp. 44–61). New York: Wiley.

Cowan, C. P., & Cowan, P. A. (1992). *When partners become parents: The big life change for couples.* New York: Basic Books.

Cramer, P. (1991). *The development of defense mechanisms: Theory, research, and assessment.* New York: Springer.

Crimmins, E. M., & Hayward, M. D. (1997). What we can learn about competence at the older ages from active life expectancy? In S. L. Willis, K. W. Schaie, & M. Hayward (Eds.), *Societal mechanisms for maintaining competence in old age* (pp. 1–22). New York: Springer.

Damasio, A. R. (1994). *Descartes' error: Emotion, reason, and the human brain.* New York: Putnam.

Deese, J. (1972). *Psychology as science and art.* New York: Harcourt Brace Jovanovich.

DeLongis, A., Coyne, J. C., Dakof, G., Folkman, S., & Lazarus, R. S. (1982). Relationship of daily hassles, uplifts, and major life events to health status. *Health Psychology, 1,* 119–136.

DeLongis, A., Folkman, S., & Lazarus, R. S. (1988). Hassles, health, and mood: Psychological and social resources as mediators. *Journal of Personality and Social Psychology, 54,* 486–495.

de Kruif, P. (1926). *Microbe Hunters.* New York: Harcourt, Brace.

de Vries, B. (1996). The understanding of friendship: An adult life course perspective. In C. Magai & S. H. McFadden (Eds.), *Handbook of emotion, adult development, and aging* (pp. 249–268). San Diego, CA: Academic Press.

Dickson, P. (1991). *Baseball's Greatest Quotations.* New York: HarperCollins.

Diener, E. (1984). Subjective well-being. *Psychological Bulletin, 95,* 542–575.

Diener, E., & Suh, M. E. (1998). Subjective well-being and age: An international analysis. In K. W. Schaie & M. P. Lawton (Eds.), *Annual review of gerontology and geriatrics: Vol. 17. Focus on emotion and adult development* (pp. 304–324). New York: Springer.

Dohrenwend, B. S., & Dohrenwend, B. P. (Eds.). (1974). *Stressful life events: Their nature and effects.* New York: Wiley.

Ehrlich, P. R. (1968). *The population bomb.* New York: Ballantine.

Elder, G. H. Jr. (1974). *The children of the Great Depression.* Chicago: University of Chicago Press. Revised 1999, Boulder, CO: Westview Press.

Erdelyi, M. H. (2000). Repression. In A. E. Kazdin (Ed.), *Encyclopedia of psychology* (pp. 69–71). New York: Oxford University Press.

Feist, J., & Brannon, L. (1988). *Health psychology: An introduction to behavior and health.* Belmont, CA: Wadsworth.

Felton, B. J., & Berry, C. A. (1992). Do the sources of urban elderly's support determine psychological consequences? *Psychology and Aging, 7,* 89–97.

Folkman, S. (1997). Introduction to the special section: Use of bereavement narratives to predict well-being in men whose partners died of AIDS—Four theoretical perspectives. *Journal of Personality and Social Psychology, 72,* 851–854.

Folkman, S., Bernstein, L., & Lazarus, R. S. (1987). Stress processes and the misuse of drugs in older adults. *Psychology and Aging, 2,* 366–374.

Folkman, S., Chesney, M., & Christopher-Richards, A. (1994). Stress and coping in

caregiving partners of men with AIDS. *Psychiatric Clinics of North America, 17,* 35–53.
Folkman, S., & Lazarus, R. S. (1988). *Manual for the Ways of Coping Questionnaire.* Palo Alto, CA: Consulting Psychologists Press.
Folkman, S., Lazarus, R. S., Pimley, S., & Novacek, J. (1987). Age differences in stress and coping processes. *Psychology and Aging, 2,* 171–184.
Folkman, S., & Moskowitz, J. T. (2000). Positive affect and the other side of coping. *American Psychologist, 55,* 647–654.
Fortenbaugh, W. (1975). *Aristotle on Emotion.* London: Duckworth.
Freeman, A., Simon, K. M., Beutler, L. E., & Arkowitz, H. (1989). (Eds.). *Comprehensive handbook of cognitive therapy.* New York: Plenum.
Freud, A. (1946). *The ego and the mechanisms of defense.* New York: International Universities Press.
Frijda, N. H. (1987). Emotion, cognitive structure, and action tendency. *Cognition and Emotion, 1,* 115–143.
Gatchel, R. J., & Baum, A. (1983). *An introduction to health psychology.* Reading, MA: Addison-Wesley.
Gatz, M., & Smyer, M. (1992). The mental health system and older adults in the 1990s. *American Psychologist, 47,* 741–751.
George, J. M., Scott, D. S., Turner, S. P., & Gregg, J. M. (1980). The effects of psychological factors and physical trauma on recovery from oral surgery. *Journal of Behavioral Medicine, 3,* 291–310.
Gergen, K. J., & Gergen, M. M. (1986). Narrative form and the construction of psychological science. In T. R. Sarbin (Ed.), *Narrative psychology: The storied nature of human conduct* (pp. 22–44). New York: Praeger.
Gergen, K. J., & Gergen, M. M. (2000). The new aging: Self-construction and social values. In K. W. Schaie & J. Hendricks (Eds.), *The evolution of the aging self: The societal impact on the aging process* (pp. 281–306). New York: Springer.
Glantz, M. D. (1989). Cognitive therapy with the elderly. In A. Freeman, K. M. Simon, L. E. Beutler, & H. Arkowitz (Eds.), *Comprehensive handbook of cognitive therapy* (pp. 467–489). New York: Plenum.
Glassman, A. H., & Shapiro, P. A. (1998). Depression and the course of coronary artery disease. *American Journal of Psychiatry, 155,* 4–11.
Glenn, N. D. (1980). Values, attitudes, and beliefs. In O. G. Brim Jr. & J. Kagan (Eds.), *Constancy and change in human development* (pp. 596–640). Cambridge, MA: Harvard University Press.
Gottlieb, B. H. (Ed.). (1997). *Coping with chronic stress.* New York: Plenum.
Gottman, J. (1994). *Why marriages succeed or fail: And how you can make yours last.* New York: Simon and Schuster.
Greenglass, E. R., & Burke, R. L. (2001). Editorial introduction. Downsizing and restructuring: Implications for stress and anxiety [Special issue]. *Anxiety, Stress, and Coping: An International Journal, 14,* 1–13.
Gross, J. J., Carstensen, L. L., Pasupathi, M., Tsai, J., Skorpen, C. G., & Hsu, A. Y. C. (1997). Emotion and aging: Experience, expression, and control. *Psychology and Aging, 12,* 590–599.
Grossack, M., & Gardner, H. (1970). *Man and men: Social psychology as social science.* Scranton, PA: International Textbooks.

Guidano, V. F. (1991). Affective change events in a cognitive therapy system approach. In J. D. Safran & L. S. Greenberg (Eds.), *Emotion, psychotherapy, change* (pp. 50–79). New York: Guilford.

Guttmann, D. L. (1974). The country of old men: Cross-cultural studies in the psychology of later life. In R. I. LeVine (Ed.), *Culture and personality: Contemporary readings* (pp. 95–121). Chicago: Aldine.

Hardin, G. (1969). (Ed.). *Population, evolution, and birth control*. San Francisco: Freeman.

Heller, K. (Ed.). (1986). Dis-aggregating the process of social support [Special series]. *Journal of Consulting and Clinical Psychology, 54*, 387–470.

Herbart, J. E. (1824–25). *Psychology as science, newly established in the basis of experience, metaphysics, and mathematics* (Vols. 1 and 2). Königsberg: Unzer.

Hestad, K., Ellertsen, B., & Kløve, H. (1998). Neuropsychological assessment in old age. In I. H. Nordhus, G. R. VandenBos, S. Berg, & P. Fromholt (Eds.), *Clinical geropsychology*. Washington, DC: American Psychological Association.

Hochschild, A. R. (1979). Emotion work, feeling rules, and social structure. *American Journal of Sociology, 85*, 551–575.

Holmes, T. S., & Rahe, R. H. (1967). The social readjustment rating scale. *Journal of Psychosomatic Research, 11*, 213–218.

Horowitz, H. J. (1986, March). Myasthenia gravis and arrows of fortune. *Hospital Practice*, 179–194.

House, J. S. (1981). Social structure and personality. In M. Rosenberg & R. H. Turner (Eds.), *Social psychology: Sociological perspectives* (pp. 525–561). New York: Basic Books.

House, J. S. (1998). Commentary: Age, work, and well-being: Toward a broader view. In K. Warner & C. Schooler (Eds.), *Impact of work on older adults* (pp. 297–310). New York: Springer.

Ingebretsen, R., & Solem, R. (1998). Death, dying, and bereavement. In I. H. Nordhus, G. R. VandenBos, S. Berg, & P. Fromholt (Eds.), *Clinical geropsychology* (pp. 177–181). Washington, DC: American Psychological Association.

Jahoda, M. (1958). *Current concepts of positive mental health*. New York: Basic Books.

James, W. (1902/1982). *The varieties of religious experience*. (1982, Harmondsworth, England: Penguin.

Janis, I. L. (1958). *Psychological stress*. New York, Wiley.

Johnson, C. L. (1983). Fairweather friends and rainy day kin: An anthropological analysis of old age friendships in the United States. *Urban Anthropology, 12*, 103–123.

Josselson, R., & Lieblich, A. (Eds). (1993). *The narrative study of lives*. Newbury Park, CA: Sage.

Jung, C. G. (1933). *Modern man in search of a soul*. New York: Harcourt, Brace and World.

Kane, R. L. (2000). Caution: Health care is hazardous to the aging self. In K. W. Schaie & J. Hendricks (Eds.), *The evolution of the aging self: The societal impact on the aging process* (pp. 183–203). New York: Springer.

Kanner, A., Coyne, J. C., Schaefer, C., & Lazarus, R. S. (1981). Comparison of two modes of stress measurement: Daily hassles and uplifts versus major life events. *Journal of Behavioral Medicine, 10*, 18–39.

Kaplan, A. (1961). Cause. *The encyclopedia Americana* (pp. 131–132). New York: American Corporation.
Keesey, J. C., & Sonshine, R. (1998). *A practical guide to myasthenia gravis*. Myasthenia Gravis Foundation of America.
Kelman, H. C. (1961). Processes of opinion change. *Public Opinion Quarterly, 25*, 57–58.
Kiecolt-Glaser, J. K., & Glaser, R. (2001). Stress and immunity: Age enhances the risks. *Current Directions in Psychological Science, 10*, 18–21.
Kim, U., Triandis, H. C., Kâgitcibasi, Ç, Choi, S-C., & Yoon, G. (Eds.). *Individualism and collectivism*. Thousand Oaks, CA: Sage.
Kitayama, S., Markus, H. R., & Matsumoto, H. (1995). Culture, self, and emotion: A cultural perspective on "self-conscious emotions." In J. P. Tangney & K. W. Fischer (Eds.), *Self-conscious emotions: The psychology of shame, guilt, embarrassment, and pride* (pp. 439–464). New York: Guilford.
Klinger, E. (1971). *The structure and functions of fantasy*. New York: Wiley.
Klos, D. S., & Singer, J. L. (1981). Determinants of the adolescent's ongoing thought following simulated parental confrontations. *Journal of Personality and Social Psychology, 41*, 975–987.
Knight, B. G., & McCallum, T. J. (1998). Psychotherapy with older adult families: The contextual, cohort-based maturity/specific challenge model. In I. H. Nordhus, G. R. VandenBos, S. Berg, & P. Fromholt (Eds.), *Clinical geropsychology* (pp. 313–328). Washington, DC: American Psychological Association.
Krause, N. (2000). Are we really entering a new era of aging? In K. W. Schaie & J. Hendricks (Eds.), *The evolution of the aging self: The societal impact on the aging process* (pp. 307–318). New York: Springer.
Krohne, H. W. (2002). Individual differences in emotional reactions and coping. In R. J. Davidson, K. R. Scherer, & H. H. Goldsmith (Eds.), *Handbook of affective sciences*. New York: Oxford University Press.
Krohne, H. W., Slangen, K., & Kleemann, P. P. (1996). Coping variables as predictors of perioperative emotional states and adjustment. *Psychology and Health, 11*, 315–330.
Kumar, V., & Eisdorfer, C. (1998). *Advances in the diagnosis and treatment of Alzheimer's disease*. New York: Springer.
Labouvie-Vief, G. (1994). *Psyche and eros: Mind and gender in the life course*. New York: Cambridge University Press.
Labouvie-Vief, G. (1997). Cognitive-emotional integration in adulthood. In K. W. Schaie & M. P. Lawton (Eds.), *Annual review of gerontology and geriatrics: Vol. 17. Focus on emotion and adult development* (pp. 206–237). New York: Springer.
Labouvie-Vief, G., De Voe, M., & Bulka, D. (1989). Speaking about feelings: Conceptions of emotion across the life span. *Psychology and Aging, 4*, 425–437.
LaMontagne, L. L., Hepworth, J. T., & Cohen, F. (2000). Effects of surgery type and attention focus on children's coping. *Nursing Research, 45*, 245–252.
LaMontagne, L. L., Hepworth, J. T., Johnson, B. D., & Cohen, F. (1996). Children's preoperative coping and its effects on postoperative anxiety and return to normal activity. *Nursing Research, 4*, 141–147.
Lawton, M. P. (1980). *Environment and aging*. Monterey, CA: Brooks/Cole.

Lawton, M. P., & Rubinstein, R. L. (Eds.). (2000). *Interventions in dementia care: Toward improving quality of life.* New York: Springer.
Lazarus, R. S. (1966). *Psychological stress and the coping process.* New York: McGraw-Hill.
Lazarus, R. S. (1983). The costs and benefits of denial. In S. Breznitz (Ed.), *The denial of stress* (pp. 1–30). New York: International Universities Press.
Lazarus, R. S. (1984). Puzzles in the study of daily hassles. *Journal of Behavioral Medicine, 7,* 375–389.
Lazarus, R. S. (1985). The trivialization of distress. In J. C. Rosen & L. J. Solomon (Eds.), Preventing health risk behaviors and promoting coping with illness. *Vermont Conference on the Primary Prevention of Psychopathology* (Vol. 8, pp. 279–298). Hanover, NH: University Press of New England.
Lazarus, R. S. (1991). *Emotion and adaptation* New York: Oxford University Press.
Lazarus, R. S. (1993a). Coping theory and research: Past, present, and future. *Psychosomatic Medicine, 55,* 234–247.
Lazarus, R. S. (1993b). From psychological stress to the emotions: A history of changing outlooks. In *Annual Review of Psychology,* (pp. 1–21). Palo Alto, CA: Annual Reviews.
Lazarus, R. S. (1996). The role of coping in the emotions and how coping changes over the life course. In C. Magai & S. H. McFadden (Eds.), *Handbook of emotion, adult development and aging* (pp. 289–306). New York: Academic Press.
Lazarus, R. S. (1998a). Coping from the perspective of personality. *Zeitschrift für Differentielle und Diagnostische Psychologie, 19,* 213–231.
Lazarus, R. S. (1998b). *Fifty years of the research and theory of R. S. Lazarus: An analysis of historical and perennial issues.* Mahwah, NJ: Earlbaum.
Lazarus, R. S. (1998c). *The life and work of an eminent psychologist: Autobiography of Richard S. Lazarus.* New York: Springer.
Lazarus, R. S. (1999a). Hope: An emotion and a vital coping resource against despair. *Social Research, 66,* 653–678.
Lazarus, R. S. (1999b). *Stress and emotion: A new synthesis.* New York: Springer.
Lazarus, R. S. (2000). Toward better research on stress and coping. *American Psychologist, 55,* 665–673.
Lazarus, R. S. (2001). Relational meaning and discrete emotions. In K. R. Scherer, A. Schorr, & T. Johnstone (Eds.), *Appraisal processes in emotion: Theory, methods, research* (pp. 37–67). New York: Oxford University Press.
Lazarus, R. S., & commentators. (2003). Does the positive psychology movement have legs? *Psychology Inquiry, 14,* 93–109.
Lazarus, R. S., & Folkman, S. (1984). *Stress, appraisal, and coping.* New York: Springer.
Lazarus, R. S., & Folkman, S. (1989). *Manual for the Study of Daily Hassles and Uplifts Scales.* Palo Alto, CA: Consulting Psychologists Press.
Lazarus, R. S., Kanner, A., & Folkman, S. (1980). Emotions: A cognitive-phenomenological analysis. In R. Plutchik & H. Kellerman (Eds.), *Theories of emotion* (pp. 189–217). New York: Academic Press.
Lazarus, R. S., & Lazarus, B. N. (1994). *Passion and reason: Making sense of our emotions.* New York: Oxford University Press.

Le Doux, J. E. (1989). Cognitive-emotional reactions in the brain. *Cognition and Emotion, 3,* 267–289.
Lerner, M. J. (1980). *The belief in a just world: A fundamental delusion.* New York: Plenum.
Levenson, J. L., Kay, R., Monteferrante, J., & Herman, M. V. (1984). Denial predicts favorable outcome in unstable angina pectoris. *Psychosomatic Medicine, 46,* 25–32.
Levenson, R. W., Carstensen, L. L., & Gottman, J. M. (1993). Long-term marriage: Age, gender, and satisfaction. *Psychology and Aging, 8,* 301–313.
Leventhal, H., Patrick-Miller, L., Leventhal, E. A., & Burns, E. A. (1997). Does stress-emotion cause illness in elderly people? In K. W. Schaie & M. P. Lawton (Eds.), *Annual review of gerontology and geriatrics: Vol. 17. Focus on emotion and adult development* (pp. 138–184). New York: Springer.
Levine, J., Warrenburg, S., Kerns, R., Schwartz, G., Delaney, R., Fontana, A., et al. (1987). The role of denial in recovery from coronary heart disease. *Psychosomatic Medicine, 49,* 109–117.
Lewis, M. (2001). Issues in the study of personality development. *Psychological Inquiry, 12,* 67–83.
Lewis, M. I., & Butler, R. N. (1974). Life-review therapy: Putting memories to work in individual and group psychotherapy. *Geriatrics, 29,* 165–173.
Lindemann, E. (1944). Symptomatology and management of acute grief. *American Journal of Psychiatry, 101,* 141–148.
Mace, N. L., & Rabins, P. V. (1991). *The 36-hour day* (Rev. ed). Baltimore: Johns Hopkins University Press.
Maes, S., Leventhal, H., & de Ridder, D. T. D. (1996). Coping with chronic diseases. In M. Zeidner & N. S. Endleer (Eds.), *Handbook of coping: Theory, research, applications* (pp. 221–251). New York: Wiley.
Magai, C., & McFadden, S. H. (Eds.). (1996). *Handbook of emotion, adult development, and aging.* San Diego, CA: Academic Press.
Magai, C., & Passman, V. (1997). The interpersonal basis of emotional behavior and emotion regulation in adulthood. In K. W. Schaie & M. P. Lawton (Eds.), *Annual review of gerontology and geriatrics: Vol. 17. Focus on emotion and adult development* (pp. 104–137). New York: Springer.
Mahoney, M. J. (1991). *Human change processes: The scientific foundations of psychotherapy.* New York: Basic Books.
Marris, P. (1975). *Loss and change.* Garden City, NY: Anchor.
Marucha, P. T., Kiecolt-Glaser, J. K., & Favagehi, M. (1998). Mucosal wound healing is impaired by examination stress. *Psychosomatic Medicine, 60,* 362–365.
Maslow, A. H. (1964). Synergy in the society and the individual. *Journal of Individual Psychology, 20,* 153–164.
May, R. (1950). *The meaning of anxiety.* New York: Ronald Press.
McAdams, D. P. (1996). Personality, modernity, and the storied self: A contemporary framework for studying persons. *Psychological Inquiry, 7,* 295–321.
McFadden, S. H., & Levin, J. S. (1996). Religion, emotions, and health. In C. Magai & S. H. McFadden (Eds.), *Handbook of emotion, adult development, and aging* (pp. 349–365). San Diego, CA: Academic Press.

Mechanic, D. (1962). *Students under stress: A study in the social psychology of adaptation*. New York: Free Press.
More, T. (1995). *Utopia* (G. M. Logan, R. M. Adams, and C. H. Miller, Eds.). Cambridge: Cambridge University Press.
Nordhus, I. H., Nielsen, G. H., & Kvale, G. (1998). Psychotherapy with older adults. In I. H. Nordhus, G. R. VandenBos, S. Berg, & P. Fromholt (Eds.), *Clinical geropsychology* (pp. 167–176). Washington, DC: American Psychological Association.
Novacek, J., & Lazarus, R. S. (1990). The structure of personal commitments. *Journal of Personality, 58*, 693–715.
Nuland, S. B. (1994). *How we die*. New York: Knopf.
Paloutzian, R. F., Richardson, J. T., & Rambo, L. R. (1999). Religious conversion and personality change. *Journal of Personality, 67*, 1047–1079.
Park, D. C. (1997). Psychological issues related to competence: Cognitive aging and instrumental activities of daily living. In W. Schaie & S. Willis (Eds.), *Social structures and aging* (pp. 66–82). Mahwah, NJ: Erlbaum.
Pedersen, J. B. (1998). Sexuality and aging. In I. H. Nordhus, G. R. VandenBos, S. Berg, & P. Fromholt (Eds.), *Clinical geropsychology* (pp. 141–145). Washington, DC: American Psychological Association.
Peterson, C. (2000). The future of optimism. *American Psychologist, 55*, 44–55.
Peterson, K. C., Prout, M. F., & Schwarz, R. A. (1991). *Post-traumatic stress disorder: A clinician's guide*. New York: Plenum.
Piaget, J. (1952). *The origins of intelligence in children*. New York: International Universities Press.
Pope, E. (2002, June). Fifty-one top scientists blast anti-aging idea. *AARP Bulletin*, 3–4.
Radloff, L. S. (1977). The CED-D Scale: A self-report depression scale for research in the general population. *Applied Psychological Measurement, 1*, 385–401.
Regnier, V. (1997). The physical environment and maintenance of competence. In S. L. Willis, K. W. Schaie, & M. Hayward. (Eds.), *Societal mechanisms for maintaining competence in old age* (pp. 232–250). New York: Springer.
Rice, P. L. (1998). *Health psychology*. Pacific Grove, CA: Brooks/Cole.
Rosow, I. (1976). Status and role change through the life span. In R. H. Binstock & E. Shanas (Eds.), *Handbook of aging and the social sciences*. New York: Van Nostrand Reinhold.
Ryff, C. D., Singer, B. H., & commentators. (1998). The contours of positive human health. *Psychological Inquiry, 9*, 1–85.
Safran, J. D., & Greenberg, L. S. (1991). *Emotion, psychotherapy, change*. New York: Guilford.
Salthouse, T. A. (1997). Psychological issues related to competence. In S. L. Willis, K. W. Schaie, & M. Hayward (Eds.), *Social mechanisms for maintaining competence in old age* (pp. 50–65). New York: Springer.
Salthouse, T. A. (1998). Cognitive and information-processing perspectives on aging. In I. H. Nordhus, G. R. VandenBos, S. Berg, & P. Fromholt (Eds.), *Clinical geropsychology* (chpt. 4). Washington, DC: American Psychological Association.
Schaie, K. W. (1994). Course of adult intellectual development. *American Psychologist, 49*, 304–313.

Schaie, K. W., & Lawton, M. P. (Eds.). (1998). *Annual review of gerontology and geriatrics: Vol. 17. Focus on emotion and adult development*. New York: Springer.
Schaie, K. W., & Peitrucha, M. (Eds.). (2000). *Mobility and transportation in the elderly*. New York: Springer.
Scherer, K. R., Schorr, A., & Johnstone, T. (2001). *Appraisal processes in emotion: Theory, methods, research*. New York: Oxford University Press.
Schooler, C., Caplan, L., & Oates, G. (1998). Aging and work: An overview. In K. W. Schaie & C. Schooler (Eds.), *Impact of work on older adults* (pp. 1–19). New York: Springer.
Schulz, R. (2000). *Handbook on dementia caregiving: Evidence-based interventions for family caregivers*. New York: Springer.
Segal, D. L., Coolidge, F. L., & Hersen, M. (1998). Psychological testing of older people. In I. H. Nordhus, G. R. VandenBos, S. Berg, & P. Fromholt (Eds.), *Clinical geropsychology* (pp. 231–257). Washington, DC: American Psychological Association.
Seligman, M. E. P., & Csikszentmihalyi, M. (Eds.). (2000). Positive psychology. *American Psychologist, 55*, 5–14.
Selye, H. (1956/1976). *The stress of life*. New York: McGraw-Hill.
Shapiro, D. (1965). *Neurotic styles*. New York: Basic Books.
Shneidman, E. (1989). The Indian summer of Life: A preliminary study of septuagenarians. *American Psychologist, 44*, 684–694.
Singer, B. H., & Manton, K. (1998). The effects of health changes on projections of health services for the elderly population of the United States. *Proceedings of the National Academy of Sciences of the United States of America, 95*, 15618–15622.
Slaikeu, K. A. (1984). *Crisis intervention: A handbook for practice and research*. Newton, MA: Allyn and Bacon. (Original work published 1944)
Snyder, C. R. (Ed.). (1999). *Coping: The psychology of what works*. New York: Oxford University Press.
Snyder, C. R., Cheavens, J., & Michael, S. T. (1999). Hoping. In C. R. Snyder (Ed.), *Coping: The psychology of what works* (pp. 205–231). New York: Oxford University Press.
Somerfield, M. R., & McCrae, R. R. (Eds.). (2000). Stress and coping research: Methodological challenges, theoretical advances, and clinical applications. *American Psychologist, 55*, 620–673.
Spiegel, D. (1997). Understanding risk assessment by cancer patients. A commentary on the Utility of Systems models of stress and coping for applied research: The case of cancer adaptation by Mark R. Somerfield. *Journal of Health Psychology, 2*, 170–171.
Staudenmeyer, H., Kinsman, R. S., Dirks, J. F., Spector, S. L., & Wangaard, C. (1979). Medical outcome in asthmatic patients: Effects of airways hyperactivity and symptom-focused anxiety. *Psychosomatic Medicine, 41*, 109–118.
Stoebe, M., Hansson, R., Stroebe, W., & Schut, H. (Eds.). (2001). *Handbook of bereavement research: Consequences, coping, and care*. Washington, DC: American Psychological Association.
Strongman, K. T. (1996). Emotion and memory. In C. Magai & S. H. McFadden (Eds.), *Handbook of emotion, adult development, and aging* (pp. 133–147). San Diego, CA: Academic Press.

Suls, J. (1982). Social support, interpersonal relations, and health: Benefits and liabilities. In G. Sanders & J. Suls (Eds.), *Social psychology of health and illness*. Hillsdale, NJ: Erlbaum.

Taylor, S. E. (1986). *Health psychology*. New York: Random House.

Taylor, S. E. (1989). *Positive illusions: Creative self-deception and the healthy mind*. New York: Basic Books.

Terman, L. M. (1925). *Genetic studies of genius: I. Mental and physical traits of 1000 gifted children*. Stanford, CA: Stanford University Press.

Tweed, D. L., Blazer, D. G., & Ciarlo, J. A. (1992). Psychiatric epidemiology in elderly populations. In R. B. Wallace & R. F. Woolson (Eds.), *The epidemiologic study of the elderly*. New York, Oxford University Press.

U.S. Bureau of the Census. (1992). *Current population reports, special studies*, P23-178RV, *sixty-five plus in America*. Washington, DC: U.S. Government Printing Office.

Vaillant, G. E. (1977). *Adaptation to life*. Boston: Little, Brown.

Vaillant, G. E., Bond, M., & Vaillant, C. O. (1986). An empirically validated hierarchy of defense mechanisms. *Archives of General Psychiatry, 42*, 597–601.

VandenBos, G. R. (Ed.). (1996). Outcome assessment of psychotherapy [Special issue]. *American Psychologist, 51*, 1005–1088.

Warr, P. (1998). Age, work, and mental health. In K. W. Schaie & C. Schooler (Eds.), *Impact of work on older adults* (pp. 252–296). New York: Springer.

Werner, H. (1948). *Comparative psychology of mental development* (Rev. ed.). Chicago: Follett.

Westerhof, G. J., & Dittmann-Kohli, F. (2000). Work status and the construction of work-related selves. In K. W. Schaie & J. Hendricks. (Eds.), *The evolution of the aging self: The societal impact on the aging process* (pp. 123–157). New York: Springer.

Whitbourne, S. K. (1996). *The aging individual: Physical and psychological perspectives*. New York: Springer.

Whitbourne, S. K. (1998). Physical changes in the aging individual: Clinical implications. In I. H. Nordhus, G. R. VandenBos, S. Berg, & P. Fromholt (Eds.), *Clinical geropsychology* (pp. 79–108). Washington, DC: American Psychological Association.

Willis, S. L. (1991). Cognition and everyday competence. In K. W. Schaie & M. P. Lawton (Eds.), *Annual review of Gerontology and Geriatrics* (Vol. 7, pp. 159–188). New York: Springer.

Willis, S. L., Schaie, K. W., & Hayward, M. (Eds.). (1997). *Societal mechanisms for maintaining competence in old age*. New York: Springer.

World Health Organization. (1948). World Health Organization constitution. In *Basic documents*. Geneva: Author.

Wright, J. C., & Mischel, W. (1987). A conditional approach to dispositional constructs: The local predictability of social behavior [Special issue]. *Journal of Personality and Social Psychology, 55*, 1159–1177.

Wulsin, L. R., Vaillant, G. E., & Wells, V. E. (1999). A systematic review of the mortality of depression. *Psychosomatic Medicine, 61*, 6–17.

Zarit, S. H., Johansson, L., & Jarrott, S. E. (1998). Family caregiving: Stresses, social

programs, and clinical interventions. In I. H. Nordhus, G. R. VandenBos, S. Berg, & P. Fromholt (Eds.), *Clinical geropsychology* (pp. 345–360). Washington, DC: American Psychological Association.
Zeidner, M., & Endler, N. S. (Eds.). (1996). *Handbook of coping: Theory, research, applications*. New York: Wiley.

INDEX